THE
EIGHTEEN-EIGHTIES
Essays

by Fellows of
the Royal Society of
Literature

———

Edited by
WALTER DE LA MARE

———

Cambridge
AT THE UNIVERSITY PRESS
1930

CAMBRIDGE UNIVERSITY PRESS
Cambridge, New York, Melbourne, Madrid, Cape Town,
Singapore, São Paulo, Delhi, Mexico City

Cambridge University Press
The Edinburgh Building, Cambridge CB2 8RU, UK

Published in the United States of America by Cambridge University Press, New York

www.cambridge.org
Information on this title: www.cambridge.org/9781107680043

First published 1930
First paperback edition 2013

A catalogue record for this publication is available from the British Library

ISBN 978-1-107-68004-3 Paperback

THE EIGHTEEN-EIGHTIES

ESSAYS

CONTENTS

INTRODUCTION

Sequels in literature are usually more dangerous than discreet. The impulse and the novelty of the initial venture cannot but have lost something of their bloom. But though this volume and *The Eighteen-Seventies* have a good deal in common—the same "idea", the same method of treatment, for example—there the resemblance between them ends; except only that the several papers in this book, as in the last, were "written for—and mostly read to—the Royal Society of Literature", and many of them by those who could ill spare the time and labour so generously devoted to them. By comparison with its predecessor, however, this collection has one signal misfortune—a change in editorship; and that, alas, will become more and more apparent as this *Introduction* proceeds. Yet even though my grace for the feast that follows cannot but fall far short of what it ought to be, that is only an additional cause of gratitude for the privilege of having been bidden to say it.

A disconcerting discovery lies in wait for the amateur explorer of any recent literary period—its refuse. The further he ventures, the more widely he surveys the scene, the more numerous, in proportion, he will find, are the books that have not only been forgotten but are now practically unreadable. And among these will be not merely the still-born, the dry-as-dust, the dejected inmates of the 2*d.* box, but many of the once smart or elegant or *outré*, of the nine-day-wonders, and of "the widely popular"—eloquent testimony to their authors' "celebrity, importance and success". They were written in that intense seclusion of self with self which is essential even to the dullest and stupidest of literary compositions, they were devoured in their tens or their thousands of copies, they had their day, they became old-fashioned, out-moded, they have perished. To all appearance they shed little influence on what was to follow them; yet it is these poor relics, simply because they served their temporary purpose, but no other, that are saliently characteristic of their day. And it is almost as difficult to discover why they are dead as it is to detect symptoms of senile decay in the brand-new volumes hot from yesterday's press.

If then it is the bad and indifferent books that date most deplorably, what of the good? Good books, however various they may be in form, style and design, contain an *elixir vitae*—a quintessence of which every great writer has the secret prescription, but which none can pass on. And though they too share in some degree in the fleeting of their day, it is this that matters least. They continue to influence and irrigate men's minds, even if it be the ultimate fate of some of them to attain the peculiar limbo of being "revered unread". "In the character of a nation inconsistency is impossible", said Buckle; and a nation's literature is its looking-glass. And as with its great men so with its great books. However original and insulated they may be, they too could have come into being only when and where they did. The signs in them of their times and of their *genius loci* become the clearer the more closely we examine them. And the more closely we examine them the richer is the reward. Movements and tendencies in letters as in life become conspicuous only in the perspective of time. It is curious to trace the river to its wellspring—in some single human soul. But though one man must originate a movement it takes many men to *make* one, and when

our glance backward deepens into a scrutiny we see not
so much the movement as the men.

So with the 'seventies, so with the 'eighties. The
one decade glided as inexorably as usual into the other
—the vast blunt stream of events pressing onward into
the vast O of temporal space—and we might assume that
the later decade would have about as much to say for
itself as the earlier. In fact, as I think the following
pages will prove, it has more. It better deserves the compliment of being called a *period*. A new life is stirring,
these are years of transition, they mark an end and a
beginning, we become conscious of a lively and refreshing breath of Spring in the air. And though the
most conspicuous flowers that presently bloomed in
that Spring were the rareties of the 'nineties—when, as
Mr Binyon has said, "it having been decided that the
close of a century must be decadent... blameless people
therefore paraded in print imaginary vices"—the
natural, the more traditional kinds, though less visible,
were at least as vigorous; and equally blameless people,
who in the later 'eighties had begun to put forth the
first green leaves of far from imaginary literary virtues,
continued to flourish for many years afterwards. Dates,
too, are obstinate and "periods" overlap; *Patience* was
produced as early as '81 and in '82 Oscar Wilde, then
aged 26 and with a sunflower in his velvet buttonhole,
was lecturing in America—when Aubrey Beardsley was
not yet in his teens. 'Ninetyisms were rife, that is, well
in advance of the calendar.

It is a temptation, perhaps, to claim too much. A sort
of loyalty, an almost paternal tenderness, springs up in
the mind towards anything that awakens one's deeper
interest. And there is always the risk of romanticizing
the past; particularly a past so near and dear and yet
so far as the years of one's childhood. To minimize the

effects of any such temptation in this volume we may
attempt to conceive what its general trend would have
been if (unlike even Mr Eliot who, if I may venture
to be specific, was in his angel infancy when, three
years before the death of Matthew Arnold in 1888,
Marius the Epicurean was published)—if all its contri-
butors had been born, say, at the turn of the century. That
being so, how would the general verdict and tribute of
"the bright young savages of to-day", in Mr Granville-
Barker's gallant phrase—those "learned and loyal
sons of the Muses"—compare with that of an equal
number of mellow octogenarians? The true poet, as
Robert Lytton decided very early in life, "must hit
hard, and speak sharply and severely, and give trouble,
and set thought going". So on occasions must the true
critic. And it is likely enough we should in the one case
have heard the laments and the objurgations of "the
child of sensibility moaning at the wintry cold", "the
breaches in his bleeding heart having been filled with
the briars of suspicion", and in the other, little but well
and fair. "Verily", and I am again quoting our Tupper,
who seems to have recalled here and there the letter, if
not the precise spirit, of Blake—"Verily the man is a
marvel whom Truth (and nothing but the truth) can
write a friend."

If, again, mere age cannot but have affected the
issue—since personal memory has a very sly finger in
the focusing of the romantic—how much more must
the individual point of view! Any such survey as this
is bound to be partial, and partial in both senses of the
word. At least a score of volumes would be necessary to
make it completely exhaustive—and exhausting. But
even at that, it is interesting to redistribute in fancy
the *subjects* of the papers in this volume among their
authors—keeping in remembrance, may be, other

authorities on the period not represented here. What, for example, would Dr Boas have said on Mr Eliot's theme; what Mr Eliot on Mrs Woods's; or Father Martindale on Ibsen; or Mr Granville-Barker on W. S. Gilbert; and Mr Chesterton on all? It may be greedy, but I hope it is not graceless to glance at such possibilities.

From any imaginary standpoint in time we can look behind us, we can look around us, and we can attempt (from *there*) to look ahead. No fewer than four of the following essays are concerned with men of letters, some of them equally renowned also as men of affairs, who were already famous in the 'eighties, and whose labours were nearly at an end. "No great man", said Ruskin, tragically enough, "ever stops work until he has reached his point of failure." And this was assuredly true of the great Victorians.

> I strove with none; for none was worth my strife,
> Nature I loved and, next to Nature, Art;
> I warmed both hands before the fire of life;
> It sinks, and I am ready to depart.

To the few of Landor's contemporaries who at the end of the 'eighties remained alive—he himself died in 1864 —the last two lines of this lovely quatrain were equally appropriate. But not so the first. It had been an age of strife and controversy, and the Victorians, whether philosophers or not, were most of them bonnie fighters. The protracted war, for example, between "science and religion", or rather theology (however nebulous the precise limitations of its field), was "drawing towards its close", though the return to the outlook of intuition or even of mere commonsense, whether simple or transcendental, which is increasingly manifest in our own day, was not yet to show itself.

Carlyle after many years' silence died in 1881, a few weeks before Disraeli, whose *Endymion* had been published the year before. Dante Gabriel Rossetti, Anthony Trollope and Longfellow followed in 1882; J. R. Green, Mark Pattison, Charles Reade, William Barnes and Sir Henry Maine in the next few years; and in 1889 Eliza Cook (whose effusions if not exactly "writ in brass" at any rate adorn a myriad tombstones of her time[1]), Charles Mackay, William Allingham, Wilkie Collins, and (on the day of the publication of his *Asolando*) Robert Browning. And though much of *Fors Clavigera* and the entrancing and unfinished *Praeterita* were also of the 'eighties, Tennyson, though he was ten years older than Ruskin, had then become the almost isolated representative of the great writers of a day gone by. He was made a peer in 1884, and during the 'eighties, apart from *The Promise of May* and *Becket*, published no fewer than four volumes of verse—the supremely characteristic "Crossing the Bar" being included in *Demeter*, which appeared in the same year as *Asolando*. Huxley died in 1895.

What active influence these individual writers continue to shed in our own day it would be difficult to discover. Some of them still abide our question—or

---

[1] And we must never "patronise the past". Faithful and tender good sense is not so common in English verse that we can afford to laugh at Eliza Cook's *Old Songs*:

> "...Old Songs! old Songs—my brain has lost
> Much that it gained with pain and cost:
> I have forgotten all the rules
> Of Murray's books and Trimmer's schools;
> Detested figures—how I hate
> The mere remembrance of a slate!
> How have I cast from woman's thought
> Much goodly lore the girl was taught;
> But not a word has passed away
> Of 'Rest thee, Babe' or 'Robin Gray.'..."

posterity's; others have won their way into a renewed
recognition; yet others seem to have suffered hardly
even a temporary eclipse.

Two supreme figures have not as yet been mentioned.
With these Fr. Martindale's paper is concerned. It is
a portrait and appreciation of the two men on whom
"popular imagination has fastened as 'Cardinals'", and
who, while utterly diverse from one another in temperament and achievement, were at one in their ardent
allegiance to the Church wherein they had both found
their haven. And though literature in itself must be
judged not by its service to any particular cause, it is
profoundly interesting to observe, as we do observe, in
Fr. Martindale's paper, no less than in Lord Lytton's
and in Mr Granville-Barker's, what aims and ideals
may be the vital incentives of the writer of any given
book other than that of making it as good a book as
he can. That banner with the strange device—art for
art's sake—looks a little bedraggled nowadays. Book
for book's sake might perhaps have worn a little better.

Seldom, for example, has the conflict in a young mind
and heart between an "irresistible passion" for poetry
and (to use a phrase that was far more familiar in the
last century than it is now) a sense of duty been revealed
as it is in Lord Lytton's essay on the work of his father.
The letter on p. 20, apart even from its intrinsic interest, is an astonishing tribute to the mind and sensi-
bilities of one who, when it was written, was still in his
early twenties. It is followed by the noble and tragic
submission in that on p. 24. History may repeat itself;
but the repetition of almost precisely the same crisis,
but with how different an emotional response, in the
lives of gifted father and son as they are revealed so
poignantly in Lord Lytton's pages is, so far as I know,
unique.

Whatever, again, may be said in disparagement of the Englishmen of the last century—in temperament, character and aim—one thing is certain. They exhibit an extraordinary variety. Nature, for them, seems scarcely ever to have used the same mould twice, and certainly not for the poets of the time. Mr Drinkwater's ironical conclusion that Martin Tupper failed in being a great poet only because he was not a poet at all might suggest a career of exacerbating pathos. Apart, however, from the hazardous attempt by the author of *Proverbial Philosophy* to finish "Christabel", which was received a little coldly, his literary career seems to have been a path of roses and with a very fair share of myrtle. And though his "homilies and rhythmicals", while continuing to amuse are unlikely ever again to edify, Mr Drinkwater none the less leaves him not only a peculiar but an endearing figure, and has shown also that he could write an easy, vivid and pleasing prose. That—innocent apparently of the faintest hope of reward—he invented the screw-top bottle and the fountain pen is an even more remarkable phenomenon than Dodgson's nictograph and postage-stamp case. In their utilitarian age indeed the idle poet had other alternatives to the thankless Muse than that of sporting with the tangles of Neaera's hair.

The remaining papers are concerned not with what had already been achieved in the 'eighties, but with what was then actually in process of achievement; and Dr Boas's is one of many affectionate and enthusiastic tributes that have lately been offered to the memory of a poet whose loyalty perhaps to his beloved island (and the want of initiative in anthologists) has to some extent obscured his finest work—such lovely things, for example, as his *Epistola ad Dakyns*.

Mrs Woods has also had the happiness of writing out of vivid recollection; of the years indeed when she herself had one of the most romantic of all experiences, that of publishing a first book. "What living poets we who were young in the 'eighties were reading" is her theme, a more defensible way than most of "penning" men of letters within the hurdles of a decade. My one regret, if I may express it, is that she has been unable to offer Coventry Patmore a closer place in her memory's affections.

The mere title of *The Angel in the House* suggests the risks its author ran. It was a lofty challenge but a challenge with a rather parochial ring, and its parochial passages are more easily memorable than its exquisite best. No one, however, can dispute its "fundamental brainwork" and Patmore on his "homely Pegasus" faced its dangers unperturbed, for he knew also that his theme was concerned with "the very well-head... Whence gushes the Pierian spring". And it was not mere arrogance—so conspicuous in that aquiline face of Sargent's vivid portrait—that enabled him at his life's end truthfully to declare, "I have written little, but it is all my best". The fact that the insensitive Victorians bought no fewer than 250,000 copies of this epic of matrimony, while suggesting that lamentable marriages were not so common with them as is generally supposed, may only add to our amusement at Honoria and her husband. So too may the confession that she was the chosen one of an "eminently fair" bevy of sixteen rivals scattered throughout Europe who had blossomed in the poet's light. But Patmore himself is smiling to himself when he says so! And the more one reads of the poem the better it becomes. There was little of the dreamer and nothing of the poseur in Patmore, as "A London Fête" alone would prove. Lines like

> A florin to the willing Guard
> Secur'd, for half the way,
> (He lock'd us in, ah lucky-starr'd)
> A curtain'd front coupé—

and "The while I tied her bonnet on" could not be
better said, though the best place for saying them may
not be a poem. Patmore often failed and Hardy did
not always succeed in assimilating the prosaic in his
verse—a prosaic that after all only thinking makes so.
But he did not attempt to poeticize it. Nor, unlike
certain "realists" who followed him, did he ever degrade
the prosaic. Moreover, as Mrs Woods points out,
alike in his earlier poems and in his magnificent Odes—
even in verses written when he was only sixteen—he was
a supreme craftsman and artist. He was also "the most
adventurously-minded of all our modern poets", and
one who will some day be given a far higher place among
his contemporaries than is his for the moment.

Mr Eliot has no definite memories of the 'eighties to
stand between himself and his two Victorians. He views
them with the quiet and steadfast eye of the critic,
weighs them in the balances, and in much finds them
wanting. In so doing he is innocent of that revulsion of
feeling which some of us who came into the world in
the 'seventies might have to confess to—in respect, at
any rate, to Walter Pater. In our youth we fall in love
at first sight with certain books, and maybe with the
authors of them; with writers perhaps as dissimilar as
Newman, Jane Austen, Emily Brontë and Poe. That
love may ripen into a lifelong and inexhaustible affection. For others we experience an early infatuation, and
I must confess that mine for Pater was much less (was
even, I am afraid, less likely to be) on account of what
he said—and it is *this* Mr Eliot challenges—than on
account of his seductive, his very unusual way of saying it.
He breathed an incantation; and from incantations one
is apt to waken more coldly disillusioned than is quite
fair to the enchanter. Such is humanity; on the one side
the hard gemlike flame...the maladies...the delicate

odour of decay and the rumour of that primrose-yellow panelling in his rooms at Oriel; on the other that entirely unforeseen tall hat and moustache. In our early contemplation of this great writer we had not perhaps "learned to manage ourselves quite perfectly". Mr Eliot indeed convicts not only Pater but even Arnold of traffic with Philistia itself, and Edward Thomas's "critical study" of a few years ago was hardly innocent of irony. Every don has his day, and assuredly "Mr Rose" of *The New Republic* had his—a day too that may yet have its morrow. As for Matthew Arnold, he would have agreed that it is only the valiant Davids of criticism who go out to meet the giants. The resounding of their smooth stones on that brazen armour not only inspires courage in the feeble, but may also serve to re-awaken their victims to a renewed activity!

Again and again in this volume it is the moral outlook of the writers under review that is most sharply questioned. Maybe in part for the very reason that it was not on their moral outlook they prided themselves least. Mr Osbert Burdett in his *The Beardsley Period* went even further: "The perversity and the corruption are upon the earlier side, and, compared with them, the Beardsley period is natural and healthy". It is a vexatious question. Getting to the roots of things—quite apart from the manure—tends to blot out the view of their flowers and green leaves and the blue sky above them. So piercing a comment, however, as "the positive content of many of Arnold's words is very small" is a shaft aimed not at anybody's morals but at the very heart of literature itself.

With Ibsen, the subject of Mr Granville-Barker's paper, we bid a rather emphatic farewell to anything in the nature of the (British) Victorian, and W. S. Gilbert, says Mr Chesterton, is "the only Englishman who understood and observed the unities of the Greek tragedy". Here, though late in the day, I am reminded of a remark made by the Editor of *The Eighteen-Seventies*. He speaks of that "intolerable gesture"—the prefatory "pat on the back". That being so, it would be indiscreet indeed to make any reference to the wit, wisdom and humour so merrily in company in the paper on Gilbert, and (all else apart) to the incisive documentation in that on Ibsen.

To turn from drama to fiction is to be swept from a softly-running river out to sea. Figures speak louder than words. If, at a moderate estimate, for every novel that was published in 1929 three novels were *written*, then, with a meagre allowance of one each, no fewer than 15,000 more or less intelligent persons were then busily engaged in writing them. And drama? Only one single play finds mention in a popular survey of the literature of the year—Whitaker's—and that play was not staged in London. There being such a vast quantity of fiction, it is no wonder there are extremes of quality. To explore in a brief space, then, the best to the worst of its "output" even in the 'eighties, including novels as salient but so different from one another as *The Portrait of a Lady*, *Robert Elsmere*, *A Drama in Muslin*, *The Romance of Two Worlds*, *Three Men in a Boat*, *Little Lord Fauntleroy* and *Called Back*, was a task only comparable with similar and almost equally desperate attempts in *The Eighteen-Seventies*. Indeed it was one only just practicable even for a lover of fiction like Mr Forrest Reid who was already familiar with the *terrain* and had long ago surveyed its every hill and valley. To rescue even one good book from oblivion is perhaps a critic's richest reward: and Mr Reid is not content with *one*. He reports progress too—of a kind: "If there is less genius in the novel of to-day, I think we may claim

that there is more science". And, in one conspicuous
respect, he tells of a change in outlook—a change
exemplified in a remark made by Rhoda Broughton in
her old age to Mr Percy Lubbock. It will be found
on p. 120. The Rhoda Broughtons of our own day
will not have to go to Paris for contrast, and fifty years
hence, it may be, England will have as drastic a Censor
as Russia, the Irish Free State and Italy have now—
where the works of Gorky, Tolstoy, Turgenev and
Dostoievski have recently been banned. Or, celestial hope, may it be that by then the "problem" will
have been exhausted, and the pioneer free to begin
again?

Fiction is literature's shortest cut to life; and though
books age differently from social and political events,
and in general much less quickly, a glance at the current
interests, activities and premonitions of the 'eighties
may help to bring its books a little nearer to us. As
regards "marginal stimulations of the Empire", the
Battle of Majuba Hill was fought and lost on 27 Feb-
ruary 1881; and that of Tel-el-Kebîr was fought and
won on 13 September 1882. The Married Woman's
Property Act was of the same year. In 1884 Gordon
was killed at Khartoum, the Franchise Bill was passed,
and two years afterwards Gladstone's Home Rule Bill
was rejected. In 1888/9 Stanley, having relieved Emir
Pasha, discovered the Congo pygmies and the Mountains of the Moon. Anarchist and dynamitard were then
terms in common use; there were Sunday riots in Trafalgar Square (and incidentally Buchanan's *God and the
Man* irradiated for one small boy his prescribed sabbatical
reading, *The Day of Rest*). The decade ended not only
with yet another successful demand to strengthen the
British Navy but also with a cartoon in *Punch* which
depicts Queen Victoria entreating her grandson, "dear

Willie", to turn his greedy eye from a posse of toy
soldiers of which he has far too many already to "these
pretty ships"!

Old volumes of *Punch* indeed may be not only in-
valuably terse and vivid recorders of the nearer past
but at the same moment disturbing reminders of the
immediate present. In June 1880 we find for example
an invocation to the Australian cricketers, which concludes:

> ...and—drinking your health—*Mr Punch* would ask, "What!
> *Can* cricket in England be going to pot?"

The chorus of *that* has not yet ceased to resound. And
so with literary matters. In the same year the jester kills
two birds with one stone in a reference to a proposal to
commemorate Lord Byron:

> ...Bad as Byron's life may have been, it can hardly be said to have
> fairly drawn down the retribution that enrols him in that ignoble army
> of martyrs, the tenants of that enlarged out-door Chamber of Horrors...
> the London Street-Statues!

And Byron reappears a few years later on the occasion
of his centenary:

> ...Englishmen seem too busy considering whether Shakespeare
> wrote his own plays, to give a spare thought to the author of *Childe
> Harold*—

for the 'eighties were responsible not only for the
foundation of the Bacon Society, but for Mrs Henry
Pott's dissertation on *Promus*, and Ignatius Donnelly's
The Great Cryptogram.

But what is apt to age and in effect perish more
rapidly than either books or events are jocular com-
ments on them. In the 'eighties *Mr Punch's* chief
butts were the lady doctor, "sweet girl graduates",
votes for women, the Bluestocking in Parliament,
divided skirts (Mrs Bloomer—who, like Wellington, Mr
McIntosh, Burke, Brougham, Boycott and Buncombe,

had the rare privilege of adding her name to the English language—died in 1894), the telephone, electricity, mashers (there is seemingly no current colloquialism for this synonym of the fop, the dude, the dandy, the spark), vaccination, the Society for Psychical Research and a Channel *Bridge*. The positive species, indeed, of humour in the 'eighties—a volume entitled *Puniana* was followed by *More Puniana*—has now a curiously domestic flavour; it is a little too early to boast of our own. Similar pleasantries refer to Miss Braddon's having boiled down *Ivanhoe* to 32 pages at a penny, to Matthew Arnold's "sootable" lecturing-suit, and the greeting given to a visitor by the wife of a newly elected working-man M.P.—

Ow d'e do, Mrs Fuzbush? Pray take a chere, M'm. Though I ham a lady now, it won't make no difference in my manners.

With that "ham" we are reminded first that the letter *h* was about this time beginning to return to its proper place in the vernacular; next that the right to impose compulsory education having been bestowed on local authorities in 1870, a "violent change" was then in progress, with the result that to-day, "for the first time in history, everybody has learned to read", and some perhaps to mark, learn and digest; and next, that while in 1868 the country could boast of only fourteen free public libraries, by 1890 there were 208, Andrew Carnegie having established the first of his benefactions to the nation in 1886: a crusade which was to cost him £10,000,000 in all. With these glorious statistics in full view, it would perhaps be a little ungracious to breathe a sigh for the benighted old illiterates of the past, who were often, though not always, as rich and racy elements in English character as are its law-less idioms in the English language.

As for the owner of the "chere" so urbanely offered to Mrs Fuzbush, it was not until 1892 that Keir Hardie became a one-man party in the House of Commons. And though the Social Democratic Federation (at first without the "Social"), the Fabian Society and the Socialistic League were all of them founded in our period, few of their most ardent adherents can have any more clearly anticipated the Labour Government of 1929 than we ourselves can foretell the possible future of a potential "party" of which the Minister of Labour and her sister Members of Parliament form at present the starry but divided nucleus.

Nor, to all appearance, was *Mr Punch* in this a seer. When, however, *apropos* of a comment of James Russell Lowell's, who returned to the United States in 1885— "There is no such tonic as Dante"—that renowned old wag suggested a series of papers on the poetic treatment of disease, with "Tupper as a sedative, Browning as an irritant, Tennyson as a demulcent and Oscar Wilde as an em—" we may not be much amused, but we are less astonished. All honour to him that he welcomed to his pages in our decade not only the author of *Vice Versâ* but also *The Diary of a Nobody*—a "small classic" which Lord Rosebery considered indispensable to the proper furnishing of any bedroom, whose Charles Pooter Mr Birrell has ranked with Don Quixote, and whose Mr Padge Mr Belloc has greeted as "one of the half-dozen immortal achievements of our time". It may be as well to add for the sake of those who have not as yet had the joy of his acquaintance that the "Nobody" of the title is not William Shakespeare in disguise.

Even at risk of tediously referring to what in part the following pages will amply explore, a brief list, however defective it must be, of the salient publications of the 'eighties may help to clarify the view. And here it is

well to keep in mind a comment on the Victorian essayists
made by Mrs Woolf in *The Common Reader*:

> They wrote at greater length than is now usual, and they wrote for a
> public that had not only time to sit down to its magazine seriously, but
> a high, if peculiarly Victorian, standard of culture by which to judge
> it. . . .

By 1890 the historians of Victorian times were com-
pleting their lifework. James Anthony Froude—responsible surely for the most destructive scrap of mis-
copying on record when he transformed "marked
veracity" into "morbid vanity"—had turned from
history to what was to prove an even more tempestuous
venture, biography; though his happiest books were
still to come. Gardiner's Collective Edition of his
History of England (1603–42) was completed in 1884;
The Great Civil War in 1891. Stubbs's *Constitutional
History of England* was of 1878. Lecky's *History of
England in the Eighteenth Century* was brought to a conclusion in 1890, while Freeman's *History of the Norman
Conquest*, concluded in 1879, was followed soon afterwards by his *Historical Geography of Europe* and *The
Chief Periods of European History*.
    Apart from works of individual authorship, the
'eighties were singularly rich in great and enduring
literary enterprises, which, unaided by a penny of public
funds, have since then been brought to a triumphant
conclusion. The *English Men of Letters* Series was begun
in 1878. The first volume of the *Dictionary of National
Biography* appeared in 1884; the first volume of the *New
English Dictionary* in 1888. Dr Wright's *Dialect Dictionary*
was to follow them in the middle 'nineties. In addition to
these there were no less than three popular "libraries"
which owed everything to the zeal of their editor,
Henry Morley. His "National Library" consisted of

no fewer than 2 1 3 admirably selected reprints at the price of threepence each.

To continue our list, the second volume of Herbert Spencer's *Principles of Sociology* was published in 1882, and *The Nature and Reality of Religion*, which he suppressed but which was re-issued without his knowledge as *The Insuppressible Book*, in 1885. Balfour's *A Defence of Philosophic Doubt* was of 1879, Caird's *The Social Philosophy and Religion of Comte* of 1885. Edward Carpenter's *Towards Democracy* and his *Civilisation: Its Cause and Cure*, Leslie Stephen's *History of English Thought in the Eighteenth Century* ('76), and his *Science of Ethics* were also of our period; so too were Sir Francis Galton's fascinating *Enquiry into Human Faculty*, and Huxley's *Science and Culture*.

As for poetry—if Mrs Woods will forgive me once more for trespassing *and* borrowing—apart from the Gallic influences clearly evident in *Poems and Ballads*, apart from the advent of Zola-ism, which was no more kindly welcomed than the author of *A Doll's House*, there was a keen revival of interest in the technique of verse as well as prose; in Andrew Lang's experiments, for example, with the old French measures and in Mr George Moore's with the new French fiction. Sidney Lanier's *The Science of English Verse*, and the invaluable essay on English metrical law appended to Patmore's *Collected Poems* were also of the 'eighties. Oscar Wilde, already the recognized high priest of aestheticism, made his literary *début* with his *Poems* in 1881—poems that deliciously fluttered the coteries but were dismissed by one uncompromising critic as "Swinburne and water"; in 1886 Mr Kipling woke to find himself famous with *Departmental Ditties*; and in 1888 *A Reading of Earth* was published, the last collection of his verse to appear in Meredith's lifetime. A few years more, and lo, *The*

Hound of Heaven, *The Celtic Twilight*, *A Shropshire Lad*; and where else shall we find six brief volumes of poetry at once so close together in time, so diverse in theme, impulse, mastery and technique and so prolific in seed?

The Nineteen-Twenties have gone their way. The Nineteen-Eighties—and into what a markless azure vacuum the phrase transports us—will enjoy a far clearer view of their literary achievement than is practicable now. Still, for bare comparison of the last ten years with a decade that is gone indeed, and as an occasion perhaps for a brief pause in our self-congratulations, even the confused catalogue that follows may be of service. The books referred to are one and all publications of the 'eighties : Seeley's *The Expansion of England*, Butler's *Unconscious Memory*, Gomme's *Folk Lore Relics of Early Village Life*, the *Fabian Essays*, Lubbock's *Ants, Bees and Wasps*, Sir James Frazer's *Totemism* (*The Golden Bough* was of 1890), W. Stanton Moses's *Spirit Teachings*, Lang's *Custom and Myth*, Gosse's *Northern Studies* (containing for England the first tidings of Ibsen), Pater's *Imaginary Portraits* and *Appreciations*, Whistler's lecture, *Ten O'Clock* (to appear again with *Whistler* v. *Ruskin* in *The Gentle Art of Making Enemies*), Dr Saintsbury's Histories of Elizabethan and of French Literature, Charles Doughty's *Travels in Arabia Deserta*, Robert Bridges's *Eros and Psyche*, Sir Richard Burton's translation of the *Arabian Nights*, *The Story of My Heart*, *The Confessions of a Young Man* and *The Twilight of the Gods*; and in fiction (again for mere mention), apart from about twelve novels by Henry James, we have *John Inglesant*, *The Tragic Comedians* and *Diana of the Crossways*, *The Mayor of Casterbridge* and *The Woodlanders*, *The New Arabian Nights* and *The Strange Case of Dr Jekyll and Mr Hyde*, *All Sorts and Conditions of Men*, *Micah Clarke*,

Plain Tales from the Hills, Dead Man's Rock, Auld Licht Idylls and *Cashel Byron's Profession.*

But all this is again to anticipate Mr Forrest Reid to whose happy lot it falls also to welcome Sherlock Holmes and his man Watson; for *A Study in Scarlet* was published in the year of Queen Victoria's Jubilee. Already the old ivied church tower with its peal of wedding bells had become a little *passé* as a happy ending: the scaffold and "the chair" were about to take its place: the heart of the writer of fiction was resigning to the head.

Many of the books mentioned above *are* literature, and that of a high creative order; some of them fall short of it, all of them in their various ways and degrees have fed or affected the minds of the present generation. There cannot but be many signal omissions in such a catalogue, some important ones are dealt with at length later, but even as it stands it is one as rich as it is miscellaneous. It is abundant proof that the writers of the 'eighties had their full share of genius, talent, enterprise and originality, though in the heat of the reaction after the war critics may have been tempted to tar the complete generation with the same dismal brush.

Societies of Literature are concerned with—literature. The vast majority of the reading public would not only smile, and possibly blush, to use the word, but would connect it at one extreme with "printed matter", and at the other with the highbrow. Still, a great part even of the intellectualist's reading is for diversion; it is an anodyne, a sip of the waters of Lethe. Happy the reader who seeks these in the masterpieces yet is not too fastidious to find them elsewhere. Not quite so richly blessed the reader who discovers them solely in the current popular press. And here a brief backward glance only at the evening newspapers of the 'eighties and of their smaller, darker, dirtier, more mysterious and not *less* delightful London cannot but be disconcerting—the *Pall Mall Gazette* (to name only the gone), the *Globe*, the *St James's Gazette* and, a little later, the sea-green *Westminster*. They were one and all partisan and yet independent; and one and all were faithful to a definite literary standard.

Literature apart, again, the reading public which in spite of, and possibly because of, broadcasting, is rapidly continuing to multiply, is a monster with seven heads, the chief sustenance of each of which may be a specific kind of best-seller. This hydra, though not then of its present bulk, was also active in the 'eighties. None the less, surely, and here I am anticipating Mr Granville-Barker, no melodrama, no farce, no "shocker", no mere novelette even of our period can have approached in cheapness, stupidity, ugliness, humbug and sneaking obscenity, the lowest order of our everyday movies and talkies. There were periodicals as witty and "shocking" as *Pick-me-up*, as vulgar as *Modern Society* and *Ally Sloper*: but they were at least English and they were in the eighteenth-century tradition. The cinematograph is mainly alien. Its fine and, in many cases, successful exceptions serve chiefly to illuminate the otherwise dingy scene. British audiences—enthusiastic admirers in the old days of the Nigger Minstrels and the Harlequinade—sit mute. That here was a cheap, easy and universal form of amusement only intensifies the tragedy. Waters, from enormously expensive reservoirs, that might have been at least reviving and refreshing have been laid on the wide world over, and as often as not the supply is putrid. Lives there the man with brow so low...?

Still, we are living in a time of scrutiny, experiment, unrest and challenge, though by no means all the ancient havens and securities are denied us. Childe Roland must be for ever setting out again, and the battlements of his dark tower, "blind as the fool's heart" in the dying sunset under the louring hills, have echoed to many challenges. To the Nineteen-Eighties their aspect may appear a little less formidable than they look at present. Whether or not, when the critics of that far day glance back in contemplation of what the writers of our own day have aspired to do, attempted to do, and done, may they in their turn temper justice with mercy. There is an ideal; it was expressed in his own Victorian fashion by Coventry Patmore in words following the sentence I have already quoted from the ten-line preface to his *Poetical Works*:

> I have written little, but it is all my best; I have never spoken when I had nothing to say, nor spared time or labour to make my words true. I have respected posterity; and, should there be a posterity which cares for letters, I dare to hope that it will respect me.

W. de la M.

POETS OF THE 'EIGHTIES

By Margaret L. Woods

I have tried very hard to catch my poets and pen them into the 'eighties; but poets are proverbially ill-regulated creatures and they will not play the game. Only a very few, like Shelley and Keats, have put all their work into a period of something like ten years. Others, like Wordsworth, Tennyson and our late Poet Laureate, have spread their activities over half a century. Baffled by this poetic perversity, I have changed the point of view and asked not what poets were writing in the 'eighties, but what living poets we who were young in the 'eighties were mainly reading. I have said living poets, because the idol of this generation was Shelley. Our admiration for Shelley was more than a literary taste, it was almost a religion. The Tennyson cult was over. We appreciated Tennyson as a poet, a great artist, but not as a thinker. Indeed his whole attitude of mind had ceased to be ours. Yet Browning, only a few years his junior, was at the height of his fame. No other poet had so strong and widespread an influence over this generation. Probably no other poet has been so widely quoted in the pulpit. His religious views were not in fact more definite than Tennyson's, but there was greater definiteness, greater frankness in their expression and a closer grapple with religious problems. But the generation of the 'eighties was less absorbingly interested in Religion than that of the 'fifties, and Browning's appeal to the Intelligentsia was not mainly religious. Ruskin had inoculated them with a passion for Italian Art and through Art with a passion for Italy, for Dante, for the Renaissance—of which Ruskin himself disapproved. To appreciate fully *The Bishop Orders His Tomb in St Praxed's* it is perhaps necessary to have a mental vision of St Praxed's and of the prelates and Popes of the period. Writers were beginning once more to turn their attention to the theatre, and although Browning early abandoned his attempt to write for the stage, his poems are essentially dramatic. His characters do not resemble the elegant lay figures of Tennyson, but stand on their feet and are vigorously alive. The realism of Browning appealed also to a generation which, unlike the preceding one, read French novels copiously, not only Balzac but Zola. It was for all these reasons that in the early 'eighties Browning Societies flourished and abounded. Some no doubt spent solemn hours in worrying over difficulties due not to obscurity of thought but to obscurity of expression. Others both read the poems and made them an avenue to the discussion of the various problems of Art, Drama, History, Human Character, set forth or implied in them.

Then there was a piquancy in the personal contrast between the two great poets of the moment, Tennyson and Browning. Tennyson, a romantic figure in his Spanish cloak and *sombrero*, represented the ideal of the Byronic generation, when poets desired to be recognized at sight as poets. Browning's unromantic, even conventional personality appealed more to a generation in which poets and painters, in England at any rate, almost invariably cut their hair and desired above all to look and behave like other people. But no generation is homogeneous and there were those who complained that Browning looked like a stockbroker and talked like a man of the world. This view of him was like a bad photograph; it had a foundation in fact but gave a false impression of the personality. His face might have been that of a man of affairs of the first order—that is a man with imagination—and he was a man of the world in the best sense. He had not only seen but observed a great variety of worlds. The poet appeared in him in an uncommon way—in this he resembled Shelley, so unlike him in all else—he was singularly sympathetic, apparently always interested in the person with whom he was conversing rather than in himself. But this interest was not invariably sympathetic. I gathered that he and that prince of *poseurs*, Oscar Wilde, had not got on very well, for Oscar said to me, with some bitterness: "From Browning's writings one would suppose that he could forgive almost any crime; but in fact he cannot forgive even the smallest social solecism".

Oscar Wilde's first volume of poems appeared early in the 'eighties. They were above the average but without force or originality, vaguely Swinburnian in matter and manner. I have never re-read them since their publication but feel sure that my opinion of them would not be raised by doing so. His real poetry was written when he had found another inspiration than that of vanity and lust, when he had drunk of the bitter cup of shame and sorrow. In Wilde's poetry there was perhaps a more marked Swinburnian tone than in that of other young contemporary poets; but Swinburne had contributed certain new elements to the poetry of the period, which in the years following the publication of *Atalanta in Calydon* it had gradually absorbed. At first there was much direct imitation of his metres and manner but by the 'eighties direct imitation was rare, although his influence was considerable. Young in years he had already become a classic in two senses. For though during the 'eighties he poured forth a considerable volume of poetry, it was his early poems that were the most read. His new publications were received with due admiration and interest but with no thrill of excitement. At the time I think his public was a little puzzled by, ashamed of its want of enthusiasm, but on looking back one perceives the reason for it. Swinburne's genius showed no development. One who knew him well says of him that "at the age of 14 many of his life-long partialities and prejudices were formed". He had "all the lyre", but the marvellous melody that he played upon it seemed little but variations upon two or three themes. The real social problems of the day were looming large on the horizon and rhodomontade about Liberty and Priests and Kings sounded hollow. In the 'eighties he changed his revolutionary for a patriotic enthusiasm, but his best work was not in this vein. He, like others, wrote rondels and it was of his *Century of Rondels* published in 1883 that Tennyson, an excellent critic, said: "Swinburne is a reed through which all things blow into music".

D. G. Rossetti stood in somewhat the same position as Swinburne, for different reasons. Not merely his best poems, but the bulk of his work had been published by 1870. Busy with his other exacting art and in poor health he died in 1882 without adding much to the volume of his poetry. But he was much read and contributed his share to the poetic movement of his time.

Another member of the P.R.B. circle to which both Rossetti and Swinburne had belonged was William Morris. So early as 1858 he had published a volume of poems entitled *The Defence of Guinevere*, containing ballads with more emotional appeal, more dramatic than anything in his later work. I would recommend the

Haystack in the Floods or the *Blue Chamber* to any young person not under a strict vow to read no poetry except that published since the War. Easily as Morris produced his poems, the many activities of his later years can have left him little time for the mere physical labour of writing the immensely long stories in which he delighted. I remember a brilliant man named Fearon who had been a schoolfellow of William Morris's at Marlborough. Games were not then regularly organized and they took long walks together in Savernake forest. During these walks Morris told Fearon a story, a serial continued from walk to walk and from term to term over a long period. At length it came to an end and Morris demanded that Fearon in his turn should tell him a long story of his own invention. Fearon, though a clever and witty boy, was incapable of producing such a story and Morris, disgusted with his incapacity, renounced his friendship. This extraordinary facility of invention was at once his strength and his weakness. It enabled him to pour out such works *à longue haleine* as the *Life and Death of Jason*, the *Earthly Paradise* and his later sagas with the utmost ease and in the midst of much other work. But it was also the source of the immense diffuseness which has caused them to fall into neglect, in spite of the many beautiful passages which they contain. Speaking of Morris and his followers at a meeting of the Oxford Browning Society I once called them the Tapestry School of Poetry. It seemed to me that this word indicated the decorative nature of Morris's work, the absence of atmosphere in it, and the unsubstantiality of its figures. *The Lovers of Gudrun* had indeed real dramatic force and feeling but these I thought it owed to the Icelandic Sagas from which the story was drawn.

William Morris was a striking figure. I remember

thinking, as I watched him stride up and down our low Oxford drawing-room, that the bulk of his head and shoulders was so great that he might have been two men more indissolubly connected than the Siamese Twins. At this time he was writing his prose socialistic romance, *News from Nowhere,* carrying on his Oxford Street business very successfully and running the Society for the Preservation of Ancient Buildings much less successfully, owing to a certain deficiency in common sense and tact. His socialism as expressed in *News from Nowhere* was unpractical and showed little understanding of human nature. I am led to this digression because in his last volume of verse there appeared a poem entitled *The Message of the March Wind* the beauty of which is impaired by the intrusion of socialistic false sentiment; for he calls on us to sympathize with the sorrows of poor working-men who have to live in towns, whereas we know that the very last thing that they wish to do is to live in the country. But could anything be more perfect than this picture of a spring evening in a Cotswold village?

> From township to township, o'er down and by tillage,
> Far, far have we wandered and long was the day;
> But now cometh eve at the end of the village,
> Where over the grey wall the church riseth grey.
>
> There is wind in the twilight; in the white road before us
> The straw from the ox-yard is blowing about;
> The moon's rim is rising, a star glitters o'er us,
> And the vane on the spire-top is swinging in doubt.
>
> Down there dips the highway, toward the bridge crossing over
> The brook that runs on to the Thames and the sea.
> Draw closer, my sweet, we are lover and lover;
> This eve art thou given to gladness and me.

Matthew Arnold was one of the veterans whose poems continued to be much read. Mentally he was a pioneer, a connecting link between two generations. His prose works no doubt played a part in giving him his fame. I think it was in the early 'nineties that I was introduced in an omnibus to an intelligent working-man who afterwards became a friend. His first remark to me was: "Are you a disciple of Carlyle?" I replied, perhaps with emphasis, that I was not. "Ah!" he exclaimed triumphantly, "then you must be a follower of Matthew Arnold." And I was ashamed to confess that I was not even that. Matthew Arnold, besides being a poet, was in his prose writings one of the pioneers of what may be called the French Movement, characteristic of the time.

One result of the keen interest felt at this time in all things French was the vogue of old French poetic forms, the ballade, the triolet and the rondel. We have seen that Swinburne wrote a *Century of Rondels*. Among lesser men, Andrew Lang was the master of this particular lyre and his *Ballades in Blue China* deserve to be better remembered. These highly artificial forms do not seem suited to the expression of deep feeling, but Charles d'Orléans and Villon have shown that the ballade at any rate can be made hauntingly sad or terribly tragic.

It may be thought that I should name George Meredith among the poets of the 'eighties, but in fact his reputation as a poet came later. Long as he had been writing, it was only in the 'eighties that he had begun to be generally proclaimed as a great novelist.

Where shall I place Christina Rossetti? By herself surely, for though by birth and association she belonged to the P.R.B. circle, in spirit she stood apart from it. In earlier days her work had been somewhat overshadowed by that of her brother, but its fame had gradually grown. *Goblin Market*, a charming phantasy

published in the 'sixties, had found not a few admirers;
then came her love songs with cadences all their own
and those religious lyrics which are her most valuable
contribution to the literature of her time. There had
been nothing like them since the seventeenth century;
yet Christina's art was not imitative but highly individual. She had an ear which guided her unerringly
through the measures of verse which must have seemed
in the 'sixties highly irregular. Both her religious and
her love poems might be accused of being too generally of a sad, even gloomy nature, but her sing-songs
for children restore the balance.

Turning from these old inhabitants of Parnassus to
those who published their first volumes of poetry in the
'eighties, one finds the decade opening with the name
of one who stands perhaps first in genius—James
Thomson. But to weigh genius in the scale is infinitely
difficult. The sparkle of a dewdrop in its day may
delight us more than the secular glow of a ruby. Yet
in sheer power of creative imagination James Thomson
undoubtedly stands above any other poet of his generation. Here again it is difficult to decide to what generation he belongs, for although his literary life may be
said to begin with the publication of his first volume of
poems in 1880, he was born in 1834. *The City of
Dreadful Night* had appeared serially in Bradlaugh's
newspaper, *The National Reformer*; not a paper in
which literary critics could have been expected to un-
earth a poet. By a fortunate accident the poem was
seen and appreciated by Bertram Dobell and others,
and Dobell succeeded, not without difficulty, in finding
a publisher for a volume of Thomson's poems, the
casual and unvalued harvest of many vagabond years.
They at once attracted attention, especially *The City of
Dreadful Night*.

By the opening of the 'eighties there had come a marked reaction from the optimism of the Tennysonian period, a wave of literary pessimism. But the pessimism of James Thomson was no matter of literary fashion. It was neither a philosophy nor a vague emotion. It was the bitter fruit of a bitter experience of life. Of Scottish birth, he had been educated and evidently not ill educated, in a Home for Scottish children. By some chance he became instructor in an Army School. At the age of twenty he loved and was beloved by a young girl who died suddenly. He is said never to have recovered from the shock of this catastrophe and it may have been the cause of his falling a victim to that foul fiend which so often chooses its prey among men who are gifted above their fellows. One surmises it to have been drink which cost him his post in the Army, which was evidently not distasteful to him. It certainly was this haunting curse which drove him about the world, from one job to another, through the next score of years. The wonder is not that his writings should have been often fraught with gloom, but that he should have been able, during so storm-tossed an existence, to produce so great a volume of poetry and so much of it of a high order.

In *Sunday up the River* and other pages of this first volume there are pleasant lyrics, such as the well-known song beginning:

> Give a man a horse he can ride,
> Give a man a boat he can sail,
> And his rank and wealth, his strength and health
> On sea nor shore shall fail.

But it is not in these that James Thomson's peculiar power is seen—his power of interpenetrating the ordinary stuff of life with weird superterrestrial phantasies—as in the poem called *In the Room*.

The City of Dreadful Night is a work of genius akin to the *Inferno* of Dante and the Hell scenes in Milton's *Paradise Lost*; to say which is not to put it on a level with these classics, but merely to describe its kind. One fundamental difference between these master-pieces and James Thomson's poem perhaps explains the fact that it has not strengthened its hold upon fame in the fifty years which have passed since its publication. Dante placed real people in his Hell, mainly people he knew and disliked. Milton, though not so directly personal, created characters in Satan and his Cabinet Ministers which one cannot but believe to have been modelled on those of men whom the poet had met in the circle of the Protector. In *The City of Dreadful Night* there are no real people, only types. Nevertheless it is a work of fine terrific imagination. Some fame, some appreciation of his powers came to James Thomson with the publication of these poems. But it came too late. He died in 1882, at the age of forty-eight.

The wave of Pessimism, itself a reaction, soon produced what may be called a back-wash in the school of Determined Cheerfulness, of which W. E. Henley was probably the originator, although R. L. Stevenson was its most popular exponent. These two young men met, both of them apparently doomed to a life of invalidism, in an Edinburgh hospital. There they cemented an alliance which was to have a considerable influence on the literary output of the later 'eighties and the 'nineties. Stevenson's was the richer imagination, but in character Henley appears to have been the leader; for it was as a leader that he was regarded by a brilliant circle of young men who gathered round him in the 'nineties. In Stevenson the Scot, Determined Cheerfulness takes on the guise of a religious Faith—as in *The Celestial*

Surgeon; in Henley it wears an air of rebellion against the Powers Above—in that brave little poem, *Out of the night that covers me*, something indeed of defiant swagger. But the Ironic Spirit is silenced when one considers how real the courage, how great the trial of these two youths of genius.

Stevenson won his laurels as a writer of stories and essays in the early 'eighties, so that when in 1885 he published his first volume of poems, *A Child's Garden of Verse*, his audience was already assured. It is the fashion to-day to talk much about the psychology of the Child. In this delightful book may be found photographically true reflections of the Child-Mind reflected in the little mirrors of small but very real poems:

> We built a ship upon the stairs,
> All made of the back-bedroom chairs—

Where is the child who has not played this game? Then the child is always like Alice in Wonderland eating her imaginary mushroom, making itself small enough to live in its dolls' house or to board its little ship:

> Oh it's I that am the captain of a tidy little ship,
> Of a ship that goes a-sailing on the pond—

Then the mysterious terrors of the night. What child has not known them? I myself when about seven years old spent part of my night—grown-up people's evening—alone in an attic approached by a dark and narrow passage which led out of a lumber-room and appeared to me to be long. During these first hours of my night I used to hear a large wild beast of some kind, probably a tiger, padding up and down that passage. It might burst the door open at any moment. There was not only fear, there was a certain pleasurable excitement in this nocturnal visitation. Many children

have fancies of the kind, especially on windy nights.
This was Stevenson's:

> Whenever the moon and stars are set,
>   Whenever the wind is high,
> All night long in the dark and wet
>   A man goes riding by,
> Late in the night when the fires are out,
> Why does he gallop and gallop about?
>
> Whenever the trees are crying aloud,
>   And ships are tossed at sea,
> By on the highway, low and loud,
>   By at the gallop goes he.
> By at the gallop he goes, and then
> By he comes back at the gallop again.

In 1888 he published another volume of poems,
Underwoods. Here too he showed himself a real poet
and one of great charm, but the volume is less distinctive, necessarily less a complete whole than the *Child's
Garden of Verse*. In the same year his friend W. E.
Henley published a volume of poems remarkable for
their originality and realistic power. The series of portraits and sketches in verse, drawn from the hospital
where he had spent so long a period of his youth,
remain among the most interesting of his poems, if, as
pure poetry, his later work surpassed them.

About this time an old poet came before the world in
a character so new that he might fairly claim to be considered as a new poet. In 1885 Coventry Patmore
brought out the complete version of *The Unknown Eros*,
of which part had already appeared in the 'seventies.
As the poet of *The Angel in the House* he had already
been popular, too popular, for a whole generation.
Among the literary he had ceased to count. *The Angel
in the House* was, like *Maud*, a novel in verse; but the
verse was not so good. It was at first universally

admired and its sales were phenomenal. New editions appeared so late as the 'seventies and even 'eighties. Other equally fluent and nauseatingly sentimental poems followed, and all had considerable sales.

Signs were not wanting in his earlier poems that he had considerable powers of description and some real aptness of style. Being an intelligent man, he grew tired of his own poetry, turned his attention to the technique of verse and completely, marvellously altered his poetic style. His *Odes* and *The Unknown Eros* are rich with harmonies which would have been deemed far beyond the reach of the poet of *Taverton Tower*. His frost-bitten laurels budded anew, but this time for a very small circle, though it consisted of those whose opinion carried weight.

It requires a sympathy with Coventry Patmore's outlook, which I lack, really to enjoy the bulk of his later poems. He had become a Roman Catholic and devoted much study to the Mystics, particularly the Spanish ones. The Southern Mysticism, which uses the language of earthly passion to describe Divine Love, is unpleasing to the normal Briton. There are in the poems of this period some whose beauty can be appreciated without questions being asked as to their inner significance, but had he written the series which he planned, in honour of the Blessed Virgin, it would probably have suffered from the too obvious influence of this exotic form of sentimentality. The only poem of the series which he did write, *The Child's Purchase*, is charming in idea and contains such fine passages as this:

> Grant me the steady heat
> Of thought wise, splendid, sweet,
> Urged by the great rejoicing wind that rings
> With draught of unseen wings,
> Making each phrase, for love and for delight,
> Twinkle like Sirius on a frosty night!

Then there is that beautiful and well-known poem, *The Toys*, which any of us can love without reservation and without being sealed of the Tribe of Patmore.

The late Poet Laureate, who so splendidly crowned his work with *The Testament of Beauty*, published his first volume of poems in 1873. They were immediately recognized, by those whose judgement counts, as the voice of a new poet, one who was going to write his name on the glorious roll of English literature. Yet there was not anything in the nature of a Bridges cult or boom. The star of Robert Bridges has risen slowly but surely from the horizon to the zenith. I myself read that first little book of poems, some years after it had appeared, with great delight. It contained many beautiful lyrics—among others, be it noted, rondeaux and triolets—*The Elegy on a Lady* and the poem *Clear and Gentle Stream*. In the 'eighties the alliance was formed between Robert Bridges and Henry Daniel of Worcester College, Oxford, the works of whose private printing press have long been the treasures of the bibliophile. Mr Daniel brought out an extremely beautiful edition of the shorter poems of Bridges printed in black-letter, also duplicated in Roman type. And the circle of lovers of these beautiful lyrics kept on widening. Dr Bridges published during the 'eighties his plays *Prometheus the Fire-Giver*, *Nero* and others and his long narrative poem *Eros and Psyche*. It was in the early years of the decade that he left London to dedicate himself entirely to his Muse, in a charming eighteenth-century house under those downs which he has so beautifully sung.

To pass from the particular to the general—What was the tendency of poetry in the 'seventies and 'eighties? In the first place the Tennysonian cult was over. It had led to over-smoothness of verse in his followers. The general idea of his period was that our verse was syllabic in structure. Tennyson was too great an artist to carry out this theory rigidly in practice, but it is my impression that he did consider the syllable the basis of prosody and that this is answerable for the smooth dullness of much of his blank verse, though he could always roll you out a sonorous line. The younger poets were looking for new forms. To take two poets of about the same age, though of very different calibre, Robert Bridges and Andrew Lang: Lang turned for his models to the French and earlier Renaissance poets; Bridges to the seventeenth-century English poets, though, as we have seen, he also wrote rondeaux and triolets.

The harmonies of verse, the technique of poetry received serious attention. Some may suppose this to be a sign of decadence, but it is evident that our two greatest masters of poetic harmony, Milton and Keats, gave great attention to the technical side of their art.

When the poetry of the late nineteenth century falls into perspective it will, I think, be seen that, putting aside the great Victorian leaders in poetry, the verse of this period is different from and generally better than the verse of the 'sixties. Of the influence of Swinburne I have already spoken. Matthew Arnold had also exercised some influence both by his experiments in short blank verse and by his beautiful use of the Spenserian stanza in his Oxford poems, although Rossetti used it in his own way as beautifully. Coventry Patmore's works illustrate the tendency of the time, the change from the fluently regular earlier Victorian to the more irregular and at the same time richer verse of the 'seventies and 'eighties.

THE
POETRY OF OWEN MEREDITH

By The Earl of Lytton

Robert, Earl of Lytton, known to literature as Owen Meredith, was born in 1831. He was the only son of the well-known novelist and statesman, and his childhood and early manhood were clouded by the domestic troubles of his parents. He inherited the literary tastes of his father and he began to write poetry before he left Harrow, at the age of eighteen, to finish his education with an English tutor in the German University town of Bonn. A year later, when he was nineteen, he entered the Diplomatic Service as an unpaid Attaché to his uncle, Sir Henry Bulwer, who was then the British Minister at Washington. In this Service the rest of his life was spent, and he served successively at Florence, the Hague, Vienna, Copenhagen, Athens, Lisbon, Madrid and Paris. In 1876 he was appointed Viceroy of India by Disraeli, and resigned this post after the defeat of Disraeli's Government in 1880. In 1887 he was appointed by Lord Salisbury as British Ambassador in Paris, which post he held till his death in 1891.

These achievements in his profession somewhat overshadowed his contributions to literature, which were nevertheless considerable. His first volume of poems *Clytemnestra and Other Poems* was published in 1855, when he was still only twenty-four, and this book was followed by others at regular intervals throughout his life. With the exception of one prose tale, *The Ring of Amasis*, his work was exclusively poetical. *The Wanderer* was published in 1858, *Lucile* in 1860, *Serbski Pesme or Love Songs of Servia* in 1861, *Chronicles and Characters* in 1867, *Orval or the Fool of Time* in 1869, *Fables in Song* in 1874. All these works were written during his father's lifetime and before his appointment as Viceroy. After his return from India, he published *Glenaveril* in 1885 and *After Paradise or Legends of Exile* in 1887. This completed the works which were published during his lifetime, but after his death two more volumes by his hand were given to the world: *Marah*, a collection of love poems, and *King Poppy*, the most serious and important work of his life.

This brief category of my father's official posts and literary productions reveals the fact that in the same man were two personalities of widely differing character, two ambitions struggling for mastery, two forms of self-expression which were never reconciled. This perpetual feud between the poet and the man of affairs provides the key to a true understanding of his emotional life, and, in the brief sketch of his personality and writings which I am about to attempt, it will be seen how his whole nature was affected by this conflict.

In early life my father's mind was completely dominated by his literary tastes. His profession was an irksome necessity. His love of poetry—both the reading and the writing of it—was an irresistible passion. His friendships were based on literary sympathies, his interests were in literature, not in politics, his tastes and his recreations were almost exclusively literary. Had he received encouragement, and been allowed to devote himself seriously to the improvement of his own technique, there is no doubt that he would

have achieved his highest reputation in the world of
letters.

The chief early obstacle to the indulgence of his
literary ambitions, and the development of his literary
talents, came from an unexpected source. It might be
supposed that his father, who was himself so pre-
eminent in literature, would have welcomed in his son
the evidence of hereditary gifts, would have shared to
the full his literary interests and encouraged him to
add fresh lustre to a name already famous in the world
of letters. This did not happen. On the contrary,
Robert Lytton received from his father letters that were
curiously critical and at times positively discouraging.
There were three grounds for Bulwer-Lytton's attitude.
The first was the not unusual want of sympathy between
age and youth. The father could appreciate neither the
opinions of his son's generation nor the forms in which
they were expressed. His test of the value of the great
poets of the past was the quality which he found in
them of expressing "the passions most common to the
human heart in all ages", but he failed to convince his
son of the soundness of this basis of his criticism, because in his letters he made use of the phrase "popular
element", which conveyed a different and objectionable
idea.

"A poet", he wrote, "who means to influence his age should aspire
to reach a wide public. This is one reason why I deplore the paramount
effect that poets who only please a few have on your line and manner.
Praised as they are by critics, Keats and Shelley are very little read by
the public, and absolutely unknown out of England. Tennyson is more
popular, because a little more complete in his way. Now take Charles
Mackay's poems. They are little praised by critics, no idols of the refining
few, but they sell immensely with the multitude—it is worth studying why.
I believe because, though they have not much elevation of subject, they
have a simplicity of style which all understand. I don't want you to go
back to old conventionalism nor write like Goldsmith, Pope, etc., but

I do want you to make a thoughtful study of all poets who are widely popular. And I think you will find that they all concur in the great laws of rhythm and harmony and in an earnest attempt to seize the most elementary, not the most refining feelings of men...."

Another reason for Bulwer-Lytton's advice to his son to put his profession before his art arose from a knowledge of the sacrifices he had himself made to achieve worldly success for the sake of his heirs. As a young man, after he had forfeited his mother's favour because of his refusal to give up the woman of his choice, he slaved himself to earn enough to keep his wife in comfort and to provide for his children. Later, after he inherited his mother's property, he had experienced the servitude which an ancestral home imposes upon its possessor and its heir. The inheritor of a long established family estate is as much bound by the obligations which it entails as the Sovereign who inherits a throne. Only those who have had this experience, perhaps, can appreciate the strength of the ties which it imposes, but those who have had the experience know that to them no escape is permitted. My grandfather knew this and was concerned that his son should not develop tastes, or become absorbed in activities that would unfit him for the duties which would in time devolve upon him. It was this motive that prompted him to recommend his son to stick to his profession and avoid the risk of becoming a literary dilettante.

"I have made for you a great position", he wrote, "I indulged the hope of refounding a House that might rank with the highest—that is a work of generations. I have done my share and my duty. But I cannot perpetuate my own ideas, and it is quite clear that my views are not yours. Be it so. I could be amply consoled if I felt sure you would be really well and happy in your own line. But I tremble for you—without any profession, 'your heart on paper and your hand in rhymes', with a sensitive nature, a very delicate organisation, and removed from that routine of life with others which is dull, no doubt, but especially needed by genius and emotional natures. It is their only chance of mental health and equilibrium."

To the arguments of his father regarding his tastes in poetry, Robert Lytton replied at length and defended his point of view in letters which showed that he had the soul of a poet more fully developed than had his father.

"With regard to masters", he wrote, "I do not deny the merits of Pope, Dryden, Byron, etc. For Byron I have a hearty admiration. But I have gone through these schools, and feel that I can never go back to them, nor do I think that any reproduction of these poets would stand or avail. I began as a child by imitating Byron. I progressed to Pope; now I have gone on. You say I have fallen foul of Tennyson, Keats, Shelley, etc. That may be very probably the case. But my notion is that it is easy to succeed in art, if we can only be quite sure that one is doing what one *likes*; one *must* follow one's sympathies. No man can say to one, 'Follow this one, or that other, for he has truth'. Better run knee-deep into a quagmire after a will-o'-the-wisp, if one feels the desire to do so, and finds pleasure in the doing of it. One is sure to find one's own way at last, I think, spite of the light being false or true. If now there be in my talk too much of other men's languages, it is because I have a strong sympathy with these certain men, and hail in their language the most correspondent expression I have yet found to my own thoughts and wants. . . .

"I assert for Poetry the highest possible mission second to that of the Bible. The poet professes to teach and uplift, to be a thinker of new thoughts, a sayer of new words. He has no business to speak below his level in order to be easily understood; he is not to be disposed of by the 'Can't understand a word of it' of some stupid dunderhead who can't understand a word of anything else. He must hit hard, and speak sharply and severely, and give trouble, and set thought going. What matter if you read the page over six times in vain, if at the seventh a light, like the soul of it, flashes out which has salvation in it? I observe that shallowness is over-valued for its clearness. People understand the brook better than the sea.

"There is a kind of poetry that is like the blowing of a trumpet; that makes one double one's fists, and feel as bold as a lion; such as Scott's, which I think first-rate of that kind, but is this to be put above poetry which penetrates to the fibres of the brain, or strikes some new thought

into your life, which perhaps revolutionises your whole moral being?
or even that poetry which creates beautiful worlds out of the dust of
daily life, and makes you see more things on a leaf on the hedge-side
than you ever before saw in the whole forest?..."

Both father and son had an equally good friend in
John Forster, and to this friend Robert Lytton was
able to write more freely than he could to his father.
Writing to Forster in January 1854, he says:

My father's theory of poetry and my own, in most respects differ
widely. I can give up my theory and accept his, and it would be pre-
sumptuous in me to say that his is not the better of the two; but then it is
not *mine*...if I cannot write as I wish to write, silence is fitter and more
soothing. To do this would be to sing from the throat, not from the
heart, to be a sham rather than a truth. Hence, so long as I continue to
jog along my own way, it follows that, despite the overwhelming
superiority and power of his mind, his advice is rather more like to pull
me off my legs, than to help me on my road.

In another letter to the same friend he develops more
fully his literary sympathies—

...After all, the intrinsic spell and magic of the poet lies somewhere
beyond and above all divisions of subjectivity or objectivity; and I think
if I had to name what is the most precious and divine part of poetry,
I should call it "suggestiveness", without which all is barren and un-
profitable. It is this that forms not the least enchantment of Shakespeare,
and I suppose that Keats meant it when he spoke (in lines which I don't
remember sufficiently to quote) of things worth more "to brood upon
than the death-doom of Empires". It is this which oozes out of every
line of Milton—it is as subtle as air, and one can't say what the secret
lies in, but now and then, through some word, there glimpses out upon
one visions and revelations of Fairyland. And the poet is a consoler and
a prophet, just in proportion as he procures you such glimpses, and
"Open Sesames" into those enchanted caves; in some sort he should
stand sponsor for us at the great fount of nature, and our souls will be
healthful and pure just as they are sprinkled with the dew of his gracious
baptism; his duty is to know our noblest part and answer for us that we
will live up to it. It is his benignant privilege to do for us just what is
elseway done by the first dew of morning, the last light of sunset, the
earliest star of evening—and when these have lost their potency, and
that which responds to them within us is in danger of drying up for want

of fit nourishment, then the poet must step in, and restore to them their
original affluence and virtue. Take such lines as these:

> Ere the high lawns appear'd
> Under the opening eyelids of the Morn.[1]

or

> —beyond the stormy Hebrides,
> Where thou perhaps, under the whelming tide,
> Visitest the bottom of the monstrous world.[2]

or such a personification as—

> While the still morn went out with sandals grey.[3]

or such a picture as the moon stopping—

> gently o'er the accustomed oak.[4]

or the curfew—

> Over some wide-watered shore
> Swinging slow with sullen roar.[5]

or of Shakespeare—

> Hot lavender...
> The marigold, that goes to bed wi' the sun,
> And with him rises weeping.[6]

or what magic in that song—

> Come unto these yellow sands, etc.[7]

And of a higher suggestiveness such lines as these:

> When you do dance, I wish you
> A wave of the sea, that you might ever do
> Nothing but that....
> Each your doing,
> So singular in each particular,
> Crowns what you are doing in the present deed,
> That all your acts are queens.[8]

or when Cleopatra calls out—

> O most false love!
> Where be the sacred vials thou shouldst fill
> With sorrowful water?[9]

---

[1] *Lycidas.*   [2] *Ibid.*   [3] *Ibid.*   [4] *Il Penseroso.*   [5] *Ibid.*
[6] *The Winter's Tale.*   [7] *The Tempest.*   [8] *The Winter's Tale.*
[9] *Antony and Cleopatra,* i, 3, 62.

or Antony—in what extremity of despair—exclaiming—

> Authority melts from me!

These lines always affect me strangely—

> Be you not troubled with the time, which drives
> O'er your content these strong necessities,
> But let determined things to destiny
> Hold unbewailed their way.[1]

And what is there that touches one above the mere words in the thought of things that
> make stale
> The glistering of this Present?[2]

or of sleep "that knits up the ravelled sleeve of Care?" But I quote at random and indiscreetly. Chaucer excels in this: Keats has mighty flashes of it that will shine against the light of any old poet, as in that fine sonnet on Chapman's Homer, and such an image as—

> Magic casements, opening on the foam
> Of perilous seas, in faery lands forlorn.

Of all modern poets, and as much as any ancient one, Alfred Tennyson, I think, abounds in it; he has set his mark upon many objects, and fenced in a great part of nature as his special property. As, for instance, "the wild marsh-marigold" that "burns like fire in swamps and hollows grey" is his flower and nobody's else's; his brother Frederick fails altogether in doing this; he does not monopolise a single association; one is tired of hearing that "the rose is red, the violet's blue" and feels tempted to ask, "Could you find nothing else in them?" and his vague impersonifications are most wearisome. I have laid down the law so lengthily with reference to these, that I am ashamed to speak of myself, though I had much to say. But it is one thing to criticise and another to perform.

The first two motives of Sir Edward Bulwer-Lytton's attitude to his son's literary ambitions were intelligible and defensible. The third is less easy to understand or to defend. He appears to have had an unaccountable jealousy of his son's success and to have feared that he might eclipse his own reputation in the

---

[1] *Antony and Cleopatra*, iii, 6, 82.   [2] *Winter's Tale*, iv, 1, 13.

field of letters. This motive is evidenced in the following
letter:

June 1. 1854.

I don't think, whatever your merit, the world would allow two of the
same name to have both a permanent reputation in literature. You would
soon come to grudge me my life, and feel a guilty thrill every time you
heard I was ill. No. Stick close to your profession, take every occasion
to rise in it, plenty of time is left to cultivate the mind and write verse or
prose at due intervals. As to your allowance, I should never increase it
till you get a step. I help the man who helps himself. What in your
letters you suggest as the road to fame, is only the lazy saunter into a
relaxed effeminate air of pleasure and egotism. It is the epicurean
looking in his rose garden, and declaring that he is cultivating philosophy.
All great natures must have some little dash of the firmer Stoic; all must
do what they don't like—for every true duty is some restraint on the
inclination. Were it not for that, do you think I should be toiling here?
Oh, no—under the orange groves of Nice writing New King Arthurs,
which none save an affectionate son would read.

This letter admitted of no argument. The pain which
it occasioned was suppressed, and Robert Lytton replied with a humility and resignation that was truly
admirable:

. . . What you have said is *quite enough*. I shall only recur in thought
to those suggestions for the future with regret that they were ever made.
I renounce them, I shall not recur to them myself in discussion. I am
quite willing to abide in the Profession and work as well and as cheer-
fully as I can in it.

If you believe what I say now, and have often said, that my chief
desire is, and up to this moment has been, to give you pleasure—at
least, if not that, to save you pain—whatever be my future, you need be
no longer uneasy, I think. . . . What you suggest I am ready to follow,
to the best of whatever may be in me. I should do so more gladly if
I thought that, by doing so, I received your affection unembittered by
a doubt.

The acceptance of his father's advice to put his profession first meant a definite abandonment of a literary
career, and from this time onwards the works which

he published were rather the expressions of a craving that refused to be stifled than the gradual unfolding of an unfettered genius.

I was only fourteen years old when my father died and it has been one of the great regrets of my life that all my serious interests date from that year. In life I only knew him as a kindly, but rather awe-inspiring divinity. The opening words of the Lord's Prayer have always recalled to me the image of the father of my childhood. He was a father I could worship and love in a dutiful sense, but not a father I could know, as he did not live in my world. His death was the first emotional shock of my life, and in the years that followed, as I learnt to know him from his poems and his letters, as I discovered the extraordinary sweetness of his character, his immense tenderness, his large heart and overflowing sympathy, I was tormented with regrets that he was no longer present to share with me the growing interests of my life, and that I could not give him in return the response which would have been so precious to him.

At the age of twelve I received an immensely long letter from him in acknowledgement of some childish verses I had sent my mother from school. It covered twenty sheets of large official notepaper, and I well remember my pride at being allowed to keep a candle in my bedroom after the lights were out, in order to read it. The letter is an interesting echo of those which my father had himself received in youth and has a bearing upon the conflict in his own life which is the main theme of my sketch. The advice which it contains is almost identical with that given to him by his father, because he in turn had then come to realize the strength of the ties which bind an owner to his ancestral property. The letter is too long to quote, but

the following extracts may serve to give some idea of
its contents:

On the whole, I think it probable that when you become a man—
and your intellect and character mature—they will find their most congenial employment and expression in some more active vocation than
poetry. And I will tell you some of the reasons (for you are now old
enough to understand them) why I also hope that this may be the case.

In the first place, when you survive me in the course of nature, you
will succeed to an estate which you will find very expensive to keep up,
while the income from it is so small that even with great economy you
will barely be able to live on it as a single man, and quite unable to live
on it as a married man with children....

In the next place, there is no money to be made by writing poetry,
however good the poetry may be....

Even if you became the greatest poet of your age, your poetry and
your fame as a poet would not furnish you with the means of keeping
up, as it will be your duty, and I hope your pride, to keep up the title,
the name, and the position in the world which in the course of time you
will inherit from your father and grandfather....It is therefore, my dear
boy, essential to your future independence and self respect, that you
should not, in any case, make poetry the sole, or even the chief, occupation of your after life....

The number of very great poets, from Homer to our own time, is so
few, that the chances are a hundred to one against any man becoming
one of them. And believe me there is no reputation less worth having,
nor any social position on the whole more contemptible than that of a
man who is absolutely nothing more, or nothing else, than a second-rate
poet....

Now, my beloved boy, don't suppose that I wish to discourage your
love of poetry or any of the feelings which at present prompt you to
write verses. On the contrary, I welcome it with satisfaction. For at
your age a dull commonplace boy would have no such inclination, and
what has most pleased me in your verses is the evidence I find in them
of a generous, tender and loving nature. That is itself a gift which you
cannot too much cherish and cultivate as long as you live. All I wish to
impress upon you is that you will have other and more important things
to do in life, and that you must not now neglect any opportunity of
qualifying yourself for the harder tasks of active manhood....

Other passages in this tremendous letter referred to
the responsibilities and obligations which I should one

day inherit, and reminded me of the public services of my father and grandfather which it would be my duty to emulate, and the whole letter stirred me profoundly. I was advised (in words identical with those used in a letter my father had received from his father at about the same age, on the subject of the choice of a public school) to keep the letter and read it again when I was older and better able to understand it. Of course, I flattered myself that I understood it fully at the time, and so far as it was intended to influence my own character, I no doubt did understand it. But what I could not then know, what I only came to realize many years later, was that in writing it my father was, once more near the end of his life, making a final suppression of the ambitions of his youth. His object was not to suppress the poet in me, so much as to justify to his own conscience the lifelong subordination to duty of the poet in himself.

Among the last poems that he wrote was one, published after his death, which gave symbolic expression to the internal conflict which had dominated his whole life. It is called *The Prisoner of Provence* and deals with the legend of the man in the iron mask—

> Is it a story I once heard told
>   In boyhood? Did I read it in my youth,
> Not understanding it till I grew old,
>   A fiction then, that now becomes a truth?
>
> Two children were they of one mother born,
>   Brethren and twins. Yet to each other they
> Were strangers ever, from life's natal morn
>   To the last moment of its dying day.
>
> The life of one was in a palace pass'd,
>   That of the other in a prison-den;
> His name was a dread secret to the last,
>   His brother's loud upon the lips of men.

The face of one to all the world was shown,
　　The other's never visible on earth.
The first was rear'd in splendour to renown,
　　The second breath'd in mystery from his birth.

　　　　　·　　·　　·　　·

One of them all men called "The Grand". He graced
　　A throne by Princes held in reverence.
The other, whom an iron mask effaced,
　　Some people call'd "The Prisoner of Provence".

　　　　·　　·　　·　　·　　·

By sad self-knowledge this full well I know,
　　And I am conscious, too, that whether they,
The twin-born brethren, did live long ago,
　　Or did not, in my life they live to-day;

Or beings like them. I divide their lot
　　With each, and keep the secret of the twain.
One brother's gaoler, though he knows it not;
　　The other's most obsequious chamberlain.

The one the world sees, talks of, thinks it knows,
　　Is named and noted. All that more or less
Men envy fate upon his lot bestows;
　　Celebrity, importance, and success.

The other breathes beneath an iron mask,
　　Suppress'd in silence, solitude and gloom,
A nameless mystery. For my lifelong task
　　Is to conceal the secret of his doom.

Because if this poor prisoner of State
　　Were free, and his true character made known,
His liberation would annihilate
　　The realm safe-guarded by his brother's crown.

Thus while one part of me, that seems the whole,
　　Lives in profusion and magnificence,
The other pines in pitiless control,
　　Lone as the nameless Prisoner of Provence.

The Prisoner of Provence—the man who lived
　　And died beneath a mask! And he, the king
Men called "The Grand"! How have their fates contrived
　　Such lights and shadows over mine to fling?

Where have I read it? Did I hear it told
   When I was young? Or dream'd it in my youth?
Is it a story of the days of old?
   Or but a fancy that reveals a truth?

I have dealt at considerable length with this conflict
of tastes and ambitions, because a knowledge of it is
necessary to an understanding of all my father's work.
Everything that he published was the expression of a
suppressed personality, and the merit of each volume
may be measured by the degree of the suppression
exercised at the time it was written. His best poetry of
the lighter kind is contained in *The Wanderer*. These
poems were written at Florence when he enjoyed an
intimate friendship with the Brownings, when his
relations with his father were cordial, before the profession which he had adopted had begun to make serious
demands upon his time, and when his literary tastes
were given a freer scope than at any other period of his
life. The love poems in *The Wanderer* have the fresh-
ness and also the passion of youth. They were written
under the stress of great emotion, and he said to
Robert Browning at the time, "God knows they ought
to be original, for they seemed torn out of my very
entrails". Though they are the expression of a restless
and unhappy period of his life, they also belong to a
period when the poet had for a time been allowed to
get the upper hand. The two years in which he had
promised his father to publish nothing and devote himself to his profession had elapsed; he felt free to express
in his favourite medium the emotions of an unhappy
experience in love, and the conscientious public servant
was for a time forced into the background. For this
reason in later life, when the poet had been definitely
subordinated to the official, he not only criticized them
unsparingly as a "produit indigeste d'une jeunesse

maladive et gaspillée", but re-wrote many of them to
the distress of those who had loved them in their
original form. They reminded him too poignantly of
the personality that chafed behind the iron mask.
Fortunately the book was republished after his death
with the original text, and the poems were rescued from
the later emendations of their author.

No extracts can do justice to the book, as the poems
have a value in the sequence assigned to them which is
lost if they are extracted singly, but two quotations
may give some indication of the spirit of these early
love poems.

The following lines are from "A Love-letter":

> I never thought to know what I have known,—
>   The ecstasy of being loved by you;
> I never thought within my heart to own
>   One wish so blest that you should share it too:
>
> Nor ever did I deem, contemplating
>   The many sorrows in this place of pain,
> So strange a sorrow to my life could cling,
>   As, being thus loved, to be beloved in vain.
>
> .   .   .   .   .
>
> I will not cant that commonplace of friends,
>   Which never yet hath dried one mourner's tears,
> Nor say that grief's slow wisdom makes amends
>   For aching hearts and desolated years;
>
> For who would barter all he hopes in life,
>   To be a little wiser than his kind?
> Who arm his spirit for continued strife
>   When all he cared to keep is left behind?
>
> But this, this only...Love in blackest woe,
>   Still lovelier than all loveless happiness,
> Hath brilliancies of joy they never know,
>   Who never knew the depth of love's distress.
>
> .   .   .   .   .

> Farewell, and yet again farewell, and yet
>   Never farewell,—if farewell mean to fare
> Alone and disunited. Love hath set
>   Our days, in music, to the self-same air;
>
> And I shall feel, wherever we may be,
>   Even though in absence and an alien clime,
> The shadow of the sunniness of thee,
>   Hovering, in patience, through a clouded time.

My other quotation is a complete love story in four lines. It also has an echo of the note on which the author had accepted the renunciation of his literary ambitions.

> Since all that I can ever do for thee
> Is to do nothing, this my prayer must be:
> That thou may'st never guess nor ever see
> The all-endured this nothing-done costs me.

My father's next volume *Lucile* was produced two years later, in entirely different circumstances. A crisis had occurred in 1858 in the unhappy quarrel between his parents. After a succession of outrageous acts, of which insanity seemed to afford the only explanation, Lady Lytton had been confined in a private lunatic asylum by her husband, who was at that time Secretary of State for the Colonies in Lord Derby's Government. The outcry caused by this action forced Sir Edward to resign his office and necessitated the liberation of his wife. The son now came to the rescue of his distracted parents and offered to take his mother abroad. The offer was eagerly accepted by his father, and mother and son proceeded to Luchon. The weeks that followed were the most miserable experience in my father's life and the innate beauty of his character alone saved him in the terrible ordeal. Though he tried his utmost to help each parent to a better understanding of the other, he only succeeded in antagonizing both. His father repaid his good offices by writing him letters of such incredible severity as to suggest that his own mind was unhinged. He even went so far as to threaten that he would not recognize his son if they ever chanced to meet! His mother also turned against him when she found that he would not take up her cause publicly, and became more violent than ever. After five months of agony he was forced to leave her, and being entirely without resources, cut off from both his parents, he joined himself to a company as a travelling artist and wandered for some weeks on horseback through the Pyrenees. It was in these circumstances that *Lucile* was composed. The poet in him once more took command, not this time by leave but in revolt. The rhythm of the poem was suggested by the action of his horse, and the best lines in it are those which describe the scenery through which he passed. The poem was for many years a favourite in America, but was less appreciated in England.

Space does not permit an analysis of the circumstances in which the works of his middle life were produced, nor a discussion of their characteristics. To his friends their favourite poems were always those that belonged to the period of their friendship, those that the author had read to them and discussed with them, and in the composition of which they seemed to have had a share. Thus Dean Farrar and Wilfrid Blunt preferred *Chronicles and Characters*, and thought this volume contained his best poetry; his daughter, Lady Betty Balfour, and Mr Elwin preferred *Glenaveril* and *King Poppy* for the same reason. His own opinions of his work are thus expressed in a letter to Dean Farrar in 1867:

Whilst I am writing, the *alito* of composition and my absorbing interest in the subject of my work make it all appear *couleur de rose* to me. The thing, whilst it is in hand, is my constant companion, "mine old familiar friend", and I feel a sort of personal affection for it. But, as soon as it is done and out of my hand, all the charm vanishes, and nearly all the interest. Scales seem to fall off my eyes; I am disposed to exaggerate all its defects; I fall into profound discouragement about it; and the thought of it soon becomes intolerable to me. Then I try to escape as fast as I can from the pursuing ghost of it, into the shelter of some new and quite different undertaking.

It is interesting to record that though he had received much discouragement himself, he extended the warmest sympathy to any young poet who sought his advice. Mr Wilfrid Blunt often said that he owed everything to my father's sympathy and encouragement at the moment of his life when he was most in need of it.

I must now say something of my father's later work, which belongs more particularly to the period covered by this volume. After a reconciliation with his father, Robert Lytton returned to his profession, and in the years that followed rose to distinction in it. He married happily, moved from one post to another, suffered the affliction of the loss in childhood of two of his sons, and enjoyed for some years the most intimate and affectionate relationship with his father. At the latter's death, in 1873, he succeeded to his title and property. Three years later he was appointed Viceroy of India. This appointment necessitated for the time being the complete abandonment of poetry, and the iron mask was firmly riveted upon the scarce resisting prisoner. Although in the interval between India and Paris the poetic side of his nature was allowed to re-assert itself timidly, the two books which belong to those years have more the character of an apology by an ex-Viceroy who could not help writing poetry, than the assertion by a poet of his right to be heard.

But during the last seventeen years of his life the imprisoned poet was finding expression in a work

which, from the very nature of it, could not be published during its author's life. This work was conceived,
and the first draft of it written, in 1874, a year after his
father's death and two years before he went to India.
It underwent many modifications and was published
after his death, with the title of *King Poppy*. It is a long
poem with a prologue and twelve cantos and it was
made the receptacle for nearly twenty years of all his
poetic ideas. The writing of it afforded him relief from
the irksome duties of his official life, and the ideas
which he packed into it were partly satirical and partly
lyrical. In the composition of *King Poppy* the poet was
allowed a free hand, but only on the condition that both
the poem and its author should be kept hidden from
the world. On this condition the poet was allowed to
pour ridicule upon the world of business and politics,
and weave at will an ideal world of his own, in which
imagination reigned supreme.

In technique and poetic diction the book gained
from the years of work bestowed upon it and the constant revision which it underwent. It contains the
humour of a nature that remained childlike to the last
and the beauty of a soul that belonged to fairyland. The
marginal notes, too, which run throughout the book
reveal their author as a master of sonorous prose. But
if the diction gained, the subject matter of the poem lost
by reason of the time spent upon it. More ideas are
crowded into it than the story warrants; the allegories
are somewhat confused, and the main purpose of the
book is too obscure. The picture I have tried to give of
the imprisonment of my father's poetic temperament
affords the key to a true interpretation of *King Poppy*,
and with the aid of that interpretation I will try and
expound the underlying purpose of the poem.

It is divided into two parts which correspond with

the dual personality of his own nature, to which I have referred. In one is described and ridiculed the world of public life with its unimaginative formulas and its pompous ceremonial, in the other is created a world of fancy for the reception of those imaginative qualities which are gradually being banished from the world of practical men. It must be remembered that the Ambassador and the Viceroy had no part in the composition of this book, beyond providing experiences for the poet to make fun of.

It is entirely the work of the poet who at one time avenges himself upon his gaoler by mockery of the world by which that gaoler is honoured, as for instance when he says:

> 'Tis easy to deceive diplomatists,
> For they, indeed, are trained to be deceived;
> And what would be the use to some of them
> Of their finessing, if it did not dupe
> The deep credulity of all the rest?

or when King Diadummianus says proudly:

> Our gallant army may with confidence
> Be counted on to beat whatever force
> Is weaker or less skilful than its own;
> And more than this no army can achieve;

and at another time reveals the fairyland in which the poet lives, accompanied by

> radiant forms,
> The fields of Fancy roaming, crown'd with flowers
> From faery gardens gloriously adorn'd
> By all the summers of the Golden Age;
> Sweet thoughts that wander, sinless as the streams
> That water'd Paradise, thro' worlds as fair
> And far away as Paradise itself;
> Bright tendernesses ever flowing from
> Unfathomable founts of sympathy;
> Beauty that time hath blemish'd not, and Love
> That life hath not dishonour'd.

One purpose of the book, then, as the author himself defined it, was "to suggest what a poor tissue of unreality human life would be if the much despised influence of the imagination were banished from it"; the other was to create a Kingdom of Consolation to which all those who are wearied with the formalities of the material world, all who suffer and toil, who are neglected or misunderstood—"life's wayworn travellers" —may turn for sympathy and consolation. Taking these two ideas together, the whole poem is worked into a sort of Golden Legend composed of the most venerable and familiar features of traditional fairy tales—an old King, a virgin child, a wrinkled dame, a shepherd boy, a sleeping princess and a palace by the sea. Each of these is worked into the poem as a symbol of some quality of the imagination—ballad poetry, tradition, art, music, love, poetry. On a lonely sea-girt island the Kingdom of Consolation is established by Phantasos— the God of Imagination—who represents the tutelary genius of men's lives. Thither finally he leads the King and the dame, the princess and the shepherd, types that have formerly played their part in the world of reality, but are now banished from it by an unimaginative generation. The material world thus deprived of all its imaginative element is efficiently governed by a puppet—a government machine being all that is necessary to fulfil the essential duties of a monarch.

With this main theme is interwoven another—the legend of the Poppy, and this double legend has somewhat obscured the story. It tells how Pluto, in whose sunless realm nothing flourishes, loved Persephone for the sake of her flowers, and how they all perished, as soon as she entered the Kingdom of the Dead, with the exception of one, a little milk-white poppy bud hid in the bosom of the Queen. Persephone, when she discovers this little one—the last of all her earthly treasures—loves it with a divine compassion and entrusts it to the care of Phantasos. The Poppy, wakening in a land of dreams, recognizes an Empire wider than the world and aspires to become its King. Demeter, in search of her daughter, comes at last to the realm of Phantasos, where the blades of corn in the rural crown of the Goddess recognize the Poppy and hail him as a lost companion. The sound of their rural voices mingles with his dreams and troubles him with a great unrest. He longs for his home on earth, and is restored by Phantasos to the living world as a messenger of consolation to suffering mortals.

> Long on Earth, an Earthly messenger I sought,
> None finding worthy of my vast design,
> Now all that failed me in this flower is found,
> A mortal fitted to receive, preserve,
> And with a boundless prodigality
> Impart to mortals an immortal gift.

The Poppy reappears on earth, and retaining consciousness of his sovereignty over the land of dreams, seeks to impart to those around him the secret of his power. The flowers are content with the beauty which they possess, birds and beasts lack nothing that they cannot obtain from the earth. Man alone appears to be discontented with his lot and to desire something more. It is to man, therefore, that the Poppy turns, hoping by the aid of that potent discontent, which is the chief attribute of humanity, to achieve his object. But he is disregarded and his power unrecognized, because he is insignificant, and so he longs for the symbols of royalty —a robe of purple and a crown of gold.

And thus it comes about, as the story unfolds itself, that the Princess in her island bower, oppressed with the thought of the crown which she will shortly have to wear, is soothed to sleep by the voice of the Poppy growing in the rock on which her palace is built. She lets her crown slip from her hand upon the Poppy's head. Finally the young shepherd boy, gazing down from the summit of the rock, makes a last desperate plunge to attain his ideal, and

> at her feet,
> Whose loveliness his life had from afar
> Divined and sought, death laid him lovingly.

> So the Poppy gain'd
> The kingly symbols he had coveted,
> A purple mantle, and a golden crown.
> But Sorrow gave him one, and Death the other.

The idea of the Poppy and the Kingdom of Consolation arose, the author said himself, from a vein of fancy which first suggested his fables. He once defined fable as "the border line between Dream and Humour", and in the Legend of Fable in *After Paradise* appears the first expression of the idea, more fully worked out later in *King Poppy*. Speaking of the life of Adam and Eve after the Fall, he tells how suspicion arose between man and beast, and how, confidence once gone, the beasts not only turned in fear from man, but turned upon each other, and thus the world became a universal battle-plain. But one refuge still is left for the gentle beasts of Paradise that were once man's familiar intimates. The Seraphim in pity sowed in the wilderness a seed from the flowers of Paradise, from which a great forest sprang up. Thither these gentle beasts departed, "and the name of their unfading forest home is Fable".

> There Justice reigns revered; there Pity shields
> An else defenceless flock; and there do they
> Their joint tribunal hold, where every cause
> That in this mortal world hath gone astray,
> And honest trial missed, by lovelier laws

Than ours is welcomed to impartial test,
All cases pleaded, be they what they may,
All rights established, and all wrongs redressed.
How far away it seems, how far away!

The conception of the forest of Fable, more fully developed into the Kingdom of the Poppy, is the creation of a new Paradise. It is not the land of shades which the Greeks pictured in their Elysian Fields; it is not the heaven towards which the Saint aspires, not the Eden forfeited by man in the dawn of creation. It belongs not to the past nor to the future, but is an ideal world accompanying the present, a world in which mankind may rest awhile and then pass on refreshed, a world in which failure and disappointment are unknown, a world of realization without effort, of enjoyment without sin.

The allegories in the poem are not very clear, but all the characters and the incidents have some allegorical significance. The Poppy's Kingdom of Consolation is meant to be something more than the analgesia induced by a narcotic. It represents a life inspired by imagination, soothed by sympathy, beautified by art, music and poetry. When Wordsworth wrote,

One impulse from a vernal wood
    May teach you more of man,
Of moral evil and of good,
    Than all the sages can,

his words had no truth from the point of view of science, no application to the experience of unimaginative man. But to the poet, who can interpret experience poetically, his words expressed a stimulating and illuminating truth.

In my father's poem Phantasos represents the inspiring divinity, the Poppy the inspired mortal. Of Phantasos he wrote, "he it is who taught the sirens the songs they sang to Ulysses, and made Mercutio acquainted with Queen Mab. Led by him, Alexander invaded the East, and Columbus discovered the West. He was the first Free-Mason, the architect of Solomon's temple, and hath left the trace of his handiwork among the shrines of Christendom, and the minarets of Islam. Sometimes graceful, sometimes grotesque; at one while sublime, at another absurd, his form is never twice the same. Many are mystified by his antics and exasperated by his whims. But to all who recognise his divinity his presence imparts freedom and joy". In fact, wherever there is true greatness, there will his influence be found. The Poppy, on the other hand, is King only of a world of feeling and he is the instrument whereby the God of Imagination offers comfort and sympathy to those who suffer or who have desires which this world cannot satisfy. He is the link between the real and the ideal, essentially mortal, yet full of the qualities which enable men to rise above themselves and their surroundings.

In my father's nature there were two strains, both of which found expression in this book. The first was a strain of pessimism which caused him to sympathize with failure and to seek consolation in the field of imagination—this is illustrated, as I have shown, in the Kingdom of the Poppy, "the fairest and the freest Kingdom upon earth", in which "all are dreamers, all are children, even the busy, even the old", and whose monarch is described as:

> Fate's master, yet man's ministering friend,
> Guide of stray'd Love's lone footsteps to the goal
> That lost on earth is in his realm recover'd,
> Feaster of famish'd hearts, rebuilder bright
> Of ruin'd fortunes, pain's victorious foe,
> Grief's comforter, joy's guardian.

The second strain was one of puritan asceticism

which had inspired the lines in the tale of King Usinara in *Glenaveril*:

> Duty's whole lesson thou hast learn'd at last
> Which in self-sacrifice begins and ends.

This strain finds expression in *King Poppy* in a separate allegory of the robe and crown. The power most easily recognized in this world is temporal power —money, the sword, the sceptre of Kings—and such power is usually obtained by the ruthless crushing of all weaker impediments in the path of its progress. But when spiritual power wishes to obtain the symbols of recognition from temporal power, it can only do so by a renunciation of all temporal gifts, and the readiness to endure martyrdom. Napoleon won his crown and sceptre by marching through blood and tears, winning glory through ruin. Christ won his glory on the Cross. Sympathy, above all human excellencies, entails suffering. This the Poppy learnt in his encounter with Typhoon; he had to win his crown and robe through suffering. As Favonius said to him when he rescued him from the fury of the storm wind,

> Never, child, never shall the hands that grasp
> The globe and sceptre, yield thee crown or robe,
> For gold is for the great, for the supreme
> The purple. Neither Pomp nor Glory grant
> To thee their emblems. But the little hand
> Of childhood opens lightly, and its gifts
> Are tendernesses which are given ungrudged.

From the hand of childhood, therefore, that shuns the harshness of unimaginative fact and believes in the truth of fairy tales, the Poppy receives the diadem of innocent delight, and from the love that leaves all for the attainment of impossible ideals, the robe of beauty —"such robe and crown as never King yet wore".

I have spoken of my father's poetry and tried to give some idea of the purpose which inspired it. I have said nothing of his public life, for that is written in the records of his time. He rose to the top of his profession and died in office. He also died pen in hand, and his last words "of love's good faith" were still wet upon the paper when death came to him, without warning and without pain.

The sadness of the poems in his last volume *Marah* which concludes with these words is explained by the fact that the worldly success which he achieved never compensated him for the sacrifice of his art which it involved. Many men have professed to despise honours and dignities which they have not achieved, power and influence which they have not enjoyed, but my father was a rare example of a man who achieved all that worldly ambition could desire, and found it unsatisfying. His verdict on life, when he came to the end of it, was—

> What is Life? The incessant desiring
> Of a joy that is never acquired;
> And instead of that joy, the acquiring
> Of enjoyments that are not desired.

As his friend, Wilfrid Blunt, truly said in an article published soon after his death, he remained to the end "essentially the man of feeling, of wit, the hunter of the ideal, the dreamer of romantic dreams, the lyric poet he was born". The truest portrait of him as he was known to his contemporaries—a man of intimate friendships, of sparkling humour, of overflowing sympathy, of exquisite tact and of profound knowledge of the world, is to be found not in his despatches, nor in his poems, but in his private correspondence which was unique, even in an age before the typewriter destroyed the art of letter writing. Only a fraction of his letters has been published, but even that fraction should suffice to enable the world to admit the truth of his friend's tribute:

His work is imperishable, but alas, how shall we perpetuate the memory of his personality which has perished from among us? This was more wonderful and rare than all his work. We can only weep and hold it dear to our hearts, for in truth he was the brightest, best and most beloved of men.

THOMAS EDWARD BROWN

Schoolmaster & Poet

By FREDERICK S. BOAS

In choosing Thomas Edward Brown as the subject of this paper, I have had a double aim. I am seeking to make a contribution to the Centenary commemoration of Brown, which fell on 5 May 1930. He is much more to me than a Victorian worthy. As a boy in his house at Clifton from 1877 to 1881 I was brought into close contact with him at an impressionable age. Through a younger brother and two nephews my family connexion with "Brown's House" has extended over nearly half a century, and I have recalled elsewhere some of my early personal memories of Brown as a Housemaster.[1] Here I am attempting to deal with the broader aspects of his scholastic and poetic work. And I thus come to the second object of my paper. The greater number of Brown's poems were published between 1881 and 1893. It was the same period that set the final seal upon his work as a schoolmaster. He may therefore, I believe, be fitly included among the representative figures of the eighteen-eighties to whom the Royal Society of Literature is during this session giving its special consideration.

Thomas Edward Brown was born on 5 May 1830, at Douglas, where his father, Robert Brown, was incumbent of St Matthew's Church. His mother was Dorothy Thompson, born in the Isle of Man, but of

[1] In *T. E. Brown: A Memorial Volume*, edited by Sir Arthur Quiller-Couch for the Isle of Man Centenary Committee.

Scottish extraction. There was thus a mingling in him
of Manx and Scottish, Keltic and Saxon, blood. He
was the sixth of her children, and when he was two
years old his father was made vicar of Kirk Braddan,
near Douglas. Here Brown's early years from 1832 to
1847 were spent, and to them he looks back in the
poem *Braddan Vicarage*, wondering

> if in that far isle,
> Some child is growing now, like me
> When I was child: care-pricked, yet healed the while
> With balm of rock and sea.

That healing influence of rock and sea was to be with
Brown to the last.

So too, in spite of Oxford and Clifton, the sense of
England as an alien, dimly descried, shore,

> The land of Edwards and of Henries, scourge
> Of insolent foemen, at the most
> Faint caught where Cumbria looms a geographic ghost.

And another dominant element in the racial medley
of these formative years was the dear brave old Scotch-
man, the man-servant John McCullogh, the Cove-
nanter who prayed that his Episcopalian "Maister", the
vicar, might stand fast on the rock of sure foundation,
to whom Brown paid such a nobly tender and humorous
tribute in the verses *Old John*:

> Old John, if in the battle of this life
>   I have not sought your precepts to fulfil,
> If ever I have stirred ignoble strife,
>   If ever struck foul blow, as bent to kill,
> Not conquer, by the love you bear me still,
>   O! intercede that I may be forgiven.
> Stern Protestant—*not pray to saints? I will*
>   To you in heaven.

At the age of fifteen Brown entered King William's
College, which has played such a great part in the

educational and cultural life of the Isle of Man. Among his contemporaries were F. W. Farrar, Thomas Fowler and J. M. Wilson, who says even of those early days that "wherever Brown was, life was fullest". At school he took a second prize for a poem, the first prize being carried off by Farrar.

In October 1849 he went to Oxford, in the position of a Servitor at Christ Church. The Servitor was a relic, soon to be abolished, of eighteenth-century class-distinctions at Oxford. The young men of wealth and fashion who held the privileged rank of Gentlemen Commoners were attended by Servitors, who, as has been said, cleaned their shoes and wrote their exercises, as the price of getting a University education.

Servitors, as is recorded by Sir Charles Mallet in his *History of the University of Oxford,* had risen to be Arch-bishops and Heads of Colleges and had included in their ranks George Whitefield and Samuel Wesley. And the position in Brown's day was less menial than in the eighteenth century. But it was galling to a proud and sensitive spirit, and it stood in the way of his career. For when in 1853 he took a Double First his servitor-ship was considered a bar to his election to a Studentship at Christ Church. Hence the night after the announce-ment of his Double First was one of the most intensely miserable he was ever called upon to endure. In the fol-lowing year he was elected a Fellow of Oriel, "the summit of an Oxford man's ambition". But the iron had entered into his soul, and I have little doubt that the Christ Church episode strengthened in him the ingrained Keltic antipathy to the conventional rule of life of the English governing class to which his poems often bear witness.

Hence it is not surprising that he "never took kindly to the life of an Oxford Fellow", and soon returned to his Island as Vice-Principal of King William's College.

It was while he held this post that in 1857 he married his cousin, Miss Stowell, in the church of Kirk Maughold so fervently invoked in the *Epistola* to his colleague Dakyns. It was doubtless the growing responsibility of a family that led Brown, as with so many others, to seek professional promotion. He had taken deacon's orders, but parochial work would never have been to his taste. So he left the Island to take up the headmastership of the Crypt School at Gloucester in 1861. The new venture was not successful. There is slight record of this period, but probably the administrative duties which fall to the lot of a Headmaster were not to Brown's taste. He could, however, indulge his love of music. "The Festival", he writes to his mother on 21 September 1862, "was a great treat. We enjoyed the Oratorio very much. It was my favourite, the *Elijah*." And one at least of his pupils at Gloucester, W. E. Henley, was to retain an ineffaceable memory of him, and "forty years on" to pay a tribute to his genius in an Introduction to the second edition of his Collected Poems (1901).

It was through his old schoolfellow, J. M. Wilson, that Brown was enabled to move to another, more congenial, sphere in the west of England. John Percival, of Rugby, was appointed in 1864 Headmaster of the new foundation, Clifton College. Wilson, who was also on the Rugby Staff, suggested Brown as suitable to take the Modern Side at Clifton, and asked him to his lodgings at Rugby to meet Percival:

I warned Brown that he must be on his good behaviour. He did not take my advice. Never was Brown so great. I still remember the Manx songs with their odd discordant pianoforte accompaniment and final shriek; the paradoxes; the torrent of fun and talk; and the stories.

Next morning Wilson asked Percival, not without anxiety, what he thought of Brown. The shrewd North countryman gave a short but sufficient answer, "Oh, he'll do".

Percival himself many years afterwards remembered another interview at Oxford when he met Brown "standing at the corner of St Mary's Entry, in a somewhat Johnsonian attitude, foursquare, his hands deep in his pockets to keep himself still, and looking decidedly *volcanic*". It is a sharp-bitten sketch, and the epithet *volcanic* is amazingly apt, at first acquaintance.

So Brown came to Clifton, to remain there for twenty-eight years as Head of the Modern Side and Housemaster. After the Gloucester episode headships had no temptation for him. Indeed in the more conventional interpretation, it would not, in my opinion, be true to say that Brown was a born schoolmaster. The routine of school life had little attraction for him, and I don't think that he had much interest in the everyday small concerns that mean so much to the average boy. Even in the letters or the poems concerned with Clifton there is curiously little reference to boys and their doings. Brown was primarily a "fisher of men". He was too large-hearted and too sincere not to "do his job", with his might and with fervour, but it was avowedly not the first thing with him. His attitude is explicitly set forth in a letter of 21 September 1893, after he had retired, to an old Cliftonian who hesitated to take up school work, because it would not give him leisure for literary pursuits:

My plan always was to recognise two lives as necessary—the one the outer Kapelistic life of drudgery, the other the inner and cherished life of the spirit. It is true that the one has a tendency to kill the other, but it must not, and you must see that it does not.

It's an awfully large order, but we really need three lives.... The pedagogic is needful for bread and butter, also for a certain form of joy; of the inner life you know what I think; the social life is required of us and must be managed.

"Needful for bread and butter, also for a certain form of joy." There, in a nutshell, is Brown's conception of the pedagogic life. The joy was in the larger aspects of the scholastic career, the fellowship with colleagues of kindred minds and tastes, the power of influencing young and receptive spirits, the communing as a teacher with fine literature and high historic issues. I cannot but feel, therefore, that in the too famous poem, *Clifton*, Brown has done injustice to himself and to his environment. It is important to notice that the earliest MS. is dated 1869, and that the first stanza then ran:

> I'm here at Clifton, grinding at the mill
>> My feet for six long barren years have trod,
> But there are rocks and waves at Scarlett still,
>> And gorse runs riot in Glen Chass—thank God!

It is possible to understand the poem as an outbreak of a Manxman's nostalgia amid the tamer beauties of the West of England, and of a mood of depression during the pioneer days of a new institution, with deeper intimacies yet scarcely formed.

> Alert, I seek exactitude of rule,
>> I step, and square my shoulders with the squad;
> But there are blaeberries on old Barrule,
>> And Langness has its heather still—thank God!

> .   .   .   .   .

> O broken life! O wretched bits of being,
>> Unrhythmic, patched, the even and the odd!
> But Bradda still has lichens worth the seeing,
>> And thunder in her caves—thank God! thank God!

Was it not misleading to publish the poem for the first time in 1893, with "thrice nine" barren years substituted for the original "six", as if it were Brown's considered verdict on his historic career at Clifton where, while one of the "squad", he had written the poems that will keep his name for ever alive, and had found true brethren of his soul?[1] Such were S. T. Irwin, the editor of his Letters, fine scholar and lover of the Muses, ever held by myself in grateful remembrance; H. G. Dakyns, translator of Xenophon, the "true Dakyns" to whom is addressed that "Epistola" in verse, one of the most deeply felt and moving of Brown's poems; E. M. Oakeley, who has recorded that in their friendship, which had no break from 1867 till "the great break" in October 1897, "music was a chief cornerstone"; J. C. Tarver, "dear Tarver", with whom he discussed modern French literature, Maupassant, Flaubert and Daudet; and F. M. Bartholomew, in whose lower-fourth form I made my entry, at the belated age of fifteen, into Clifton scholastic life.

There is nothing finer in Brown's letters than his tribute to this best type of duty-loving public-school master after his death:

> Such a combination of virtues I never expect to see again in any man as God gave us in Bartholomew.... Simple and sage—simplicity, I imagine, the grand note, simplicity of motive rather than of action, a very deep and rare simplicity. His loss is beyond all losses that I can conceive. Clifton was twined around his very heart: his life was Clifton.

And the sonnet appended to this letter proves that Brown, who in 1869 could speak of "grinding at the mill" at Clifton, had realized a quarter of a century later

---

[1] I have to thank Miss Ethel Brown, a daughter of the poet, who was present when this paper was read before the Royal Society of Literature, for sending me afterwards, and allowing me to print here, an unpublished extract from Brown's Diary, written after his summer holiday in Keswick in 1891, which is conclusive evidence of his real feeling for Clifton towards the close of his career there:

"Clifton, after all, holds what has been most precious to me in my life, to Clifton then let me devote what remains."

that the school was the reflection of a Platonic arche-
type:

> and so you constant taught
> This earthly Clifton, loved Bartholomew.
> Bides yet a Clifton in the chiefest Heaven,
> The αὐτο-Clifton God has made for us,
> Serenely placed, divinely bright and fair.
> Sometimes unto our noblest hearts 'tis given
> To see its circuit broad and luminous:
> He saw it, and he found it, and he's there.

Among others not so prominent in Brown's letters and
poems who helped to model the earthly Clifton nearer
to the "idea laid up in Heaven" were such original
thinkers as T. W. Dunn and C. E. Vaughan, scientific
pioneers like W. T. Tilden, W. A. Shenstone, and
G. H. Wollaston, and the heads of the "military and
engineering side", H. S. Hall and F. H. Stevens. With
such a staff of "all the talents" and with Brown as chief
lieutenant on the Modern Side, the two successive
Headmasters, Percival and Wilson, made it their aim
to combine in Clifton the traditional ideals and studies
of the older public schools with the newer subjects that
were claiming a place in the curriculum, and with the
specialized work necessary for entrance into the Services and other professional careers. The same aim,
broadly speaking, was being pursued in the other chief
scholastic foundations of the mid-nineteenth century,
Marlborough, Haileybury, Wellington, Radley and
Rossall. The second half of that century is therefore one
of the fateful periods in English education, and by the
'eighties the new movement may be said to have come
to maturity. With the twentieth century arose another
problem, the expansion of Secondary School education
in the day schools.

The best proof of the stimulus of the Clifton teaching
is found in the long roll of worthies who have passed

from the school. It has given to the army Earl Haig,
Field-Marshal Birdwood, Sir Francis and Sir George
Younghusband; to Parliament the late Speaker, Mr
J. H. Whitley, Lord Buxton and Sir Thomas Inskip;
to the Universities Sir Herbert Warren, Sir Charles
Firth, Sir Arthur Quiller-Couch and Professor H. H.
Turner; to Literature and the Bar Sir Henry and Sir
Francis Newbolt. The list might easily be extended,
but I will add only two who were members of Brown's
own House, Charles Cannan, the late distinguished
Secretary of the Clarendon Press, and Dr A. G. Little,
the well-known authority on mediaeval history.

Thus we come back to Brown himself. As I was on
the Classical Side I never had him as a form-master,
and cannot speak of his teaching from personal experience. There is a remarkable tribute to it by a well-
known old Cliftonian, Dr Horatio F. Brown, who
attended one of his history classes.

His was the most vivid teaching I ever received: great width of view
and poetical, almost passionate, power of presentment. For example,
we were reading Froude's *History*, and I shall never forget how it was
Brown's words, Brown's voice, not the historian's, that made me feel
the great democratic function which the monasteries performed in
England; the view became alive in his mouth....I should say that his
educational function lay in "widening"...there was a whiff of the
great world brought in by him.

And it is a different testimony to Brown's versatile
teaching power that my brother-in-law, Dr S. G. Owen,
though primarily a classic, attended a class that he
held in Hebrew, and thus won a prize for Divinity.

But though Brown was not my form-master, I, of
course, heard his talks to our House, his speeches at the
annual House Suppers, and (as a VIth form boy) his
conversation when he came in to mid-day dinner in
"hall". In everything that he said he showed the com-

mand of apt and easy vocabulary which is familiar to
readers of his letters. One episode will bear repetition,
though Brown was here addressing not his own House
only but all the boarders at one of the Sunday evening
gatherings in Big School, which were among the
pleasantest features in our life at Clifton. He took
"Hymns" as his subject, and perturbed some of his
colleagues by giving play to his caustic wit. I can still
remember him rolling out, in parody of an easily
recognizable type of hymn, the couplet

> And for every pot of jam
> Praise, O praise, the great I Am.

He gave somewhat faint praise to Heber's "From
Greenland's icy mountains", which we happened to
have sung before his address, and denounced its musical
setting. The memory of that Sunday evening, in or
about 1880, rises before me as I read Brown's letter to
Irwin of 3 December 1893: "Religious poetry lies open
to so many dangers. *Hymns Ancient and Modern* show
the ghastly results only too manifest". And while ex-
tolling Heber's lines beginning, "Thou art gone to the
grave, but we will not deplore thee", he could "spare
the buoyancy" which might have been utilized in
another "From Greenland's icy mountains".

But even in that old enemy of mine, who does not recognise the
artist? "Waft, waft, ye winds, His story"—no—then I give it up.
A true child of genius for all that. He did not live to be a Charles
Wesley, nor could he perhaps ever have become that. One Charles
Wesley, sir, and no other.

I wonder, as he wrote this characteristic appreciation
of the best poetic work of "the old Evangelical School",
in contrast with the insincerity and sentimentalism of
some other hymnologists, if his mind went back to that
memorable Sunday evening in Big School.

But there are some Saturday evenings in our own House which have even a better title to remembrance. More than once Brown delighted, and somewhat mystified, us by reading out, with all his peculiar force and fire, narrative poems in an unfamiliar dialect. He said nothing about their authorship, and it was only after I had left Clifton, that I learnt that the boys of Brown's House—*O fortunatos nimium, sua si bona norint*—had had the privilege of hearing some of the *Fo'c's'le Yarns* from the lips of their creator, and in part before they had reached the outside world. For though *Betsy Lee* had appeared in 1873, and other poems had been printed in a local newspaper or in semi-private booklets, it was not till 1881 (in which year my life in Brown's House ended) that Brown made a definite approach to the general body of readers by the publication of the first series of *Fo'c's'le Yarns*. In this volume *Betsy Lee* was reprinted, with three other narrative tales in verse, *Christmas Rose, Captain Tom and Captain Hugh*, and *Tommy Big-Eyes*. A second series followed in 1887, entitled *The Doctor and other Poems*, and a third in 1889, *The Manx Witch and other Poems*.

In *Fo'c's'le Yarns* we have Brown's most distinctive, though perhaps not his finest, poetic achievement. It was his aim

> To sing a song shall please my countrymen;
> To unlock the treasures of the Island heart.

The stranger, if he lent a favouring ear, would be welcomed:

> Natheless, for mine own people do I sing,
> And use the old familiar speech.

This speech is a form of local dialect. I don't know how philologists would label it, but it may be broadly described as a homely type of vernacular English with an admixture of phrases derived from the original Manx tongue of the Island. It is not a speech that appeals to everyone. Thus Professor Saintsbury in the *Cambridge History of English Literature*, vol. XIII, ch. VI, assails it as "not a real dialect, but an ugly or bastard patois or rather jargon of broken-down Celtic and the vulgarest English". And even those who cannot accept so harsh a judgment must admit that Anglo-Manx is not such a natural instrument of the Muses as that Anglo-Irish speech, whose liquid rhythms began, also in the 'eighties, to find their mouthpiece in Mr W. B. Yeats. But it is the most convincing proof of Brown's genius that from what on other lips might have been a "scrannel pipe" he drew such authentic and such varied harmonies. And all this in one of the simplest of metrical forms, the rhyming couplet with four beats, which is used throughout the three series of *Fo'c's'le Yarns*. With skilful and subtle art, which is hidden under the home-spun diction, Brown continually varies the rhythm of his couplets and prevents it from becoming jog-trot or monotonous. With apparently effortless ease he can make it completely malleable. It adjusts itself, without jolt or jar, to all purposes—narrative, description, dialogue, reflection, characterization. That is the hall-mark of the born story-teller in verse from the time of Chaucer downward, and it is a gift that the Muse has too often withheld from her otherwise favoured children.

The Yarns are held together by the figure of Tom Baynes, "old salt, old rip, old friend", into whose mouth they are put. Outwardly he was modelled on a Peel sailor, but in essence he is Brown himself, or that part of him which was "the Kelt a good deal hardened and corrupted by the Saxon". These are his words in a letter of 4 November 1882 to J. R. Mozley, which continues: "That is Tom Baynes, that is myself in fact. I never stopped for a moment to think what Tom Baynes should be like; he simply is I...so when I am alone I think and speak to myself always as he does". The events and experiences associated with Tom Baynes in *Betsy Lee* and other of the Yarns are, of course, imaginary, but the "old salt" in his humour, his tenderness, his breadth of sympathy, his justice of outlook on men and things is a dramatic projection of his creator, who was known (I am told) as Tom Brown in the Island. Don't we hear the very voice of Brown when Baynes in *Betsy Lee* cries out against the rules and regulations of a "Sailors' Home"?

> A bell for dinner and a bell for tay,
> And a bell to sing and a bell to pray,
> And a bell for this and a bell for that,
> And "wipe your feet upon the mat!"
> And the rules hung up; and fined if you're late,
> And a chap like a bobby shuttin' the gate—
> It isn' raisonable, it isn':
> They calls it a Home, I calls it a Pris'n.

And near to Tom Baynes stands "Pazon" Gale, a brother in spirit, however apart in calling and class. Pazon Gale was drawn mainly from Mr Corrin, vicar of Kirk Christ, Rushen, in the South of the Island, whom Brown called "quite the dearest and noblest old man I ever met". But there were blended in the character traits from Brown's father, as Wordsworth's "Happy Warrior" unites features of his sailor brother and of Nelson. He is one of that noble company of the cloth, Chaucer's "povre persoun", Fielding's Parson Adams, Goldsmith's Vicar of Wakefield, who are in the world yet are unspotted by it. Such are not all who wear clerical livery:

> For there's pazons now that's mortal proud,
> And some middlin' humble, that's allowed.

And there's pazons partikler about their clothes,
And rings on their fingers and bells on their toes:
And there's pazons that doesn' know your names,
"Shut the gate, my man", and all them games.
And there's pazons *too* free—I've heard one cuss
As hard and as hearty as one of us.
But Pazon Gale—now I'll give you his size,
He was a simple pazon, and lovin' and wise.
That's what he was, and quiet uncommon,
And never said much to man nor woman;
Only the little he said was meat
For a hungry heart, and soft and sweet,
The way he said it.

Round Tom Baynes and Pazon Gale jostle in the
various Yarns a motley crowd of Manx sailors, miners
and farmers, doctors and lawyers, mothers and wives,
girls of high and low degree, "childer", and such
strongly individual figures as the Manx witch and the
hypocritical "Local". It is only for natives of the Isle
of Man to say how far local types are here embodied,
but even the "stranger" can realize the vigour and
variety of the portraiture. And though he may have
seen little or nothing of the Island, he can appreciate
how skilfully Brown varies the scenic background of
the tales from Douglas to Castletown, from the Sherragh
Vane "up Sulby glen" to the Laxdale lead-mines, with
now and then a shift to the mainland, Liverpool or
London, and occasional glimpses of still more foreign
parts.

But with all their differences of detail the chief
Yarns have the same basic theme of star-crossed love—
the rivalries of wooers, the pride and credulity of
parents, the machinations of cheats and hypocrites,
delay or defeat, the union of twin souls. Thus is the
first of the Yarns, *Betsy Lee*. Tom Baynes has loved the
girl from childhood, but when her parents suddenly

come into money they encourage the suit of the spruce lawyer's clerk who has brought the good news. By a lying charge of immorality the clerk forces Tom to take ship for abroad, and by a report of his death during his two years' absence kills the broken-hearted Betsy. At her grave Tom meets his treacherous rival, and is about to strike him down, when he sees in his eyes that he too is broken-hearted:

> And he looked—aw, the look—"Come, give us your hand!"
> I says—"*Forgive you?* I can! I can!
> For the love that was so terrible strong,
> For the love that made you do the wrong".

Love, if only it be real, however it may have gone astray, has still its indefeasible claim and reconciling power.

In *The Manx Witch* the course of true love is hindered by superstition and spite. The two miners, Jack Pentreath and Harry Creer, are rivals for the hand of Nessy Brew, who favours Jack. But the girl's aunt, "Missthriss" Banks, a woman of doubtful reputation, "the blackest wutch on the Islan'", comes between the pair with her evil arts, and persuades Harry that it is he whom Nessy loves. This leads to a fight between the suitors, stopped by Tom Baynes, who advises them to shoot the witch with a silver bullet made of shillings melted down. Though this does not work, she disappears mysteriously, and it is not till two years afterwards that her body is found in a disused shaft of the mine, into which she had fallen. Not till then does Nessy yield to Jack's entreaties, and marries him with Harry as best man.

The poem is, in the main, compact of dark moods and darker arts, but there are flashes throughout of Brown's more jovial humour, as in the account of a lovers' society, with its strict code among rival wooers.

> Now it appears they were signin'
> Articles—I think there were nine in—
> *Rules*—is it? I don't care—
> Rules then—that they'd run it fair;
> No chap to take advantage lek
> Over the rest; and the smallest speck
> Lek it would be of encouragement—
> Lek a word or a nod—then this here gent
> To kermoonicate it to the lot
> Under penalties to be shot,
> For all I know, or hung as high
> As Haman, if he tould a lie.
> Honour bright! I seen the book
> Years after, and even a look
> Was down, and how much was countin' for it
> 'Longside of the chap that gorrit.

A look with a smile in chapel from the fair one counted two marks, while her sharing of a hymn-book with him gained the lucky gallant no less than seven.

Captain Tom and Captain Hugh has in it some of the features of a home-spun *Romeo and Juliet*, with the rivalries, and cross-purposes, of two Manx houses. The Castletown captains have been inseparables from boyhood—

> Where the one was, the other would be,
> And stickin' mortal close, and backin'
> One another up, whatever was actin—

and have married two sisters living in cottages side by side. All is harmony till

> The years went by, and the childher grew
> And the ouldest boy of Captain Hugh
> Fell in love with the ouldest gel
> Of Captain Tom—aw, terrible!

The two mothers are delighted, and so is Captain Tom, when he gets the news on coming back from Ireland:

> he slapped the thigh
> And come ashore in a blaze of joy.

But Captain Hugh hears it from the two mothers with
chilling indifference and silence:

> just a spit,
> And a puff o' the pipe to see was he lit,
> And his hand on his chin and his eye on the say;
> So the women had to go away.

This is the first rift in the lute. And there is worse to
follow. Captain Tom is chosen, in preference to Captain
Hugh, to sail a new schooner, and Hugh, in the bitterness of his heart, and egged on by drunken uncle
Ballachrink, takes to racing the schooner with his
smack. Obsessed with a jealousy that has turned to
madness, he refuses in a gale to reef the sails of his
craft, knocks Ballachrink overboard, and grapples with
his son, Hughie, till the smack founders. Captain Tom
rescues Hughie, but Captain Hugh defeats the attempts to save himself. And with what may be called an
inverted *Romeo and Juliet* conclusion, it is over the
bodies, so to speak, of the elders that the lovers are at
last united:

> And poor Annie, you know, and the fond she was
> Of Uncle Hugh; but lost is lost,
> And that's a fact, and, do what you will,
> The world must go on, and it's good and it's ill—
> So married the chap, and what'd prevent her?
> Married him that very winter.

In *The Doctor*, as in *Betsy Lee*, parental pride and
tyranny bring love to a tragic close, but the tale moves
in a higher social sphere. And though the Prologue and
the later Acts of the drama are laid in the Island, the
central, significant episodes take place in London. It
was these that had turned the charming, clever young
Dr Bell into the broken-down, drunken medico who
had found a retreat in a lonely Manx farm. He had
been introduced when a young practitioner by a doctor

of established reputation to a baronet, who would not dispense with his services. Sir John was a widower, with an only daughter, who fell in love with Dr Bell. His older colleague, inflamed with jealousy, spies upon the pair, and brings the baronet on the scene when they are having a secret rendezvous at a ball:

> And then, "Look there, Sir John, look there!"
> *Look there*, indeed. Ah, the close! the close!
> And the four lips makin' the one red rose—
> Somethin' worth lookin' at, I'll swear!
> Aw, a beautiful pair! a beautiful pair!
> "Rascal, scoundrel, villain, thief",
> Aw, the rose was broke—aw, every leaf.

The girl is banished to the Continent, where her lover seeks in vain to find her. He retires to a small farm in the Isle of Man, and marries the farmer's daughter who nurses him to life through an epidemic of cholera. As the years pass his wife dies, his elder children leave him, but the youngest, Kitty, is the pride of his life. One day a yacht puts into the bay and the Doctor is called to a lady dangerously ill aboard.

> But when she seen him she gave a cry
> And "Oh you're come to see me die!
> Oh, Edward! oh, perhaps it's as well—
> Oh, Edward Bell! Oh, Edward Bell!"
> And he fell on his knees, and he bowed his head;
> "Harriet! Harriet!" he said;
> But the Lady Harriet was dead!

But again all is not lost. There is love at first sight between Kitty and Lady Harriet's son, Harry Combe. He was back in the Island the very next month,

> And not long about it and axed her straight
> Would she be after marrying him.

These illustrations from four of the Yarns, though they do not cover the full range of Brown's narrative art, indicate his methods and leading motives as a story-teller in verse. He deals with primitive emotions, and elemental things—love and hate, jealousy and fear, broken hearts and shattered lives. These modern tales of Manxland have something of the stark quality of the mediaeval sagas of the greater island in the Arctic seas. But they close on the notes of forgiveness, reconciliation and hope.

But the Doric flute of the Island was not Brown's only poetic instrument. There have been singers, of whom Burns is the most illustrious, who can make immortal music in their native dialect, but who become flat when they turn to standard English. Brown was *doctus utriusque linguae*. His purely English poems show him as master of an Attic style, lucid, polished, fastidiously exact. I doubt if anyone would have believed, on purely internal evidence, that the writer who had been content with the four-beat couplet for thousands of lines in *Fo'c's'le Yarns* could have shown in the more limited field of his English verse such an astonishing virtuosity of craftsmanship. Brown seems able to do what he likes with words, rhymes, and metre. There are the eight-lined stanzas of *Old John*, with their arresting short double-rhyming line at the close of each stanza; the ten-lined stanzas, with their intricate rhyming scheme, addressed to his godson "Childe Dakyns"; the more fluid structure of the strophes to the "Childe's" father, with the haunting refrain, "Three places, Dakyns", or of the metaphysical musings in *Dartmoor*, and of the sketches and character-studies in *Roman Women*. Here and elsewhere the rhythm is fitted to the mood, and the right word is chosen with a felicity that owes most to Brown's inborn flair for verbal expression and something to his classical training and that assiduous study of French and Italian literature to which his letters bear witness.

A few of the English poems, including *My Garden*, *The Schooner* and *Opifex* have won their way into the anthologies and are widely known. I have spoken above of some of those that deal with early memories, with Manx scenes and characters, with Clifton friendships, with visits to Clevedon, Lynton and elsewhere. It had not yet become the fashion for schoolmasters to spend their holidays in Swiss winter sports or Mediterranean cruises. And in spite of Brown's enthusiasm for continental writers, he did not often cross the Channel. But a visit to Rome in the winter of 1879–80 resulted later in one of his most characteristic poems. It is a series of sketches of "Roman Women" with whom this "merman from the Northern sea" became as enraptured as with the tongue they spoke—among them the woman

> Round-ribbed, large-flanked,
> Broad-shouldered (God be thanked!),

who is bidden cling to the man she loves, "grow to him, make noble boys for Italy". And another, how different!

> Ah! naughty little girl,
> With teeth of pearl,
> You exquisite little brute,
> So young, so dissolute....
> Ah, child, don't scoff—
> Yes, yes, I see—you lovely wretch, be off!

And then in cruel contrast with his tenderness to all types of Roman womanhood, his caustic exhortation to the Englishwoman whom he meets on the Pincian Hill, the embodiment of all the conventions:

> I know your mechanism well-adjusted,
> I see your mind and body have been trusted
> To all the proper people:
> I see you straight as is a steeple;

> I see you are not old;
> I see you are a rich man's daughter;
> I see you know the use of gold,
> But also know the use of soap-and-water;
> And yet I love you not, nor ever can—
> Distinguished woman on the Pincian!

It is true that we owe her a debt for that, in our bleak island,

> You gave us stalwart scions,
> Suckled the young sea-lions...
> For this and all His mercies—stay at home!
> Here are the passion-flowers!
> Here are the sunny hours!
> O Pincian woman, do not come to Rome!

We seem almost to hear an echo of the voice of Byron, the exile in Italy, arraigning the fossilized religiosity of English society under the Regency. The Pincian woman is to Brown the type of the formalism which was in his eyes the antithesis to, the negation of, what was truly spiritual. It was not by precept and rule, it was not even through the working of the intellect, that the ideal was reached. As he wrote in arresting words, "genius is intellectual not moral. For instance it seems probable that the greatest genius in the Universe is the Devil".

Of Brown's mental wrestlings with ultimate problems there is a significant record in the poem *Dartmoor*, where "Homo", the man, as he gazes upon a gorgeous sunset, agonizes to know what it means:

> Is it ironical, a fool enigma,
> This sunset show?...
> Or is it more?
> Ah, is it, is it more?

He reproaches the Creator for His tantalizing reticence:

> Call you this *speech*?
> O God, if it be speech,

Speak plainer,
If Thou would'st teach
That I shall be a gainer!
The age of picture-alphabets is gone
We are not now so weak;
We are too old to con
The horn-book of our youth. Time lags—
O, rip this obsolete blazon into rags!
And speak! O, speak!

And in the second part of the poem the "Demiourgos", the maker of the Universe, does speak, not to solve the riddle, but in strangely plaintive accents to remind the Man that he is too self-centred, that he must take his share with all created things:

Ah, then
You only think of men!
But I would have no single creature miss
One possible bliss.
And this
Is certain: never be afraid!
I love what I have made.

In the daring sweep of its imagery, in its passionate intellectualism *Dartmoor* is a survival of the "metaphysical" school at its best, and seals Brown of the tribe of Donne, whose rediscovery, however, dates later than his day.

The interdependence of man and nature, the all-embracing and redemptive power of love—these are the bases of Brown's conception of life and the world. And they became his, not by the exercise of the pure reason but by instinct and intuition during his hours of solitary communion while he walked over the Clifton Downs. It is the exaltation, the vision, of the true mystic that thrills through those lyrics, unique of their kind, in which Brown lays the scene in Heaven. It is he alone who knows that

> When Wesley died, the Angelic orders,
>   To see him at the state
> Pressed so incontinent that the warders
>   Forgot to shut the gate,

and who creeps in and hears what passes between God and the organist.

It is he who

> Was in Heaven one day when all the prayers
> Came in, and angels bore them up the stairs,

and saw the "great sorter" set apart for the Master a hedgeling rose, "the first prayer of a little child". It is he who has had sure intelligence that all is well in Heaven with the poor Manx "innocent", Chalse a Killey:

> And now it's all so plain, dear Chalse,
> So plain—
> The wildered brain,
> The joy, the pain—
> The phantom shapes that haunted,
> The half-born thoughts that daunted—
> All, all is plain,
> Dear Chalse!
> All is plain.

It is he who is present when another Manx half-wit, the unchaste Catherine Kinrade, confronts before the divine judgment seat her harsh eighteenth-century episcopal persecutor—

> None spake when Wilson stood before
> The throne—
> And He that sat thereon
> Spake not,

till from the lips and eyes of Catherine, now made perfect woman, there flowed

> A smile that lit all Heaven; the angels smiled;
> God smiled, if that were smile beneath the state that glowed
> Soft purple—and a voice:—"Be reconciled!"

So to his side the children crept,
And Catherine kissed him, and he wept.
Then said a seraph:—"Lo! he is forgiven".
And for a space again there was no voice in Heaven.

Thus from one of the ugliest episodes in Manx annals Brown drew inspiration for the greatest of his apocalyptic poems, which enshrines the quintessence of his creed.

In July 1892 he resigned his Clifton mastership and returned to his island, which he again made his home, though he declined the offer of the Archdeaconry. Letter-writing, lecturing, and contributions to Reviews occupied most of his time. But it was fitting that the last scene came at Clifton. On 29 October 1897, he was addressing the boys of Tait's House, where he was staying, when he had a sudden seizure from which he never recovered consciousness.[1] He was buried beside his wife in the churchyard of Redland Chapel, across the Downs.

Ah, did you once see Shelley plain,
And did he stop and speak to you?

In my years in "Brown's House" I saw "Shelley plain". I came as a schoolboy into contact with a man of genius. He was not the only poet whom the Public Schools could claim in the last decades of the nineteenth century. William Johnson Cory, the delicate lyrist of *Ionica* (1858) remained as a master at Eton till 1872. Edward Bowen in 1886 published that volume of Harrow songs, including *Forty Years On* and *Willow the King*, which has found echoes in hearts far beyond

---

[1] An ambiguity in a sentence in vol. II, p. 231, of S. T. Irwin's edition of the *Letters* has led me in *The Contemporary Review*, June 1930, and Sir A. Quiller-Couch in his Centenary *Memoir*, to state in error that Brown was speaking to the boys of his old House.

the Hill. E. D. A. Morshead at Winchester issued in 1881 his notable translation of the Aeschylean trilogy of *The House of Atreus.* And doubtless there were other contemporary scholastic devotees of the Muse. But Brown stands above them in a class apart. There are many Victorians whose laurels are by now somewhat faded. But the fame of Thomas Edward Brown, schoolmaster, letter-writer and poet, was never higher than in this, his Centenary year, and will prove, as I believe, imperishable.

THE SIBYL AND THE SPHINX

Newman and Manning in the Eighties

By FATHER MARTINDALE

Sibyls, once upon a time, were very important persons, and so were Sphinxes, the Cumaean Sibyl in particular, and I mean of course especially the Sphinx beside the Pyramids, not the exotic monster that Oedipus got mixed up with. The Sibyl was very difficult to manage, and Apollo had a deal of trouble not only to inspire her but to make her talk such sense as people could assimilate. Then the advance of scholarship relegated the poor Sibyl into the world of elegant myth, till to-day, when out she has come again, and you cannot read treatises on Hellenistic, or late-Judaic, or imperial-Roman religion or society without finding the Sibylline books continually mentioned, their interpolations, their conflations, their origins and influence. As for the Sphinx, which fascinated my boyhood, I used to think that Herodotus, who had so much to say about the Pyramids, never mentioned that great Beast because it had frightened him too much. Then I began to surmise that he had thought it merely a "very large sphinx" and had not been impressed. When I first saw it, neither was I impressed—till my perfectly revolting guide showed me how some Government department had begun to mend the left-hand side of its wig, but had not finished even that. . . ."It is not good to touch It", he said with a quite genuine shudder. The Sphinx began to reassert its spell. I believe that it may genuinely have affected the minds of countless generations of Egyptians.

The rather tawdry title of this paper is due to the words "Sibyl" and "Sphinx" having quite honestly come into my head when I was asked to think once more about Newman and Manning. Newman uttered ambiguous oracles, scattering his ideas rather as the Sibyl so annoyingly threw her leaves all over the windy cave, save when now and again, just like her, he said something so devastatingly to the point that the recurrent Aeneas, worshipping or defying him, stood paralysed. Then, despite the *Apologia*, he suffered a true period of eclipse. But now he has reappeared, and has shone out upon a wider world than ever; first, a French world; then a German one; and I think he is destined to re-dawn even upon England, which does not like ideas at the best of times. As for Manning, who has ever felt quite sure about him? He received a funeral comparable with Wellington's, but people almost at once began to say that he was very dead. Purcell's book gave a *prima facie* justification to the thesis that Manning was posthumously negligible, that he had never really achieved or been anything great; indeed, that he wasn't a "nice" man at all. Superficial, unscrupulous, untrustworthy. Manning's star went wan. But now, I think, the clouds are clearing off it. He is at least something of a mystery. Was he a great citizen after all, a great churchman, a great man? As he sits there, very old, a mere skeleton, beside his roaring fire, what is his real mind? Who knows? At least he is not like the Sphinx as it squats smiling at the august and rising sun, providing a problem as to what it is thinking about only so long as you do not realize that it isn't thinking at all. Manning had a true mind about men and life, and even now it is hard to be quite sure what it was.

First, however, did these two men belong to the 'eighties at all? Well, Newman died in 1890, Manning in 1892. But was their work over a good ten years before? Certainly for ten years Newman had published nothing but an essay or two. Manning had done many things, some massive enough at the moment, like settling the Dock Strike. But not for these is he remembered. Popular imagination definitely has fastened on these two men as "Cardinals", and they received their Hats in 1879 and 1875 respectively. In different ways, their influence was, in the 'eighties, not only at work, but being recognized.

First, then, as to Newman hidden away at Edgbaston. Not that I can provide new anecdotes about what passed within that Sibyl's cave. Dean Church's pages on "Cardinal Newman's Naturalness", in vol. II of his *Occasional Papers*, are said to offer all that might supplement the last two chapters of Mr W. Ward's *Life of Newman*. An old friend of Newman's, who forbids me to mention his name, agrees so thoroughly with the Dean that he writes to me that

Newman carried the art of being ordinary to perfection. He was singular in nothing. He took his food, his recreation, went about his ordinary duties, conversed without any mannerisms whatsoever. He had no foibles, no crotchets. The best testimony to this is the absence of good stories about him such as there are about Manning and Ullathorne, for a good story generally implies some effort on the part of the subject to make his personality felt. What surprises me...is Newman's patience under annoyances of the kind which do try old people, such as noise, being kept waiting, forwardness on the part of young people, etc., and the absence of any demand upon those about him for small attentions to his comfort. I could give instances, but they would be so trivial upon paper. As he was, I believe, naturally quick-tempered, he must have disciplined himself to an unusual degree to preserve a bearing of habitual courtesy and gentleness under all circumstances. Then as his strength

failed, he was never peevish or querulous. He was spared any great
physical pain but not the deprivations of great old age. He ceased to be
able to say Mass, to see to read, and even lost the sense of touch to the
extent that he could hardly use his rosary. For a long time before he
had ceased saying Mass he used to sit with a missal for "caecutientes"
trying to learn the Canon by heart in the hope that some day he might
trust his memory.

I have quoted this paragraph out of gratitude to the
writer, and because it may still be needed to efface
finally the picture of Newman moping his last years
out, something of a clerical Mrs Gummidge, twitching
with nerves, wincing beneath criticism, lamenting a life
of failure. Again and again have I seen that picture
offered, and at one time I feared that it might bear even
a little likeness to reality. It does not. Newman, sensitive of course, even petulant now and again, sometimes tart enough even upon paper, never collapsed
like that. It had never been petty things that made him
suffer. Indeed, save perhaps quite towards the end,
I think he really began to feel himself, as Cardinal,
officially, justifiably, a "force" within the Church, and
he was desirous of acting as such.

When the renaissance Pope exclaimed (so they say)
that "God has given us the Papacy—let us enjoy it",
he at least implied that it was a post of maximum op-
portunities. Newman, once Cardinal, could at least
theoretically be Pope. In gentle banter, they asked him
what he would do did he become so. He recalled that
one Pope had been elected at ninety-three, and had
done much work. *His* work, he declared, would be to
appoint various commissions, scriptural especially and
historical, which should prepare and advance yet more
work for his successor. You see whither his thoughts
were travelling. All his life Newman had been of extreme generosity in suggesting to other people the work
he thought they could do, and in helping them to do it.

When you rather irritably feel, at times, that Newman was obsessed by "Oxford", it is worth recalling that one of the best features of the best Oxford is the amazing and self-effacing readiness of its most accomplished scholars to put all their treasures at the disposal of young men who may possibly be able to profit by some part of them. Such at least was my happy experience. Newman wrote endless little letters, read manuscripts, added tiny touches which vitalized dead pages, lifted the mediocre into excellence—for none of which he could win any glory, from none of which he stood to gain, save, no doubt, affection and almost adoration.

He himself did, during this period, a little patristic work, and published an article on "inspiration" which was less fortunate in its formulas than in its principles; but, as we see, he would have wanted to get that work done by a great number of men, on a very large scale, in the way in which papal authority could so supremely stimulate and sanction. He would have been pleased by the way in which things have developed since his day. Even, he began to have parts of his own work translated into Latin, so as to give their ideas wider circulation without running the risk of seeing himself mistranslated into those modern languages which he could not control, since his knowledge of them was slight. But as ever, he entertained his desires for the sake of other men; always realist, he took little interest in the advance of science for its own sake. He visualized those many minds which were gravitating towards the accepting of the Catholic Fact, and then were rebuffed by some departmental misunderstanding or ignorance. He guessed also how great was the strain upon many a Catholic mind which felt as though new knowledge was setting away from, or proving hostile to, the old beliefs.

His desire was to feed more and more human thoughts and facts into the Church's Mind, so that her eternal thought and judgement might work upon them, and that she might hand back her supernatural, absolute and universal Truth without men having to fear that her authorities did not know all that others knew, or were unable to sympathize with and appreciate them. All his life Newman had been (we are often reminded) sovranly conscious of two luminous facts—God, and himself. He never had doubted but that God communicated Himself to man, and had done so uniquely and definitively through Jesus Christ; and he had come to hold that Christ's own message reached men authoritatively by means of the Catholic Church; but never, he knew well, did God, or Christ, or Church, profess to do the whole work *instead* of man, albeit it was done wholly on behalf of man. "Qui te creavit sine te, non te salvabit sine te." The whole process of enlightening, sanctifying, saving, was co-operative, vital, and *therefore* developmental.

Newman therefore was like a man who had the chance of living in a beloved country, or of talking about it, or of making a map of it. Above all, obviously, he wished to live there! He liked to make word-pictures of it, but he could not do so because he *was* living in it. He did not care much for the map-making, and not at all for the policing of it.

Again, he *could* make anatomical charts, if he liked, of man, and even, if I may say so, of God; but accurate as they might be in their two-dimensional way, he did not care for them. He had always preferred the far harder task of meeting and portraying the floating, increasing, shrinking, never-the-same creature, man, and of portraying—not a floating, evanescent God, for God is immutable, but man's mysterious knowledge of God, in which there is both an element absolutely endurable, and one which is fluid. Hence, in reality, both the *Essay on Development*, and the *Essay in Aid of a Grammar of Assent*. (Note in each case the word "essay", usually omitted, perhaps always in the latter case.) He exposed himself to every shaft. In the *Grammar* he wished to describe the way in which the living man assents, not to define the way in which an abstract mind assents. That had been done a thousand times in text-books of psychology, whose value he did not dispute; but he was working at something different. An illustration from ethics. Text-books of ethics necessarily deal with the "four-square" man, the man "as such" who never existed and never will. Such a man must be thought of as devoid of heredity, environment, temperament, crystallized errors of the mind, unknown yet ever-operative complexes in the will and the emotions. Hence a confessor, dealing with one man, will never dream of weakening as to principle, but will—please God—be endlessly imaginative, sympathetic; gentle without softness; flexible yet not invertebrate; firm but never rigid; comforting but not complaisant. What the confessor must do—difficult task, God knows!—with the individual suffering, sinning, endeavouring, mys-teriously vibrant will, Newman was trying to do for the mind—the mind, not the floating loose and angel-mind; nor even free to reason logically without inter-ference, but engaged on its business of understanding more and more truthfully, with ever better certainty, both helped and hindered by the data of humanity, for the total human *datum* both holds the truth and hides it; is its vehicle, and its veil. Hence Newman heard himself called a fanatic and a sceptic, a geometrician and an impressionist, a Kantian, a Cartesian and a scholastic, an intellectualist and a voluntarist—not that

the word, I think, was then accessible; but Newman has
been claimed since then by schools that gave a lop-sided
importance to the will in matters of belief, especially in
France about twenty years ago. So, when French modern-
isms came into prominence, and kept invoking Newman,
there was an attempt to get him condemned at Rome.

But oh! how wise was Rome not to condemn Newman because of that sort of thing! And indeed, during
the 'eighties, Newman, engaged in sympathetic discussion with Mr Wilfrid Ward, and in sharp dispute
with the Congregationalist Principal Fairbairn (who
urged that Newman had become a Catholic as a refuge
from scepticism), was reopening the topic that lay at
the back, in reality, of the *Grammar of Assent*—how
"real" assents came into existence.

As for the *Essay on Development*, one ought to remember that Newman anticipated Darwin. Not that
the general theme of "development" in doctrine was
anything new to Catholic thinkers, the Fathers, especially certain Greek ones, were full of it. None the less,
since the religious revolutions of the fifteenth and
sixteenth centuries, the intangibility and immutability
of doctrine had been far further to the fore. Yet I suppose in all men's hearts lurks the hope-against-hope that
things are getting better. And again, that we live in a
world at least to some extent orderly, not haphazard,
spasmodic, but rationalizable. Hence quite ordinary
folk were pleased with the Darwinian theory, and no
one would have been worried about it had not the headlong atheist or even liberalist fastened on it in order to
disprove the existence of a Creator or at least of His
special interventions in the history of mankind. But
even others went too fast and too far. They would have
found it disappointing to diagnose that mankind im-
proves but in patches, degenerates in whole groups at

a time, moves by zigzags, in spirals, even in tilted spirals so that a group even while progressing may be lower at any given moment than it had been. So with very great rapidity the Darwinian hypothesis was transferred to all sorts of areas for which it was never meant, such as general history, psychology, religion; rigid laws of progress were formulated, all of which have had to be revised. So meanwhile anyone who talked of development in doctrine became increasingly suspected. Those who were to say, when speaking of the *Grammar*, that Newman was trying to show how you could regard yourself as believing when you really were not, already said that he was merely seeking a way of justifying the obvious difference between contemporary and primitive Christianity, so as to be able to say that the two things were the same, whereas they clearly were quite different. Despite Newman's most elaborate rules for discriminating between what developed, remaining the same, and what changed into something specifically different, when French Modernism, already alluded to, still troubled to mask itself or grimaced as orthodox, you heard the name of Newman insanely coupled with that of Loisy. But just as Newman loved to see the vague perception, the surmise, even the clear notional assent "becoming" the real assent of the whole man, without dreaming that the intellectual fact was not specific in its nature and underivable from matter, so, as he watched history, he delighted in the interplay of forces, pagan, Jewish, Christian, and to see the unified, solid, yet exquisitely, iridescently growing Thing; but he would have shrunk appalled—his whole life, antiliberalistic in its very fibre, would have quivered back in pain—from the suggestion that no special separate supernatural influx had entered the world both in the Mosaic revelation and in the Christian one.

It seems to me precisely here that Newman, passing through his double period of testing and trial, and having experienced a twofold rehabilitation, has shown himself most of all—I say no more, "Sibylline", but, prophetic, much as the Hebrew prophets were. For these saw certainly the immediate and actual, and spoke of it, but saw therein—or so spoke as to enable us to see therein—a future both proximate and remote. Ours is the remoter future to which Newman spoke. During those years that he spent at Edgbaston, a vision of Newman was forming itself owing in part to the accelerated currency and intensified sanction that his Cardinalate had given to his ideas—a vision of scarlet and silver, of fragility and force, of almost terrible spirituality emphasized fantastically by his nearness to that city which even then was heading towards the production of the word and idea of "Brummagem". Not the anxious or exhilarated Newman of the Tracts, not the restless, fighting, always conquered Newman of the Irish University, the Oxford Oratory episodes; not the dazzling exultant Newman of the *Apologia* had the tacit but permeating influence of the Newman of the 'eighties. And I think that we are now at a moment when science itself is making it almost impossible for us to fail to distinguish between the carnal, the incarnate, the discarnate; between what is natural to and in this cosmos, and the supernatural; nay, between matter, soul, and God. But if between these disparates we also detect a harmony in process of construction, why, then maybe there is no one who can help us so efficaciously as Newman, both to appreciate it and the more rapidly to accomplish it.

I look forward to a philosophical survey which shall include not only Ionian thought, Platonic and Aristotelian thought, but later Alexandrian philosophy,

Thomistic and post-Kantian, and indeed, Indian, Hebrew, Persian and Arabian thought, and modes of thinking, from none of which can eighteenth and nineteenth century thought be altogether, or at all, disconnected. In this, Newman cannot but be found in his place in a vitally continuous movement. A vital movement, because he would be seen not as defying the best in the past, nor even juxtaposed to it, but as belonging to it and by means of his personal vitality even revivifying it and thereby vitalizing our generation and others not yet born. It may be that the writings of Fr. Przywara contain for the first time an orderly display of material, patristic, mediaeval, and Newmanic, sufficient to inspire the comprehensive genius we are needing, to attempt the colossal task.[1]

A recent sympathetic writer (Mr J. L. May, in his *Cardinal Newman*, Geoffrey Bles, 1929) says that Manning was a man of his own day, and died with it. Even were this half true, it would provide me with an excuse for leaving myself so little space in which to speak of him. But I cannot admit that it is true. Mr Denis

---

[1] See *J. H. Kardinal Newman: Christentum: Ein Aufbau aus seinen Werken:* 8 Bändchen; Herder, Freiburg, 1922. A patristic scholar, ardent admirer and acute critic of Newman. His German is said to be such as to puzzle even his compatriots. His ideal however is recognizable in the peroration of a chapter called: "Kant-Newman-Thomas", in *Dringen der Gegenwart*, Augsburg, 1929: "By his unifying conception of God's relation with the world (*Gott-Welt-Spannung-Ein*) not only did the great Aquinas first create a polarity of thought, which thereby inspired all subsequent 'polarities', and therewith Newman's own polarisation of intellect and will, but this 'polarity' of Newman's is, taken as an item in the history of thought, nothing else but the fresh renascence of the scholastic polarity of intellect and will. In this personal union of the great thought of the Middle Ages and the great thought of modern times, in this organic unity of St Thomas *and* Newman, as opposed to the self-destroying alternative: St Thomas *or* Newman: proper to the Modernism-Integralism disease—that climax of modern infirmity—is expressed, as in a personal symbol, the Mission of Catholicism to Philosophy—*Tibi Dico, Surge!* 'I say to thee, Arise!'"

Gwynn has recently written a book suggesting that
Cardinal Wiseman was the greatest of those three
Cardinals. Who can estimate human greatness? But
anyhow, Wiseman, whom I deeply admire, would have
agreed that without Manning he would have been de-
frauded of more than half of the fruits of his labour;
and again, without Manning, Cardinal Vaughan, who
followed him, would have been in a thousand ways
crippled or shackled. Nor must Vaughan be thought
of as a mere follower. His association with his predecessors was organic and vital and in no way degenerate.
I venerate Vaughan. When, in the recitation of my
Breviary, the *Benedicite* bids me call on "all holy and
humble men of heart", it is of men like Vaughan or
Challoner that I think. Theirs may be the most enduring
work. Yet without Manning, Vaughan might have done
but little. Had he followed Errington, heaven knows
what he could have done, despite the humility and even
holiness of Errington.

When Newman heard of Manning's election, he saw
in it a proof that Rome was not afraid of converts as
such, and acknowledged that Manning had "a great
power of winning men when he chooses"—as witness
the election itself!—but "whether he will care to win
inferiors, or whether his talent extends to inferiors as
well as superiors, I do not know". Newman added that
personally he had always got on better with inferiors
than superiors. I do not think that this was due to his
needing flattery and homage; but I think that he did
need to be loved—at times, you would almost say, to
be petted; but he needed real love, and he won it, and
this implies that he was himself able to love. *Cor ad
cor*. Manning's "sphinxishness" has produced the
dogma that love was quite left out of him. The adequate
symbol of this used to be, the complete obliteration of

the memory of his wife. He would not remember her
—he ended by forgetting her as everyone else did. The
late Baron F. von Hügel gave publicity to what should
for ever end that myth at any rate. Manning kept her
letters, and, every night till near the end, took them out
of their shrine. The fact remains that Manning's method
of self-control and of controlling other men created the
impression of lovelessness. I am sure that he had what
may be called the love of the will—a passionate pity,
above all, and I suggest that Canon E. St John's book,
*Manning's Work for the Children: a Second Chapter in
Catholic Emancipation*, be read; that his speeches against
the Slave Traffic be recalled; and that you realize that
he and he really alone solved the problem of the Dock
Strike in 1889 far rather by an appeal to decent emotions than by reason or a very accurate knowledge of
conditions. Yet I ask myself whether Manning could
have played with a baby; what a slave would have
experienced had he been transferred to Manning's
guardianship; what would have been the effect of an
evening spent by Manning in, say, a sailors' club, an
average sergeants' mess, when there was no crisis on.
You are forbidden *odium malevolentiae*—you must never
hate anyone so as to wish him ill; you are not forbidden
to think that a man is abominable or detestable. I think
Manning had much "love of benevolence" for men
towards whom he felt no personal affection. I think that
Manning was un-English in this—that from time to
time he could be witty, but never could he tolerate a
sense of humour. They say that in the Saints pity and
love destroy the sense of humour. It were bad logic to
assert that when pity and love have destroyed a sense
of humour, you find a Saint; but the two propositions
at least overlap. I do not think, in short, that Manning
had, or rather allowed himself to experience, the love

ME   6

that is called love of affection. Perhaps he could not, in so far as he was a Catholic personage. I think he had been too bruised by his submission to the Thing he was sure he ought to submit to, so to love it, at any rate in England. For the *Res Catholica* he would have made any sacrifice, and have been glad to do so; to the representatives of that Universal Thing within this island, and at his point in history, sacrifice might seem to be demanded, but could not be delighted in. It had hurt him too much to become a Catholic, for him to be able to love the poor little Catholic world into which he came, or to allow himself to love any more the cultured Anglican world that he left. Hence he became a rigid Catholic, no less limitedly afraid of, resentful of, Oxford, than Newman was (also limitedly) hypnotized by it; just so much deluded by his vision of a Catholic University in London as Newman probably was by that of an Oratory in Oxford (the only point upon which they *both* made the *same* mistake was, the appetite of Catholics for higher education in or out of a university); and as out-of-love with the traditional Catholics as Newman learned to be in love with them—though you might have thought that Manning, the diplomatist, would have courted and won over his predecessors and that Newman, delicate don, would have flinched from the bluff, inartistic, non-Hellenist, non-patristic fox-hunting agricultural Communion-four-times-a-year Catholic squire and his corresponding cleric. As a matter of fact, Newman had the sense to appreciate these sober, patient, unassuming men, who handed the little Catholic lamp forward through fog-smothered generations. Manning was always rather apt to quench the flickering wick; sometimes, if a reed was bruised, he broke it. Ullathorne, *h*-less mystic, cabin-boy-Archbishop, peace-loving Benedictine ready to fight more

than any other one Englishman for the rectification of
our unbelievably atrocious treatment of Australian convicts, was assimilated by Newman as never Grant or
Errington could be by Manning.

Possibly philosophers and even historians speak too
slightingly, rather snobbishly, of "the man of the
moment". After all, if the man fails his moment, there
is a gap and a dislocation. It is not at all certain that
some other man will arise to replace him: the whole
future may be affected by his failure. Notice that in
the Catholic evolution of England the "hereditary"
Catholics were in no way dislodged by Manning. He
took over the government from one of them, only to
hand it over to another. But should you suggest that
this applies after all only to England, and that Newman
has become in a sense international, I must suggest
that I think that Manning's influence abroad, in a very
concrete yet fundamental affair, has been very wide and
is enduring. I have no time to describe his gravitation
towards what his enemies called socialism during the
last years of his life. He was assimilating and expressing
ideas concerning society that certainly startled many,
moderate as they would now be held. Now Pope Leo
began his wonderful series of social encyclicals in 1878
and wrote the last of them in 1901, but the supremely
important one, *Rerum Novarum*, on the "condition of
the working-classes", appeared in 1891. The Pope
wrote to tell Manning that the encyclical was coming;
he wrote again in April, very anxious about its accurate
translation. To what extent Manning had been in touch
with the admirable Cardinal Mermillod, who with his
associates prepared so much of the material for Leo's
encyclicals, I cannot find out, nor the extent of his
association, if any, with men like de Mun or Ketteler.
His active correspondence went more towards Ireland

and the United States, especially during the troubles created around Henry George. It remains that Leo said that his 1880 encyclical was, really, Manning's. "It was he who gave me the idea of doing something for the slaves. He is a man of vast views, and his conversation is full of suggestion. I have written this encyclical in consequence of my talks with him." An American archbishop said that Manning's mind was an image of Leo's; not resplendent as Leo's mind, but yet an image of it. It would be perfectly unfair to suggest that these two men, Pope and Cardinal, merely "sensed" the decline of privilege and authority, the arrival of the masses, and wished to anticipate a *débâcle* by "getting democracy on to the side of the Church". Much that Leo said was extremely unpalatable even to English socialists; and no one will accuse Manning of undervaluing authority, even when purely human. Each was using eternal principles, balancing partial truths with supreme impartiality. A twofold parallel occurs to me. During the recent War, Pope Benedict, a man of lucid mind if ever there was one, wrote more than once upon the situation, and in particular his Peace Note. At the time I was being allowed to see German, Austrian and Turkish papers. I remember that they clamorously asserted that the Note had been fabricated in Paris and in London, just as we said that it was imposed by Berlin and Vienna. It held a perfect balance, and could not, therefore, be other than unpopular; but how have the nations now settled down towards acknowledging its justice, even though they will not, or cannot, logically apply it! Again, during our General Strike, Cardinal Bourne published a statement which without any doubt at all saved England from all manner of tragedies and much bloodshed especially in the North and in Wales. It was quoted everywhere. But forthwith he balanced what seemed to one party its lop-sidedness by a sermon on the miners which those who control publicity were very careful not to quote. None the less, it made its way through our Catholic world, and would that the rest of the world realized what a difference that makes! I feel sure that this side of Manning, and his influence—less separately visible, perhaps, because more co-operative than Newman's was—have not yet been sufficiently studied or estimated. After all, in our modern world, ideas underlie action as they always did. Who supposes that mere taxation, mere Court-Supremacy, sufficed to bring about the French Revolution? Who was at the bottom of the Russian one? Tsars? No, but students and men of academic mind. And Russia, for so long silent and supplying no ideas at all to Europe at large, is, whether we like to acknowledge it or no, pumping ideas more than any other country is into contemporary brains. If we disapprove of Russia, we must realize that we can only counter her by the creation of a different Mind; crude in many ways as were the social ideas of the 'eighties, very imperfect as was Manning's acquaintance with sheer facts, we might do much worse than study, develop and apply the ideas which he, along with, and in the wake of, Leo so vigorously propagated.

Manning published not a few works in the 'eighties, and a little, I am reminded, later on. *Pastime Papers* appeared posthumously in 1893. I have loyally re-read some of Manning's works, and I confess myself surprised. His ecclesiastical writings I find excellent within definite limits, but intolerably dull. (I say "ecclesiastical", not "spiritual".) He accumulates authorities who all repeat much the same thing—that was the point—and in my heart I think he thought that this was the proper thing to do in such documents; it displayed tradition—it *was* the tradition—and I cannot help feeling (to my own discredit, maybe) that he liked to show, and thought it prudent to show, that he could do this as well as anyone else. The convert, the practical man, the governor, had also to be recognized as sound in, and learned in, theology. (Every now and then, I have felt that Newman wanted to do something in the line of "Catholic devotion" for the sake of the devout Catholics among whom he had come, and not quite from an interior fountain of emotion. The hymns in the *Dream of Gerontius* are not traditional-Catholic at all, Catholic, but utterly Newman. And how characteristic is the intimidated quatrain:

> O Mother-Maid, be thou our aid
> Now in the opening year,
> Lest sights of earth to sin give birth
> And bring the tempter near.

But nothing, nothing, will make me believe in the spontaneity of some of his other hymns.)

Manning, in his ecclesiastical writings, was the teacher of his clergy; the admirable repeater of formulas (in which he thoroughly believed) rather than the prophet (like Jeremiah) unable to control the "fire in his bones" if he refrained from speaking. The Sphinx, during the intolerable tedium of the centuries, must have said a number of excellent conventional things to the priests who offered sacrifice around it. However, the Inquisitor in Mr G. Bernard Shaw's *St Joan* suffered terribly because he was so *fair* (at least I think he did), and Manning too could suffer, but especially with those for whose misdoing he could discern so many an excuse— I confess, that he saw few excuses for the shortcomings (as he conceived them) of his clergy. "Begin from the Sanctuary!" Sometimes they found, as Francis Thompson was tempted to, his shoulder (if *that* were Christ's!)

too "high to lean thereby". I insist, not one sentence
that rings *insincere* will you read in Manning.

He wrote, however, two other sorts of literature, so
to call it, nor do I use the word in Verlaine's sense, who,
when he remarked that "tout le reste" was but literature, implied that you might disregard it. He wrote or
had written spiritual works, and his passionate personal
notes reveal what was *in* him when he thus externalized
himself so much as he could. He wrote on the Holy
Spirit, and on the Sacred Heart of our Lord. A Spirit,
and a Heart. In an article like this, I do not wish to
enlarge on this topic. But it must never be forgotten
by anyone who chooses to study and to speak about
Cardinal Manning. The "fire in the bones" was there.
Not a hint of the bland Eminence who did not really
believe in anything *much*; nor of the inhuman, academic
Authority who did not know how to love or suffer. The
rather ornate, super-respectable, Ashmolean Museum
of which you are, for a moment, tempted roughly to say
that "it's all wrong" (not reflecting that at any rate it
stands up and is watertight, and that's not nothing),
turns out to have been built of lava, and you are permitted to peer into the volcano from which it spouted,
and within which still glow the molten materials that
afterwards solidified. The very immobility of the
Sphinx, and its suave smile, suggest that it has pounced,
and is apt to do so again at any moment. There are
teeth behind the smile: but (to return to Manning)
there is gentleness within the suavity no less than the
austerity.

As for the third category of writings, his letters,
these are full of a vivacity which (naturally) is lacking
in either of the other two. Many of these were public,
like the brief article (really a letter) to the *Weekly
Register* in 1881 on *La Dame aux Camélias* which had

been played in London. Other letters were of course private. "You ladies are torpedoes, not legislators!" He wrote then as he talked, when at ease. He was writing, as usual, on his knee, and dropped a pen. Someone picked it up. "Don't do that; life is too short to be spent in picking up pens." And he took another from a bundle near him.

He threw his letters, when written, on to the floor. "Samuel Wilberforce", someone said, "threw his into an open umbrella, when he travelled by train."

"Ah—if he'd never done anything worse than that...!"

He liked Gregorian chant. "But look at the Roman churches, Eminence!" "Too true. And what is the result? Victor Emmanuel in the Quirinal!"

"*Only* seventy cases? But think—seventy little children's tears dried; seventy little children's pains stopped. It is *glorious*!"

I ask myself in what way this interior vivacity and also tenderness are below those of Newman. Perhaps, not at all. But Manning, in his public capacity, had to suppress so much. Hence part of his sphinxishness. But had not Newman to suppress many and poignant things? Alas, yes. But I think he in his position was able to express, too, more than Manning could, in prose. Manning never could have let himself write the covering letters to the *Apologia*. Hence Manning really felt irritated by Newman's self-expressiveness. I forget on what occasion Manning announced that what was wrong with Newman was "temper—Temper—*Temper*!" His voice rose shrill and shriller. Meanwhile, Newman felt himself quite justified in exhaling his soul in violin-music, and had been skilled to be wine-taster to his College. I doubt if ever he felt the need to regret it or to fail to be amused and pleased by the memory.

Perhaps Manning would have frozen it away. Hence while each wrote a prose of great lucidity and indeed dignity, each from time to time also wrote a prose that must be called superfine journalism; but even so, the endless variety of Newman's work is still an enchantment and a lesson, despite the nonsense Mr George Moore talked (and there too was bile!) about it. Silvery and yet sonorous; of a childlike simplicity, yet sublime. Newman was almost French in making you think that sentences so limpid could secrete nothing very special. Manning was not at all French, but, rather, Latin; and yet...when all is said and done, he was hopelessly English; he adopted every Italian pronunciation of his Latin, chirped his *c*'s and so forth; yet when he spoke at Rome, genial smiles spread over the faces of the assembled Fathers.

Remember then especially that Manning wrote two books, one, the *Temporal Mission of the Holy Ghost*, one, the *Internal Mission of the Holy Ghost*. Having had his mind turned, about 1841, to the fact that he seldom spoke about God's Holy Spirit, he dwelt perpetually upon that subject. "From that day I have never passed a day without acts of reparation to the Holy Ghost." "He has been the chief thought and devotion of my whole life." "To Him almost palpably I owe everything." Manning was quite sure that the Holy Spirit was energizing quite as much in the current of exterior things as in those of the mind and of devotion. Also, he was sure that the Holy Ghost used human instruments. "It has been decided by the Holy Ghost and by Us", wrote the Apostles, in words that you would hardly find, I think, in any Papal document. And such is the Christian mystery. Man is not merely animal, nor angel merely. Christ, Catholic dogma teaches, was not God, spectrally disguised as man, or even using a

man as an "animated tool", nor yet a mere man ex-
ceptionally like to God. He was true God, true man,
one person. Ever since His coming the Catholic
Church conceives itself as truly Christ's Body, no less
divine than human, and as human (with all the consequences of that) as divine. If you read Manning's
own Notes and Diaries, you will find how clear he was
both as to his own humanity and to that of those with
whom he dealt, and to the obscure yet indubitable
action of the Spirit—an action no less really individual
and interior, than social and external. If Newman saw
luminously God and Self, Manning saw these, and the
world at large as well. Hence let us not quarrel with
him if he visualized Newman as eider-downed in
Edgbaston, whereas he himself was "fated" to be ever
in the limelight, on the platform, and defending the unpopular cause. Newman seemed to him flitting about
in literature, mummified in patristics, exhaled into compromises, adjustments, suggestions; whereas he himself
had to concentrate on strategics, tactics, the Map,
because Christ was walking, not only on Gennesareth,
let alone Nile or Indus or Euphrates, but on Thames.

Manning was no opportunist merely—he was not,
religiously, like a man who should think we can retain
the sympathy of New Zealand by playing carillons in
Hyde Park: nor Newman an idealist merely, as one who
dreams that we will retain that of Australia because
some Australians still call England "home". Newman,
if I may quote myself (Preface to *The Spirit of Cardinal
Newman*; Burns and Oates, 1914), "attenuated and
frail, yet magical, magnetic, electrical...elusive and
subtle", was "to the very end the almost savage foe
of cant, humbug, and untruth; a man of silvery whispers,
swift glances, birdlike exquisiteness of touch and presence, yet utterly human, homely, playful; majestic, too,

quelling and imperial", whom you will find—all of whom I think you will find, in the rhetoric and ecstasy, colloquial and sublime, of the *Dream of Gerontius* written so long before the august approach of Death summoned him to his final purification and salvation. As for Manning, please do not think me impertinent or silly if I recall that in 1892 he died on the same day as the Duke of Clarence and Avondale, heir to the throne, and that I heard of this when I, a mere boy, was also sick of influenza. Childish simplicity! But still, I was impressed by the death of the English prince; but even then felt that another prince had died who represented the only dynasty that has never failed, nor can fail. At Harrow, I spent hours reading the *Apologia*, and Manning's *Essays*. I met with imperishable ideas. I met also with much that seemed even then old-fashioned, queer, and irritating. This, I forget; the men, I cannot.

Manning, to speak very crudely, found himself set between two Cardinal Archbishops who were stout— Wiseman was very stout indeed and florid, and endured criticisms when his ill-health, had it been known, would have provoked quick sympathy. A shrinkingly sensitive man in some ways, he exulted in the pageants of the Church, and was easily taken for an overbearing prelate. Cardinal Vaughan looked "magnificent" too; he was taken as being "haughty"; some people wondered why he could not be "jolly" like his mercurial brother Bernard; others professed themselves glad he was not, and preferred his stately progress across a scene far narrower, none the less, than Manning's was. Not till his "life" was written, had the world the slightest conception of his spirit of interior humility, penance, and prayer. Between these massive men stalked Manning, aquiline, even hawk-like, quite terrible when he wanted to rebuke a priest (which, when summoned to Manning's house, priests usually foresaw his doing), or even a lady for her frock. The thin, rectilinear lips could shape themselves into several sorts of smile, but they say that no one can remember his laugh—anyhow, no hearty laugh, such as that which would set Wiseman rocking. Still, still, he is the Sphinx! If you can cry, surely you should be able too to laugh. He met a small boy whom he asked "what his father was". The boy said: "A carpenter". Manning was shaken to the soul. "I had met a carpenter's son. My Lord was once a little servant like that boy....Oh", he exclaimed, almost in tears, to the Nonconformist minister he was talking to, "what depths of love there were in Christ!"

I will dare to say that, while there was about him, certainly, in his house, on official occasions, all the rigidity that there is in royal Courts, and more than that simplicity which can belong to royalties "off duty", there never was about him that tiny touch of sheer *vulgarity* which almost always spoils great human occasions or even personages. I conclude, therefore, that he must have been a very great man, who had not learned to manage himself quite perfectly. I take it that where the Spirit is, and where there is a Heart, there should be ease even in anguish, sweetness even in majesty. Possibly, since during his career he did not complete full harmonization of himself, we, who can but estimate what such careers display, may never understand him properly. But we should understand enough to be sure that the discords were resolvable, and are, perhaps, by now, fully resolved.

THE PLACE OF PATER

By T. S. Eliot

Although Pater is as appropriate to the 'seventies as to the 'eighties, because of the appearance of *Studies in the History of the Renaissance* in 1873, I have chosen to discuss him in this volume because of the date 1885, the middle of the decade, which marks the publication of *Marius the Epicurean*. The first may certainly be counted the more "influential" book; but *Marius* illustrates another, but related aspect of Pater's work. His writing of course extended well into the 'nineties; but I doubt whether anyone would consider the later books and essays of anything like the importance, in social history or in literary history, of the two I have mentioned.

The purpose of the present paper is to indicate a direction from Arnold, through Pater, to the 'nineties, with, of course, the solitary figure of Newman in the background.

It is necessary first of all to estimate the aesthetic and religious views of Arnold: in each of which, to borrow his own phrase against him, there is an element of *literature* and an element of *dogma*. As Mr J. M. Robertson has well pointed out in his *Modern Humanists Reconsidered*, Arnold had little gift for consistency or for definition. Nor had he the power of connected reasoning at any length: his flights are either short flights or circular flights. Nothing in his prose work, therefore, will stand very close analysis, and we may well feel that the positive content of many words is very small. That

Culture and Conduct are the first things, we are told; but what Culture and Conduct are, I feel that I know less well on every reading. Yet Arnold does still hold us, at least with *Culture and Anarchy* and *Friendship's Garland*. To my generation, I am sure, he is a more sympathetic prose writer than Carlyle or Ruskin; yet he holds his position and achieves his effects exactly on the same plane, by the power of his rhetoric and by representing a point of view which is particular though it cannot be wholly defined.

But the revival of interest in Arnold in our time— and I believe he is more admired and read not only than Carlyle and Ruskin, but than Pater—is a very different thing from the influence he exerted in his own time. We go to him for refreshment and for the companionship of a kindred point of view to our own, but not as disciples. And therefore it is the two books I have mentioned that are most readable. Even the *Essays in Criticism* cannot be read very often; *Literature and Dogma*, *God and the Bible*, and *Last Essays on Church and Religion*, have served their turn and can hardly be read through. In these books he attempts something which must be austerely impersonal; in them reasoning power matters, and it fails him; furthermore, we have now our modern solvers of the same problem Arnold there set himself, and they, or some of them, are more accomplished and ingenious in this sort of rationalizing than Arnold was. Accordingly, and this is my first point, his Culture survives better than his Conduct, because it can better survive vagueness of definition. But both Culture and Conduct were important for his own time.

But Culture has three aspects, according as we look at it in *Culture and Anarchy*, in *Essays in Criticism*, or in the abstract. It is in the first of these two books that Culture shows to best advantage. And the reason

is perfectly clear: Culture there stands out against a
background to which it is contrasted, a background of
perfectly definite items of ignorance, vulgarity and
prejudice. As an invective against the crudities of the
industrialism of his time, the book is perfect of its kind.
Compared with Carlyle, it looks like clear thinking, and is
certainly clearer expression; and compared with Arnold,
Ruskin often appears long-winded and peevish. Arnold
taught English expository and critical prose a restraint
and urbanity it needed. And hardly, in this book, do
we question the meaning of Culture; for the good
reason that we do not need to. Even when we read that
Culture "is a study of perfection", we do not at that
point raise an eyebrow to admire how much Culture
appears to have arrogated from Religion. For we have
shortly before been hearing something about "the will
of God", or of a joint firm called "reason and the will
of God"; and soon after we are presented with Mr
Bright and Mr Frederic Harrison as foils to Culture;
and appearing in this way between the will of God and
Mr Bright, Culture is here sufficiently outlined to be
recognizable. *Culture and Anarchy* is on the same side
as *Past and Present* or *Unto this Last*. Its ideas are really
no clearer;—one reason why Arnold, Carlyle and
Ruskin were so influential, for precision and complete-
ness of thought do not always make for influence.
(Arnold, it is true, gave something else: he produced
a kind of illusion of precision and clarity; that is,
maintained these qualities as ideals of style.)

Certainly, the prophets of the period just before that
of which I am supposed to be writing excelled in
denunciation (each in his own way) rather than in construction; and each in his own fashion lays himself open
to the charge of tedious querulousness. And an idea,
such as that of Culture, is apt to lead to consequences

which its author cannot foresee and probably will not like. Already, in the *Essays*, Culture begins to seem a little more priggish—I do not say "begins" in a chronological sense—and a little more anaemic. Where Sir Charles Adderley and Mr Roebuck appear, there is more life than in the more literary criticism. Arnold is in the end, I believe, at his best in satire and in apologetics for literature, in his defence and enunciation of a needed attitude.

To us, as I have said, Arnold is rather a friend than a leader, or if a leader, only as a stimulus to proceed. He was a champion of "ideas" most of whose ideas we no longer take seriously. His Culture is powerless to aid or to harm. But he is at least a forerunner of what is now called Humanism, of which I must here say something, if only to contrast it and compare it with the Aestheticism of Pater. How far Arnold is responsible for the birth of Humanism would be difficult to say; we can at least say that it issues very naturally from his doctrine, that Charles Eliot Norton is largely responsible for its American form, and that therefore Arnold is another likely ancestor. But the resemblances are too patent to be ignored. The difference is that Arnold could father something apparently quite different—the view of life of Walter Pater. The resemblance is that literature, or Culture, tended with Arnold to usurp the place of Religion. From one point of view, Arnold's theory of Art and his theory of Religion are quite harmonious, and Humanism is merely the more coherent structure. Arnold's prose writings fall into two parts; those on Culture and those on Religion; and the books about Christianity seem only to say again and again—merely that the Christian faith is of course impossible to the man of culture. They are tediously negative. But they are negative in a peculiar fashion:

their aim is to affirm that the emotions of Christianity can and must be preserved without the belief. From this proposition two different types of man can extract two different types of conclusion: (1) that Religion is Morals, (2) that Religion is Art. The effect of Arnold's religious campaign is to divorce Religion from thought.

In Arnold himself there was a powerful element of Puritan morality, as in most of his contemporaries, however diverse. And the strength of his moral feeling —we might add its blindness also—prevented him from seeing how very odd the fragments might look of the fabric which he knocked about so recklessly. "The power of Christianity has been in the immense emotion which it has excited", he says; not realizing at all that this is a counsel to get all the emotional kick out of Christianity one can, without the bother of believing it; without reading the future to foresee *Marius the Epicurean*, and finally *De Profundis*. Furthermore, in his books dealing with Christianity he seems bent upon illustrating in himself the provincialisms which he rebuked in others. "M. de Lavelaye", he says in the preface to *God and the Bible*, with as deferential a manner as if he were citing M. Renan himself, "is struck, as any judicious Catholic may well be struck, with the superior freedom, order, stability, and religious earnestness, of the Protestant Nations as compared with the Catholic." He goes on complacently, "their religion has made them what they are". I am not here concerned with the genuine differences between Catholic and Protestant; only with the tone which Arnold adopts in this preface and throughout this book; and which is in no wise more liberal than that of Sir Charles Adderley or Mr Roebuck or "Mr Tennyson's great broad-shouldered Englishman". He girds at (apparently) Herbert Spencer for substituting *Unknowable* for *God*;

quite unaware that his own Eternal not ourselves comes
to exactly the same thing as the Unknowable. And when
we read Arnold's discourses on Religion, we return to
scrutinize his Culture with some suspicion.

For Arnold's Culture, at first sight so enlightened,
moderate and reasonable, walks so decorously in the company of the will of God, that we may overlook the fact that
it tends to develop its own stringent rules and restrictions.

Certainly, culture will never make us think it an essential of religion
whether we have in our Church discipline "a popular authority of
elders", as Hooker calls it, or whether we have Episcopal jurisdiction.

Certainly, "culture" in itself can never make us
think so, any more than it can make us think that the
quantum theory is an essential of physical science: but
such people as are interested in this question at all,
however cultured they be, hold one or the other opinion
pretty strongly; and Arnold is really affirming that to
Culture all theological and ecclesiastical differences are
indifferent. But this is a rather positive dogma for
Culture to hold. When we take *Culture and Anarchy* in
one hand, and *Literature and Dogma* in the other, our
minds are gradually darkened by the suspicion that
Arnold's objection to Dissenters is partly that they do
hold strongly to that which they believe, and partly
that they are not Masters of Arts of Oxford. Arnold,
as such, should have had some scruple about the use of
words. But in the very preface to the second edition of
Literature and Dogma he says:

The *Guardian* proclaims "the miracle of the incarnation" to be the
"fundamental truth" for Christians. How strange that on me should
devolve the office of instructing the *Guardian* that the fundamental
thing for Christians is not the Incarnation but the imitation of Christ!

While wondering whether Arnold's own "imitation"
is even a good piece of mimicry, we notice that he employs *truth* and *thing* as interchangeable: and a very

slight knowledge of the field in which he was skirmishing should have told him that a "fundamental truth" in theology and a "fundamental thing" in his own loose jargon have nothing comparable about them. The total effect of Arnold's philosophy is to set up Culture in the place of Religion, and to leave Religion to be laid waste by the anarchy of feeling. And Culture is a term which each man not only may interpret as he pleases, but must indeed interpret as he can. So the gospel of Pater follows naturally upon the prophecy of Arnold.

Even before the 'seventies began Pater seems to have written, though not published, the words

The theory, or idea, or system, which requires of us the sacrifice of any part of this experience, in consideration of some interest into which we cannot enter, or some abstract morality we have not identified with ourselves, or what is only conventional, has no real claim upon us.[1]

Although more outspoken in repudiating any measure for all things than man, Pater is not really uttering anything more subversive than the following words of Arnold:

Culture, disinterestedly seeking in its aim at perfection to see things as they really are, shows us how worthy and divine a thing is the religious side in man, though it is not the whole of man. But while recognising the grandeur of the religious side in man, culture yet makes us eschew an inadequate conception of man's totality.

Religion, accordingly, is merely a "'side' in (*sic*) man"; a side which so to speak must be kept in its place. But when we go to Arnold to enquire what is "man's totality", that we may ourselves aim at so attractive a consummation, we learn nothing; any more than we learn about the "secret" of Jesus of which he has so much to say.

[1] In quoting from *The Renaissance* I use the first edition throughout.

The degradation of philosophy and religion, skilfully initiated by Arnold, is competently continued by Pater. "The service of philosophy, and of religion and culture as well, to the human spirit", he says in the 1873 conclusion to *The Renaissance*, "is to startle it into a sharp and eager observation." "We shall hardly have time", he says, "to make theories about the things we see and touch." Yet we have to be "curiously testing new opinions"; so it must be—if opinions have anything to do with theories, and unless wholly capricious and unreasoning they must have—that the opinions we test can only be those provided for our enjoyment by an inferior sort of drudges who are incapable of enjoying our own free life, because all their time is spent (and "*we* hardly have time") in making theories. And this again is only a development of the intellectual Epicureanism of Arnold.

Had Pater not had one gift denied to Arnold, his permutation of Arnold's view of life would have little interest. He had a taste for painting and the plastic arts, and particularly for Italian painting, a subject to which Ruskin had introduced the nation. He had a visual imagination; he had also come into contact with another generation of French writers than that which Arnold knew; the zealous Puritanism of Arnold was in him considerably mitigated, but the zeal for culture was equally virulent. So his peculiar appropriation of religion into culture was from another side: that of emotion, and indeed of sensation; but in making this appropriation, he was only doing what Arnold had given licence to do.

Marius the Epicurean marks indeed one of the phases of the fluctuating relations between religion and culture in England since the Reformation; and for this reason the year 1885 is an important one. Newman, in leaving

the Anglican Church, had turned his back upon Oxford.
Ruskin, with a genuine sensibility for certain types of
art and architecture, succeeded in satisfying his nature
by translating everything immediately into terms of
morals. The vague religious vapourings of Carlyle, and
the sharper, more literate social fury of Ruskin yield
before the persuasive sweetness of Arnold, who at
least made a statement for a generation. Pater is a new
variation.

But we are liable to confusion if we call this new
variation the "aesthete". Pater was, like the other
writers I have just mentioned (except Newman), a
moralist. If, as the *Oxford Dictionary* tells us, an aesthete
is a "professed appreciator of the beautiful", then there
are at least two varieties: those whose profession is most
vocal, and those whose appreciation is most professional.
If we wish to understand painting, we do not go to
Oscar Wilde for help. We have specialists, such as
Mr Berenson, or Mr Roger Fry. Even in that part of
his work which can only be called literary criticism,
Pater is always primarily the moralist. In his essay
on Wordsworth he says:

> To treat life in the spirit of art, is to make life a thing in which means
> and ends are identified: to encourage such treatment, the true moral
> significance of art and poetry.

That was his notion: to find the "true moral significance
of art and poetry". Certainly, a writer may be none the
less classified as a moralist, if the morality he finds is
suspect or perverse. We have to-day a witness in the
person of M. André Gide. As always in his imaginary
portraits, so frequently in his choice of other writers as
the subjects of critical studies, Pater is inclined to
emphasize whatever is morbid or associated with
physical malady. His admirable study of Coleridge is
charged with this attraction.

More than Childe Harold (he says of Coleridge), more than Werther, more than René himself, Coleridge, by what he did, what he was, and what he failed to do, represents that inexhaustible discontent, languor, and home-sickness, that endless regret, the chords of which ring all through our modern literature.

Thus again in Pascal he emphasizes the malady, with its consequences upon the thought; but we feel that somehow what is important about Pascal has been missed. But it is not that he treats philosophers "in the spirit of art", exactly; for when we read him on Leonardo or Giorgione, we feel that there is the same preoccupation, coming between him and the object as it really is. He is, in his own fashion, moralizing upon Leonardo or Giorgione, on Greek art or on modern poetry. His famous dictum: "Of this wisdom, the poetic passion, the desire of beauty, the love of art for art's sake has most; for art comes to you professing frankly to give nothing but the highest quality to your moments as they pass, and simply for those moments' sake", is itself a theory of ethics; it is concerned not with art but with life. The second half of the sentence is of course demonstrably untrue, or else being true of everything else besides art is meaningless; but it is a serious statement of morals. And the disapproval which greeted this first version of the Conclusion to *The Renaissance* is implicitly a just recognition of that fact. "Art for art's sake" is the offspring of Arnold's Culture; and we can hardly venture to say that it is even a perversion of Arnold's doctrine, considering how very vague and ambiguous that doctrine is.

When religion is in a flourishing state, when the whole mind of society is moderately healthy and in order, there is an easy and natural association between religion and art. Only when religion has been partly retired and confined, when an Arnold can sternly remind us that Culture is wider than Religion, do we get "religious art" and in due course "aesthetic religion". Pater undoubtedly had from childhood a religious bent, naturally to all that was liturgical and ceremonious. Certainly this is a real and important part of religion; and Pater cannot thereby be accused of insincerity and "aestheticism". His attitude must be considered both in relation to his own mental powers and to his moment of time. There were other men like him, but without his gift of style, and such men were among his friends. In the pages of Thomas Wright, Pater, more than most of his devout friends, appears a little absurd. His High Churchmanship is undoubtedly very different from that of Newman, Pusey and the Tractarians, who, passionate about dogmatic essentials, were singularly indifferent to the sensuous expressions of orthodoxy. It was also dissimilar to that of the priest working in a slum parish. He was "naturally Christian"—but within very narrow limitations: the rest of him was just the cultivated Oxford don and disciple of Arnold, for whom religion was a matter of feeling, and metaphysics not much more. Being incapable of sustained reasoning, he could not take philosophy or theology seriously; just as being primarily a moralist, he was incapable of seeing any work of art simply as it is.

Marius the Epicurean represents the point of English history at which the repudiation of revealed religion by men of culture and intellectual leadership coincides with a renewed interest in the visual arts. It is Pater's most arduous attempt at a work of literature; for *Plato and Platonism* can be almost dissolved into a series of essays. *Marius* itself is incoherent; its method is a number of fresh starts; its content is a hodge-podge of the learning of the classical don, the impressions of the sensitive holiday visitor to Italy, and a prolonged flirtation with the liturgy. Even A. C. Benson, who makes as much of the book as anyone can, observes in a passage of excellent criticism:

> But the weakness of the case is, that instead of emphasising the power of sympathy, the Christian conception of Love, which differentiates Christianity from all other religious systems, Marius is after all converted, or brought near to the threshold of the faith, more by its sensuous appeal, its liturgical solemnities; the element, that is to say, which Christianity has in common with all religions, and which is essentially human in character. And more than that, even the very peace which Marius discerns in Christianity is the old philosophical peace over again.

This is sound criticism. But—a point with which Dr Benson was not there concerned—it is surely a merit, on the part of Pater, and one which deserves recognition, to have clarified the issues. Matthew Arnold's religion is the more confused, because he conceals, under the smoke of strong and irrational moral prejudice, just the same, or no better, Stoicism and Cyrenaicism of the amateur classical scholar. Arnold Hellenizes and Hebraicizes in turns; it is something to Pater's credit to have Hellenized purely.

Of the essence of the Christian faith, as Dr Benson frankly admits, Pater knew almost nothing. One might say also that his intellect was not powerful enough to grasp—I mean, to grasp as firmly as many classical scholars whose names will never be so renowned as that of Pater—the essence of Platonism or Aristotelianism, or Neo-Platonism. He therefore, or his Marius, moves quite unconcerned with the intellectual activity which was then amalgamating Greek metaphysics with the tradition of Christ; just as he is equally unconcerned with the realities of Roman life as we catch a glimpse of them in Petronius, or even in such a book as Dill's on the reign of Marcus Aurelius. Marius merely *drifts* towards the Christian Church, if he can be said to have any motion at all; nor does he or his author seem to have any realization of the chasm to be leapt between the meditations of Aurelius and the Gospel. To the end, Marius remains only a half-awakened soul. Even at his death, in the midst of the ceremonies of which he is given the benefit, his author reflects "often had he fancied of old that not to die on a dark or rainy day might itself have a little alleviating grace or favour about it", recalling to our minds the "springing of violets from the grave" in the Conclusion to *The Renaissance,* and the death of Flavian.

I have spoken of the book as of some importance. I do not mean that its importance is due to any influence it may have exerted. I do not believe that Pater, in this book, has influenced a single first-rate mind of a later generation. His view of art, as expressed in *The Renaissance,* impressed itself upon a number of writers in the 'nineties, and propagated some confusion between life and art which is not wholly irresponsible for some untidy lives. The theory (if it can be called a theory) of "art for art's sake" is still valid in so far as it can be taken as an exhortation to the artist to stick to his job; it never was and never can be valid for the spectator, reader or auditor. How far *Marius the Epicurean* may have assisted a few "conversions" in the following decade I do not know: I only feel sure that with the direct current of religious development it has had nothing to do at all. So far as that current—or one important current—is concerned, *Marius* is much nearer to being merely due to Pater's contact—a contact no more intimate than that of Marius himself—with something which was happening and would have happened without him.

The true importance of the book, I think, is as a document of one moment in the history of thought and

sensibility in the nineteenth century. The dissolution of
thought in that age, the isolation of art, philosophy,
religion, ethics and literature, is interrupted by various
chimerical attempts to effect imperfect syntheses. Religion became morals, religion became art, religion became science or philosophy; various blundering attempts
were made at alliances between various branches of
thought. Each half-prophet believed that he had the
whole truth. The alliances were as detrimental all
round as the separations. The right practice of "art for
art's sake" was the devotion of Flaubert or Henry
James; Pater is not with these men, but rather with
Carlyle and Ruskin and Arnold, if some distance below
them. *Marius* is significant chiefly as a reminder that
the religion of Carlyle or that of Ruskin or that of
Arnold or that of Tennyson or that of Browning, is not
enough. It represents, and Pater represents more
positively than Coleridge of whom he wrote the words,
"that inexhaustible discontent, languor, and home-
sickness...the chords of which ring all through our
modern literature".

MINOR FICTION IN
THE 'EIGHTIES

By Forrest Reid

Having promised to write a paper on the fiction of the 'eighties, I foresee that my task may prove difficult. I do not wish to concentrate on the scene and the conditions, because in that case I should merely be reproducing in less lively colour the pictures already so brilliantly painted of the 'seventies. The 'seventies and 'eighties practically form a single period; the scene and conditions undergo no striking change prior to the 'nineties; therefore I think my best plan will be to choose certain representative authors and through them try to give as comprehensive a view as may be of a very heterogeneous mass of material.

It is an artless method, but considering the extent of the ground to be covered I can think of no better. To put it mildly, a great many novelists were busy in the 'eighties, so busy that with not a few two novels a year appears to have been the normal rate of production, and it is to be remembered that two novels then meant five volumes, more often six. True, I have read a considerable number of these books, but most of them I read long ago, so that they are now but the veriest phantoms, floating in a mist of associations real and imaginary, the hour and the place—window-seat or walled garden, river or seashore, winter fire or summer sun—often emerging in far more vivid detail than the author and his work. I do not know why I should find it so much easier to remember where and when I read this or that book than to remember (beyond a mere general sense of happiness or unhappiness and a few detached scenes and characters) its contents, but so it is. I was brought up in a house full of novels, most of them belonging to the 'seventies and 'eighties, and in my teens I read with an appetite not easily sated: moreover I read honestly, pronouncing the words and never skipping, so that I somehow feel a great deal more should have remained than actually has. I read all the descriptions of sunsets provided so liberally and conscientiously by William Black. Unlike the descriptions of Thomas Hardy and Victor Hugo (between which I found a mysterious affinity), they created absolutely no impression on my mind, because, I think, they had created very little upon his. Still, I read them, though after three or four books I reached the conclusion that Black was not to be one of my authors, and for no better reason, I'm afraid, have not included him in my present survey. I read all the moralizings provided by novelists with a "purpose" or a "problem", but there was less virtue here, "problem" novels possessing at that time a curious fascination for me.

It was in 1883 that Olive Schreiner, with *The Story of an African Farm*, produced what must have been among the earliest of these; that is to say, of the modern variety, for of course there had been the experiments of Charles Reade and Wilkie Collins. But it was *The Story of an African Farm* which paved the way for the *Yellow Asters*, *David Grieves*, and *Heavenly Twins* of the 'nineties. Miss Schreiner, if she stood a little apart from the band of feminine novelists associated with the New Woman, nevertheless practically invented her. The Woman's Rights novel, the Religious Doubts novel, the Sex novel—seeds of all these

were wafted from her farm in Africa, to produce a
variegated crop of fictions bearing such titles, discon-
solate or provocative, as *A Superfluous Woman, A
Sunless Heart, The Woman Who Did*—works widely
discussed at the time, and which it would be difficult
by any effort of imagination to reanimate to-day. As
novels the interest they excited was violent and brief.
They annoyed Andrew Lang; they gained the sympathy if not the admiration of Thomas Hardy; they
left the small aesthetic camp indifferent. And of them
all *The African Farm* alone to some extent survives,
because of the genuine fervour behind it. It is not a
book to be re-read. If we have read it and cared for it
in the old days, it will be wiser to leave it at that. Even
in the 'eighties its appeal must have been mainly to
youthful readers, with whom the generosity of its spirit
would outweigh crudities of form and characterization. To myself the book appealed profoundly, and in
an ancient copy lying on the table before me quite
a jungle of marked passages remains to show me where
I was moved, if not, alas, to show me why. My favourite
chapter must have been that containing the allegory of
the Hunter and Truth, since this is pencilled from
beginning to end, while Lyndall's dissertations on the
rights and wrongs of women get not a single mark.
I must confess I still prefer the allegory to the dissertations, though what chiefly strikes me now is that so
few of these marked passages have any connexion with
the story. As I view them at present, they are a mere
series of technical blots—views, reflections, aspirations,
which had the dubious merit of coinciding with my
own. Yet I can see, too, that they would not have been
nearly so effective had I simply come across them in a
book of essays or sermons. This in fairness must be
granted to the author. Her story created the state of

mind most likely to prove receptive to her "message". There was art in it—or possibly I should say inspiration —but the book was not conceived as a work of art. It was an indictment, a sermon, a confession of faith, an appeal for justice, anything you like but a work of art, and as it stands it is an odd mixture of caricature and reality. Bonaparte Blenkins, the serio-comic villain, is not a real man; he bears, in fact, though sadly degenerated, a distinct resemblance to Mr Punch: Waldo —my own dear Waldo—is not a real boy; and Lyndall, I am afraid, though she was the author's darling, is not a real girl. What *is* real is Olive Schreiner, and where she identifies herself with her characters the fundamental feelings ring true. The humanity of the book is unmistakable. The author packed between its covers everything she had to say: she was not afraid to let herself go, not afraid to gush; it was all infinitely more personal, infinitely more confidential than most autobiographies.

So far as I am aware it struck a completely new note. I think it was George Meredith who read and accepted the manuscript for Messrs Chapman and Hall, but it certainly was not because he saw in Miss Schreiner a disciple. As a matter of fact, to accept *The African Farm* showed considerable courage, more than had been displayed by James Payn when he read and refused *John Inglesant*. The book reflected a new spirit which had begun to manifest itself among more serious novelists but which so far had received scant encouragement from their critics. It was before everything a book of revolt, a demand for freedom, though all that Olive Schreiner herself was interested in was the social question. But in other quarters the demand was based on aesthetic grounds. The novelist felt himself to be hampered: there were subjects of profound interest he was only allowed to treat dishonestly, if at all. There arose a clamour for what a character in one of Henry James's stories calls "the larger latitude". The ironic little masterpiece in question, *The Death of the Lion*, was perhaps rather cruel, since it must have been difficult not to associate Guy Walsingham, the author of *Obsessions*, with a lady who, also writing under a masculine pen-name, had attracted a good deal of attention just then. Both *Keynotes* and *Discords*, though I have read neither, I suspect to be experiments in "the larger latitude"—which phrase, I need scarcely add, means latitude to write with frankness of the relations of the sexes. It was bitterly opposed, and among the most acrimonious of the opposers were several of our novelists themselves, notably Mrs Oliphant, who attacked the later tales of Thomas Hardy with a virulence that leaves us gaping. Everybody has heard of the storm created by the publication of *Tess* and *Jude*, but much earlier than this, the love scenes in *Two on a Tower* had been censured as unpleasantly suggestive, while *The Return of the Native—The Return of the Native* of all books—had been described in the pages of a prominent literary journal as "betraying the influence" of decadent French fiction. Earlier still, and still more amazingly, Wilkie Collins had contrived to offend the innocents. There would be little point in reviving these ineptitudes were they not the outward and visible signs of a widespread spiritual prudery. An editorial note which appeared in *The Graphic* of 30 January 1875 reveals the remarkable state of mind that had been created by an attitude of excessive moral vigilance.

In last week's instalment of *The Law and the Lady* the following paragraph, which occurs on page 83, column 2, was printed thus:— "He caught my hand in his and covered it with kisses. In the indignation of the moment I cried out for help". In the author's proof the passage stood as follows:—"He caught my hand in his, and devoured it with kisses. His lips burnt me like fire. He twisted himself suddenly in the chair, and wound his arm round my waist. In the terror and indignation of the moment, vainly struggling with him, I cried out for help". The editor of this journal suppressed a portion of the paragraph on the ground that the description as originally given was objectionable. Mr Wilkie Collins having since informed us, through his legal advisers, that, according to the terms of his agreement with the proprietors of *The Graphic*, his proofs are to be published *verbatim* from his MS., the passage in question is here given in its original form.

One up to Wilkie! we may think, but this was not to be the last word. Our editor perfectly foresaw *his* opportunity, and sure enough, when *The Law and the Lady* had run its course as a serial and was issued in three volumes, *The Graphic*, instead of the customary review, simply printed beneath the title of the work an apology to its readers for having provided them with a tale the true nature of which had only been discovered after its first chapters were in print. Possibly the apology was sincere; possibly moral feelings really were wounded; in any case it was inevitable that a point of view so narrow, so *stupid*, should lead to a reaction, and in the 'eighties the backward—or forward—sweep of the pendulum had already begun. Quite apart from the *African Farm* and its defence of the New Morality, the early novels of George Moore and George Gissing were experiments in naturalism. True, in the case of Gissing there was to be no tampering with the proprieties, and even the naturalism remained far from unqualified. But George Moore showed a less conciliatory spirit, and in his very first story, *A Modern Lover*, published in 1883, through the mouth of Harding the novelist he produced his manifesto. "We do not always choose what you call unpleasant subjects, but we try to go to the roots of things; and the basis of life, being material and not spiritual, the analyst inevitably finds himself, sooner or later, handling what this sentimental age calls coarse."

Gissing, I think, never handled what any age, however sentimental, could call coarse, but he had a passion for the sordid (founded on dislike) and even when it was not necessarily in his subject a kind of flatness in his style produced a drab and dispiriting effect. The novels are devoid of charm, and the monotonously despondent tone somehow suggests a low vitality. Behind them is neither a lyrical nor a dramatic impulse, nor the impulse of the natural story-teller. It is work we must respect; he never wrote a cheap nor an insincere passage; but in all these novels of lower middle-class life I cannot recall a single beautiful line. And it is not because of the subjects. In the slum scenes of *The Princess Casamassima* Henry James used material quite as sordid, but there was joy in the making of the book, and his genius infused its darkest pages with the spirit of life and beauty. The value and meaning of a subject obviously must vary with what we bring to it, and it seems to me that Gissing brought little beyond the knowledge of the historian and the student of social problems. His incidents are presented in a curiously muffled fashion; there is never a sharp detonation. Moreover, he never really learned the technique of naturalism: in his method he was anything but an innovator.

> She proceeded to eat a supper scarcely less substantial than that which had appeased her brother's appetite. Start not, dear reader; Alice is only a subordinate heroine.

> Oh, the gravity of conviction in a white-souled English girl of eighteen! Do you not hear her say these words?

He does not realize that it is just such tiresome little apostrophes that prevent us from hearing her. I must confess it seems to me odd that Gissing's desire to write a realistic novel should have carried him no further than it did, that his experiments should have stopped short with the matter, leaving the manner to look after itself. There were models with which he must have been acquainted. Whether one approved of the story or not, surely it was plain that the method of *Madame Bovary* had a good deal to do with its extraordinary effect of reality, and whether one liked that method or not, surely it proved the advantage of possessing *a* method. But whatever other changes were taking place in the fiction of the 'eighties, whatever other activities were astir, except in the work of Henry James and George Moore the technique of the novel remained practically stationary. The authors' annoying "asides" continued to come crashing through the illusion like stones through a sheet of glass. And sometimes these "asides" extended for pages. Only too frequently, indeed, in the average novel of the period, they were there for no other reason than that they *did* extend for pages, and so helped to fill out the compulsory three volumes. Lengthy discussions (dialogue only by courtesy) fulfilled a similar purpose. Any convention is a drawback, but the three-volume convention was a disaster. Most of the novels of the 'eighties are too long. Even where he does not quite shamelessly resort to padding we see the author deliberately slackening his pace because he must not reach the end too soon. And the faults we find in the lesser writers are present also in the works of the masters. If there is less genius in the novel of to-day I think we may claim that there is more science. And the writing *is* less stilted. The moderns, I dare say, err on the other side, but let me give an example of what I mean. One of the chief merits of the novels of Rhoda Broughton is the vivacity of the dialogue, but re-read a page of that dialogue merely

changing "have not I?" and "do not you?" to "haven't
I?" and "don't you?", and note the result:—the
actual sound of the voices immediately begins to reach
us. After making allowance for the modifications that
must have taken place in our speech, I think it will
hardly be denied that in the average modern novel the
writing is more flexible than it was in the 'eighties, that
the novel itself contains less surplusage, that it does, in
short, show an advance in craftsmanship. True, the
question instantly suggests itself—Does the average
novel either of the 'eighties *or* the nineteen-thirties
matter? And if not, what is the position? In the
'eighties Henry James, Hardy, Meredith and Stevenson
were all writing, while from America came several
brilliant and charming novels by W. D. Howells, and
at least one masterpiece, *Huckleberry Finn*.

The 'eighties are sufficiently removed to enable us
to obtain a kind of Pisgah view of them. Looking back
across that stretch of half a century we *can*, for our
present purpose, see our novels and novelists divided
into groups or schools—the realistic, the romantic, the
pastoral. On the other hand, when we come to consider the more outstanding works with an idea of
seeking relationships with the past or future our time-
scheme presents an oddly broken line. Thus, though it
is not fanciful, perhaps, to point to a relationship
between W. H. Mallock's *New Republic*, published in
1877, and Mr Aldous Huxley's *Crome Yellow*, published in 1921, what have we in between? Casting
backward from *The New Republic* we arrive at *Headlong
Hall* and *Nightmare Abbey*, which constitute, I suppose,
the fountain-head. Again, Baring-Gould's *Mehalah* has
nothing in common with the rural tales of Thomas
Hardy, but a great deal in common with *Wuthering
Heights*. *John Inglesant* may have derived something

from *Esmond*, but the historical romances of Stanley Weyman, "Q", and Conan Doyle owe far more to the tales of Dumas than to *The Cloister and the Hearth*, while one of the most brilliant books of our whole decade, one of the least popular and at the same time most likely to survive, Richard Garnett's *Twilight of the Gods*, goes straight back to *Vathek*. As for the modern mystery story, how can we compare it with *The Moonstone* or *The Woman in White*?—and still less is it comparable with the tales of the Irish novelist, Sheridan Le Fanu, that so strangely underestimated writer, whose work at its best has a streak of genius running through it and hovers on the edge of a rather dreadful kind of poetry.

Probably the most popular novels of the late 'eighties and early 'nineties were the romances. I do not include *John Inglesant* among them, because, though it certainly was popular and a romance, it was essentially a spiritual confession, a novel of ideas, very nearly as much so as *Marius the Epicurean*, and spirituality is hardly the distinguishing quality of *King Solomon's Mines, Dead Man's Rock, A Gentleman of France*, or *The White Company*. It was, I venture to say, Andrew Lang, who to a large extent created the vogue of the romantic school. For Lang could make a reputation, or at any rate sell an edition, in a way no critic can to-day. And he loved these books—loved them so well that they seem to have had the power to blunt his critical faculty, which could be fastidious enough in other directions. The actual writing did not appear to matter so long as there were plenty of fights and adventures. Of course it must have mattered really, but he could close his ears to the most slipshod style if the story was of the kind he fancied. I remember reading a novel by Hume Nisbet, dedicated to Lang "by special permission", which struck me even

at the age of fourteen as a little crude. The comic
passages—as is usually the case—were particularly ex-
cruciating, and Lang, whose own humour was so
charming, must have loathed them. Still he *would* have
these books, and nobody dared to contradict him. His
prestige, his learning, his wit and his irony were too
formidable: in the heyday of his influence not a voice
was raised in revolt, and even timid disagreements
were larded with compliments. He could be generous
when it pleased him. He wrote charmingly of Rhoda
Broughton, with a graceful half affectionate playfulness
which conveyed at the same time a perfect appreciation
of her talent. Yet (and it might be in the same article)
he would ridicule a tale of Tolstoy's without having
troubled to read it; he described *Esther Waters* as the
unfortunate production of an Irishman without humour,
and dismissed Hardy's *Tess* in tones of magnanimity
that must have been infuriating. He infuriated Henry
James, though he had praised *Washington Square* and
done Miss Annie P., or Daisy Miller the honour of
bringing her into his delightful book of epistolary
parodies, *Old Friends.* But it was the early James Lang
liked, the James who, largely on the strength of *Daisy
Miller*, actually for a few years achieved popularity. If
he disapproved of the subject of a book or the point of
view of a writer, no sincerity, no subtlety of treatment
could win his praise, while if the subject were to his
taste he could tolerate almost any treatment. On the
other hand, when both subject *and* form pleased him—
then, even in the case of such exotic writers as Edgar
Poe and Gérard de Nerval, he became the most sensitive and sympathetic of critics. But he was whimsical,
Puckish, sometimes not without a hint of cruelty in his
wit, and his taste in fiction remained to the end the
taste of a schoolboy who is good at games.

Whether we attribute it to "freakishness" or to an odd insensibility, with the solitary exception of Stevenson, the more important novelists of his generation had very little for which to thank Lang. Even his appreciation of Rhoda Broughton's work we cannot help suspecting to be in part at least due to friendship. Elsewhere he shows not the slightest sympathy with her kind of novel. His treatment of it is to play with it like a cat with a mouse, giving delicate but painful taps at the style, plot, and characters, before the final pounce that finishes it off. But for Rhoda Broughton he reserved another method. Miss Broughton did not, we are told, in conversation at all events, take her novels very seriously, and this in itself would appeal to Lang. That she must have taken them seriously in one sense, however, that of being profoundly moved by what she was writing at the *time* of writing, is obvious. The emotion behind them must have been genuine since it still lives. She founded her own school and carried it on through the 'seventies and 'eighties—the school that is, for me at least, permanently associated with Bentley's Favourite Novels, fat dark green books, the contents of which had usually first been serialized in *Temple Bar*. I once planned to read them all, and I think must have come pretty near to succeeding. In the Bentley tradition, after *Not Wisely but too Well* and *Cometh Up as a Flower*, Rhoda Broughton had it very much her own way till the late 'eighties, when Miss Corelli was admitted to the fold, and promptly upset everything, capturing the public by the irresistible baits of melodrama, and an occultism that smacked of the Egyptian Hall. Rhoda Broughton's popularity had distinctly waned when in 1890 she published *Alas!*, though she still, in that novel, kept to the manner which had made her famous. In *Belinda*, which belongs to

1883, she had to my mind reached the highest point of her attainment. She had been writing then for seventeen years, and without losing any of her early zest had acquired more restraint. The love scenes in *Belinda* have all the old power, but it is now under firmer control, and her wit and humour, I think, are more abundantly in evidence here than in any other of the tales. The interest of *Belinda*, as indeed of all the novels of her first period, is frankly and almost exclusively erotic, but it is clean and healthy, and the passion does come through; there are no young women in fiction more genuinely in love than Rhoda Broughton's. What they experience, I admit, is largely an infatuation of the senses, and only a physical infatuation, I suppose, could work the physical havoc which brings more than one of these heroines to an early grave. The heroes are of tougher fibre; *they* survive all right—superb animals, glorious in strength if ugly of feature. This worship of brawn no doubt is carried to a point where to the weakling it may become on occasion just the least bit trying. The male whose interests are intellectual is so exclusively used as a foil to some Herculean numskull. We see him wrapped in overcoats and mufflers, an umbrella tucked under his arm, and galoshes on his large flat feet. There is something ruthless in the way the physical infirmities of Belinda's husband, Professor Forth, are kept before us. They acquire in the end a kind of moral quality, become a part of the general despicableness of his character—its meanness, selfishness, joylessness, and narrow-mindedness. For not only is the intellectual male usually depicted as unsound in wind and limb, but he is also denied any compensating graciousness of manner, and above all his loves are as feeble as his muscles. Not for him splendid, reckless passions, and it is by the capacity for experiencing an overwhelming passion that man in these novels is judged. True, in the tales of her second period, Rhoda Broughton worked gradually away from this point of view (her sense of humour was so strong that this perhaps was inevitable once the emotional impulse had begun to die down), but in the earlier, and to my mind distinctly superior novels the hero, whatever the hue of his moral character, whether he have the black reputation of Colonel Stamer (in *Not Wisely but too Well*) or the innocent record of "a non-reading, hard-rowing, foot-balling, cricketing" youth like David Rivers, Belinda's lover—the hero, whatever his virtues or vices may be, *must* be endowed with two transcendent physical qualities, a superb body and a capacity for fierce and devouring passion.

Miss Broughton's attitude in all this, if perfectly comprehensible, is none the less unusual—unusual, that is to say, in its outspokenness. And if to-day we find in her love scenes a remarkable abandon, what effect were they likely to have produced on readers of the 'eighties, accustomed to heroines of an angelic modesty and decorum? The books were read and adored, but they were also banned and banished as coarse and unmaidenly. They were not actually "wicked"—"wickedness" was reserved for Ouida, and naturally there were no "brown, painted harlots" in Miss Broughton's pictures of county society; but she was all the more dangerous because her characters were human. "I began my career as Zola", she remarked in her old age to Mr Percy Lubbock. "I finish it as Miss Yonge. It's not I that have changed, it's my fellow-countrymen."

Rhoda Broughton had little sense of style and her habit of writing in the historic present was not without its inconveniences; but her books had the warmth of life in them, and their success was deserved. Moreover, considering the narrow range of subject, the variety we find in these for the most part tragic love dramas is surprising. It springs from the fact that the love motive is felt so intensely that fresh incidents and situations have never to be sought for, but spring up spontaneously in the writer's imagination. Nothing quite like these books had been done before, though only too much was done afterwards, one of the most popular imitations, *Comin' thro' the Rye*, on its first anonymous appearance having been actually attributed to Rhoda. The irrepressible F. C. Burnand parodied her in *Punch*, and this burlesque novel—*Gone Wrong*, by Miss Rhody Dendron—later appeared in book form with a cover design by Linley Sambourne. To *Punch*, also, Du Maurier contributed portraits of "splendid ugly men". But these were jests of honour, tributes to her popularity, the novels are not in the least absurd, and the reader to-day, should he return to them, will laugh and cry in the right places.

The best comment on her own early fictions Miss Broughton supplied herself when an old woman (she died in 1920). So at any rate I take her last story, *A Fool in Her Folly*, to be. In this posthumous tale it seems to me she deliberately showed the other side of the medal. Surely there have crept some memories from the past into her half satiric, half sympathetic portrait of Charlotte. It is just such a novel as *Not Wisely but too Well* that Charlotte in her enthusiastic innocence embarks upon, and the manuscript of which so shocks her parents that they burn it and she has to write it all over again from memory. *Love* is the title of Charlotte's work, a volcanic love her theme, her hero a dark, passion-scarred man. This hero, when half way through the second version of her novel, she meets in the flesh.

Bill Drinkwater is Colonel Stamer of *Not Wisely but too Well* reduced to reality. Like Stamer, like the hero of Charlotte's own novel, Bill is a black sheep, but there is this important difference in Miss Broughton's new presentment of the type, that his failings are no longer veiled in a romantic glamour, but particularized. Bill was expelled from Eton, a similar result followed when he was sent to an Army tutor in Yorkshire, and his later career has been marked by a trail of unsavoury episodes. Upon Charlotte, however, the true significance of these vulgar little affairs is lost. She bathes her lover in the transforming light of imagination—and through his passion for *her* sees him achieving redemption. Alas, this time the sheep really is black; so far from en-nobling her hero, poor Charlotte, having kept a tryst with him at a lonely shanty on the downs, narrowly escapes from a worse misfortune than the disillusion-ment in which her grand passion ends.

"Rhoda", says Mr Percy Lubbock, "to the end of her life, wore an air of the eighteen-seventies; myself I have seen her, a generation later, with a trailing gown and a parasol and a croquet-mallet, contriving to wield all three at once with effect; and though it was difficult to think that she was the creator of her gushing Joans and Nancies and Belindas, she evidently came to us from their time and place; and if she hadn't written her novels she had lived in them, in that high-coloured England of big houses and big meals and big families." Certainly the big houses and big meals and big families form part of the charm of the novels. The very appear-ance of these, with their steel-engraved frontispieces, carries us back to a more homely, more leisurely, mellower age. I can myself, or so I fancy, recall it—not dimly, but brokenly—in such isolated pictures as impress themselves, usually quite inexplicably, on a child's mind. For that age died slowly, and more slowly, I dare say, in Ireland than in England. There are no crinolines in my pictures (nor for that matter in Rhoda's), which are of the mid-eighties, but there are crinolettes and parasols and spotted veils and small toque-like hats and trailing gowns, all in my mind still inextricably bound up with earliest visions of feminine beauty; and it was thus that Miss Broughton's heroines were apparelled. I confess I admire them. I admire the world they lived in. If I could I would sweep away nearly every invention of the intervening years— motor-cars, wireless, aeroplanes, movies, talkies, re- taining only the guileless gramophone, and even that I would sacrifice to be rid of the rest. The frontispieces to the novels seem to me charming: I have an affection for big houses; while anybody who has been brought up in one must know that big families are the best. Miss Broughton's is the "county" world, and I like that too. Probably there are London scenes in her books but I do not remember them; for me the novels have a countrified and familiar aspect over which I would gladly linger.

If I am to cover my ground, however, I must pass to other books and other scenes, and the London scene will do as well as any, sophisticated, worldly, amusing, as we find it in the work of W. E. Norris.

The career of Norris began thirteen years later than that of Rhoda Broughton; he was really of our decade, his first novel, *Mademoiselle de Mersac*, having been published in 1880; and certainly I came to his work later. There were no novels by Norris in our house, and I have forgotten how I procured *Miss Shafto*, *A Bache- lor's Blunder*, *Major and Minor* and the rest. But they were in Bentley's list, and for me that was sufficient; never can a publisher have inspired greater faith. Here

there can be no doubt about origins: whatever value
we may set on the achievement, it is plain that Norris
got his idea of the novel from Thackeray. His fiction
is the fiction of a man of the world, well-bred, detached,
not taking himself or his work over-seriously, deploring,
rather, any emphatic display of emotion; amused, at
times mildly cynical, but always kindly. He tells a
story of course, but it is as little startling as he can make
it, and there is only just enough *of* it to hold together
an easy-going comedy of manners. Norris does not invariably end his fable with a wedding, but tragedy is
as little in his line as mystery or melodrama. What he
chiefly relies on, and what is the main source of our
enjoyment, is his lightness of touch, and this is particularly happy in his drawing of those idle, clever young
good-for-nothings, who constitute by far the most
amusing portraits in his gallery. We cannot call them
villains, still less can we call them heroes, these young
gentlemen of expensive tastes and slender if any means,
whose engaging imperturbability and deplorable morals
enliven the pages of Norris's best novels, and who, we
cannot help suspecting, were regarded by their creator
with considerable affection. Probably they really *are*
villains, for they live by their wits and on their friends
—sometimes, alas, their friends of the opposite sex.
Moreover they are utterly selfish; their intelligence,
their wit, and their graces of person and manner being
employed solely to gain their own disreputable ends.
In spite of this, the charm they exercise upon long-
suffering relatives and friends is completely convincing,
because we feel it ourselves. They have a playful, ironic
humour which passes easily into insolence when nothing
is to be gained by politeness. On the other hand, they
never indulge in self-pity, above all never whine when
misfortune overtakes them, never lose their composure

in the most trying circumstances. They take risks and abide by their luck. They are not in the end allowed to triumph, but even when detected and exposed they have a delightful habit of leaving the virtuous both looking and feeling extremely foolish. Philip in *No New Thing*, whose fortunes we follow from early boyhood till his marriage with Signora Tommasini, the great operatic contralto, fat, *passée*, good-natured, nearly old enough to be his grandmother, but with heaps of money, is a typical Norris youth. His career is little more edifying than that of Mr George Moore's "modern lover", but then he is so much more tolerable as a man, and so infinitely more amusing as a companion. We *feel* his attractiveness, whereas we have to take Lewis Seymour's for granted, since it depends apparently entirely on his good looks.

Norris wrote with an always dangerous and eventually disastrous facility. Possibly the rate of his production did not exceed that of Anthony Trollope, but his range was very much narrower, and his talent far less robust. He never lost a certain grace of manner, but he forced his gift, and the early liveliness failed under the strain of over-production. *Thirlby Hall, The Rogue, Adrian Vidal, No New Thing*—he wrote, I dare say, a score of novels as good or nearly as good as these, and perhaps another score that do not fall immeasurably below them, but the four I have mentioned contain everything that will be found in the rest. They are, I suppose, what used to be described as "society novels". They deal with a world in which even a bachelor cannot live comfortably under two or three thousand a year and in which titles are plentiful as daisies. For the more familiar picture of English middle-class life we may turn to Mr Anstey's two serious novels, *The Giant's Robe* and *The Pariah*.

Or rather to one of them, for though *The Giant's Robe* has some delightful humour and a tragic and exciting plot, it is of the later book I really wish to speak, tragic and enthralling also, but with a tragedy more subtle and a plot less in evidence. *The Pariah* is an admirable novel, standing far above the average fiction of both its day and ours, far too good to be forgotten. The portrait of Allen Chadwick, the loutish, undersized, uneducated, uncomely, cockney youth, who wakes up one day to find himself a rich man's son, is a delicate and beautiful study, to some extent anticipating that of Kipps. But all the circumstances of the story are different, and Allen's temperament is both less adaptable and more sensitive. Transplanted into an environment where he is disliked and looked down upon; blundering, shy, by no means clever—the innate kindness and generosity of his nature are belied at every turn by his unfortunate speech, manner, and appearance. Hectored and bullied by a coarse-grained father who desires to make a gentleman of him while not understanding very clearly what a gentleman is, and to this end has married an aristocratic but impecunious widow who (with an eye to the advancement of her own brood) is careful, beneath a veil of apparent sympathy, to keep her stepson's shortcomings constantly in view; despised and disliked by his stepbrothers and sisters, Allen in the end is turned adrift; the cuckoo tactics succeed, the pariah is eliminated. The tragedy is quiet, with from the first a kind of hopelessness in it; and for all its pathos there is never a false note of sentimentality. I do not know that the novel attracted any particular attention. It was not what was expected, and therefore probably aroused disappointment. Mr Anstey had the bad luck to write in his first story a book which was ever afterwards to be associated with his name, so that no matter what new ground he broke up, to the public he remained and still remains the author of *Vice Versâ*. I can think of no other explanation for the neglect of his later books. After all, *Tourmalin's Time Cheques* is quite as original and amusing as *Vice Versâ*. So are *Under the Rose*, *The Travelling Companions*, and all that series of stories in scene and dialogue beginning with *Voces Populi* and ending with *Lyre and Lancet*.

With the exceptions of those two masterpieces, *The New Arabian Nights* and *The Twilight of the Gods*, the only experiments in the fantastic I can recall belonging to the 'eighties are Mr Anstey's. *Vice Versâ*, *The Tinted Venus*, *A Fallen Idol*, *Tourmalin's Time Cheques*—these endearing tales, in which the quaintness of the situations is exquisitely opposed to the realism of the talk and characterization, act upon one's spirits like sunshine upon a barometer. They are true flowers of the comic genius, and each is, into the bargain, the work of a born story-teller. Observation, invention, an exquisite sense of human absurdity, and a gift for writing dialogue with a mimetic skill that creates the very illusion of the speaking voice—all these qualities have kept them as fresh to-day as when they were first published.

The extremely slender thread, with a few knots tied in it, each representing a group of novels, by which I have tried to guide myself through a far too intricate subject, brings me at last to that particularly home-grown product, the pastoral novel. Here, close to the soil, we breathe the very smell of England, and here, in the works of Thomas Hardy, we find the English genius, a little earthy perhaps, but spontaneous, strong, triumphant, in its supreme gift of poetry. And in the work of those less famous writers with whom I am alone concerned there is an equally strong local flavour. There are flashes of poetry in the novels of Richard

Jefferies—*Greene Ferne Farm*, *Amaryllis at the Fair*, *The Dewy Morn*—though all three are failures. Jefferies, in truth, apart from his power of description, was but poorly equipped as a novelist. He had little gift for creating character, little inventive power, little sense of construction, and his technique was more artless even than that of most of his contemporaries. He wrote one masterpiece, *Bevis*, but *Bevis* was a book about boys, a dream of his own boyhood, everything in which sprang from memory, a love of nature, and an inexhaustible joy and patience in noting the details of the natural scene. And even *Bevis* he did his best in the last chapters to spoil. Fortunately that was impossible, yet anybody with the slightest feeling for the novel form must have seen that the book really ends when Bevis and Mark return from New Formosa. It was published in 1882 in the conventional three volumes and failed. Later it was mutilated and the abridgement published in one volume, with pictures, to attract a juvenile audience. Finally it was reissued in the present century as Jefferies wrote it, and this third appeal was at least moderately successful. It seems to me to be the best book about boys ever written, with the possible exception of *Huckleberry Finn*: in fact, in its own line, I believe it to be unsurpassable. At the same time I feel much less certain that it is the best boy's book. There is no need to ask what the modern boy, under the spell of Mr Edgar Wallace, would think of *Bevis*, but I can remember what I thought of it in my own boyhood, and I thought it dull. Yet Bevis is a real boy, and apart from his taste for killing things lived exactly the kind of life I liked most. For some inexplicable reason it was the human, the personal appeal I found wanting. Bevis himself was too detached and self-centred. I never cared for him in the way I cared for George Manville Fenn's heroes. Unlike them, he refused to be woven into my own imaginings; therefore the book left me cold, and I doubt if at that time I finished it.

It was the only story Jefferies ever wrote into which he was able to put his whole heart, and this in itself indicates his limitations as a novelist. He knew far more about Bevis and Mark and Pan the spaniel, and was far closer to them than to his mature heroes and heroines. They were a part of wild nature, and it was wild nature, not human nature, he loved and understood. He was far more interested in the building of the raft, the exploration of the lake, the lessons in swimming and sailing, even in Pan's private exploits, than in the love business of his grown-up fictions.

Greene Ferne Farm, published in 1880, is typical of these. It is a short novel, less than three hundred pages of big print; it contains a few beautiful passages and two or three good chapters; but Jefferies' individual note, the note that is carried right through *Bevis*, sounds only intermittently.

Mr Ruck, very big and burly, was shaped something like one of his own mangolds turned upside down: that is to say, as the glance ran over his figure, beginning at the head, it had to take in a swelling outline as it proceeded lower. He was clad in a snowy-white smock-frock, breeches and gaiters, and glossy beaver hat.

This costume had a hieroglyphic meaning. The snowy smock-frock intimated that he had risen from lowly estate, and was proud of the fact. The breeches and gaiters gave him an air of respectable antiquity in itself equivalent to a certain standing. Finally the beaver hat—which everybody in the parish knew cost a guinea, and nothing less—bespoke the thousand pounds at the bank to which he so frequently alluded.

"Hur be a upstanding girl, that Margaret Estcourt. A' got a thousand pound under the will."

"And the Greene Ferne Farm when the widder goes."

"Five hundred acres freehold, and them housen in to town."

"A' be a featish-looking girl, yon."

"So be May Fisher; but a' bean't such a queen as t'other. Margaret walks as if the parish belonged to her."

"If a' did, her would sell un, and buy a new bonnet...."

The sound of singing came from the open door under the tower hard by.

"Dall'd if it bean't 'I will arise.'"

"'S'pose us had better go in."

In such a passage can we not hear the echo of another voice, that of the author of *Under the Greenwood Tree*? Those chapters, too, in which Margaret and Geoffrey, the undeclared lovers, are lost on the downs at night, might have been conceived by Hardy, though here it is Jefferies who is writing. They find shelter in an ancient tomb or dolmen, and possibly it is this which recalls the scene, written more than ten years later, where Angel Clare and Tess flee from justice across Salisbury Plain. True, no cloud of doom hangs over Jefferies' lovers, no ironical President of the Immortals makes sport of them; it is only that both scenes impress upon us the same sense of a vast lonely space and of immemorial time in contrast with the pitiful fragility of human life. We are face to face with earth and sky and night, conscious of an immense silence through which the mysterious voices of nature reach anxious questioning ears. And in the simplicity of treatment there is a kind of grave instinctive poetry, a beauty Greek in spirit if not in form, and which is utterly alien from and beyond the reach of "fine writing".

Still, when all is said, *Greene Ferne Farm* remains a very minor performance, and in the same year, 1880, there had appeared a much more remarkable novel of rural life. Baring-Gould's half-forgotten tale, *Mehalah*, if not a great book is at least a memorable one. It would be memorable if for nothing else than that the author of it is, I suppose, Emily Brontë's only disciple.

In its subject, in its principal characters, in its conception of love as a kind of spiritual or demoniac obsession, in its violence, in its wild and lonely setting, *Mehalah* inevitably reminds us of *Wuthering Heights*. The likeness, indeed, if it forms part of the book's fascination, is also its misfortune. *Mehalah* is powerfully written; set it among any group of novels of the better class and it will stand out as a bold, striking, and picturesque work; the one comparison it can *not* survive is the comparison it forces us to draw.

For it is not, as *Wuthering Heights* is, born of the spirit. It has everything else, everything but just this unanalysable quality, this quality which cannot be imitated, the bright naked flame. *Mehalah* is good prose fiction, but *Wuthering Heights* belongs to the world of great poetry—is of no school, betrays no influences; were it the only novel in existence it could hardly be a thing more unique and isolated.

On its own plane, however, *Mehalah* is worthy to survive. The time is 1780 or thereabouts, the scene the glittering, desolate Essex salt marshes, the subject a passionate and unrequited love. How far Elijah Rebow, consciously or unconsciously, may have been derived from Heathcliff does not matter. He never appears to us as a kind of dark fallen angel (and how far *that* aspect depended on the fact that Emily Brontë was in love with her hero it would be useless to seek, though one can guess that under a certain type of examination he would emerge as the projection of a repression). Rebow, if he was suggested by Heathcliff, nevertheless is *not* Heathcliff: much less is Mehalah Catherine Earnshaw; and the author's realization of his characters remains throughout clear and consistent. Rebow is as violent and ruthless as Heathcliff, as constant in his love, while the passion that consumes him is as

9-2

absorbing and as clean as Heathcliff's; spiritualized, one might think, by its very intensity. He rants at times, but so does Heathcliff. Both are ready to commit any action that may bring them nearer to their heart's desire; both are revengeful, implacable, and in most directions unscrupulous. And Mehalah is Rebow's soul-mate as Cathy is Heathcliff's. But a sharp divergence here is given to the march of the drama, for Mehalah hates and defies Rebow and loves the worthless, easy-going George. To get the girl into his power Rebow sticks at nothing. He betrays Mehalah's lover to the press-gang, robs her and her widowed mother, plots against them, buys up their impoverished farm, burns the house down over their heads, and finally, by lying, scheming, and violence, gets them beneath his own roof at Red Hall. This gaunt red-brick house, standing bare and bleak and lonely above the level of the marsh, without a tree to shelter it, and where, in the cellars under the paved floor, Rebow keeps his maniac brother chained like a wild beast—this house is in itself a Brontë conception. The whole theme of the book might well have scared off anybody but a Brontë, and by what miracle it escapes melodrama I do not know. That it does escape it, however, is I think unquestionable. And the story unrolls itself before us against a background of water and sky. The smell of the sea is in it, the brown salt weed drying on the flats, the sound of oars and of boats being launched and beached, the cry of wild duck and curlew, now and then the report of a gun: and though it is not a tale of smugglers and we are not told of a single cargo that is run, smuggling somehow is going on all round us.

There are faults, glaring enough—passages of false rhetoric, passages of stilted dialogue, antiquarian and other tiresome digressions: Mrs de Wit's allusions to

her son's "galliwanting" become trying; the characters
sometimes say the wrong thing, or the right thing in
the wrong way; but in the great dramatic moments
the style becomes strangely clarified, and so living and
moving is the whole conception that faults are no sooner
perceived than they are forgotten. What is the secret of
the emotional force that strikes through such a book as
Mehalah and holds us, for it is rarely to be found in
modern fiction? Is it that the novelist of to-day cares
less for his characters, regards them largely in the light
of "copy"—cares less for everything?

Mehalah was a rather odd book for a parson to have
written, even though he did not intend to sign it.
Where rustic religion is concerned the tone if not
cynical is completely disillusioned.

> Mrs de Wit was a moralist, and when nearly drunk religious.
>
> "I always make a point to believe the worst. I'm a religious person,
> and them as sets up to be religious always does that."
>
> The "dearly beloveds" met in the Lord's house every Lord's day to
> acknowledge their "erring and straying like lost sheep" and make
> appointments for erring and straying again.

There is not the slightest attempt to point a moral,
to preach or to pray. The attitude to women is to say
the least unflattering, and such an episode as that of the
curate's children and the bat is in the spirit if not the
manner of Mr T. F. Powys.

Just one more book I should like to mention, not
because it is characteristic of our period—for really it
would be more in place in a paper on the 'nineties—
but because it has never, I think, met with anything
like the appreciation it deserves: and after all it *was*
published in the 'eighties, in 1887, appearing first
anonymously in *Temple Bar*, and then in a single slender
dark blue volume. (I am ending up, you see, fittingly
if quite unintentionally, with yet another Bentley book:

"that wise old publisher", as Miss Corelli called him when he accepted *A Romance of Two Worlds*.) *A Village Tragedy* by Margaret L. Woods is a realistic pastoral novel, but it is a work of infinite delicacy, written in a simple lucid prose that is in itself a joy, rare then and rare to-day. The tragic plot is simple as the writing, the characters lowly—the hero being almost inarticulate—but in spite of its gloomy shadows there is a beauty in this love tale that approaches the idyllic. Beauty and sadness alike spring in some measure from the youth of the lovers, their pathetic inexperience if not innocency, for Annie and Jesse are really little more than children when they are thrown into each other's arms —Annie the farm drudge, and Jesse the work-house boy, now working on a farm too. The disaster is not of their making; it is the result of the cruelty, prurience, and stupidity of their elders, for there has been nothing but friendship between them when the girl in the middle of the night is dragged out of bed and thrust out of doors by her suspicious and half-drunken aunt and mistress. She seeks shelter, naturally enough, in the boy's cottage, but it is an unfortunate step, and her aunt sees to it that it shall be irretrievable. It may be objected that in the misinformation that prevents Annie and Jesse from getting married, in Jesse's long illness, and in the railway accident which kills him just when at last there seems to be a chance of happiness—it may be objected that in such a sequence of accidents, all unfortunate, there is a hint of the arbitrary; and it cannot be denied that the dice have been heavily loaded against Annie and Jesse, though no more heavily than in many a novel of Hardy's. Still, the little book remains of a rare distinction, and takes rank amongst our very finest pastoral novels.

Like *Mehalah*, it is among those that ought, if out

of print, to be reprinted. *A Village Tragedy, The Pariah, Mehalah*—if I were reissuing a selection of novels of the 'eighties I should begin with these three. But I should not end there: there are others—at least a score —whose ghosts would haunt me reproachfully if I did. Fifty years! A man considers himself only middle-aged at fifty, yet for a book it is far beyond the allotted span. The thought might well awaken in the most self-confident author a mood of chastened melancholy. Luckily youth is untroubled with such thoughts, or I dare say nobody would think it worth the bother to begin to write, which would be a pity. It is only when we see the books we ourselves have once so enjoyed— or perhaps even written—dropping into oblivion, that a spirit of tenderness towards the past is aroused. Let us cultivate it, without neglecting the present. It may one day—who knows?—breathe some faint friendly whisper among our own dry bones.

GILBERT AND SULLIVAN

By G. K. Chesterton

No institution was so supremely typical of this section of the Victorian era as that product of the partnership of Gilbert and Sullivan, commonly called the Savoy Opera. Nowadays everybody is talking about the Victorian era, especially those who would persuade us that their minds are wholly fixed on the future. Unfortunately, it is also true that those who defend the Victorian era are quite as unjust to it as those who attack it. They both make the mistake of supposing that, because it was a phase of the English character, it was solid or stolid; whereas the English character is moody and very subtle. On the one hand the futurists, with the ignorance naturally produced by exclusive contemplation of the future, talk of the Victorian Age as merely limited and timid, a system of restrictions and respectabilities. The truth is, of course, that it was emphatically the Liberal Age, perhaps the first and perhaps the last; certainly believing much more in the intrinsic claim of Liberty than does the age of Mussolini and Mr Pussyfoot Johnson. On the other hand, the reactionaries are driven by reaction to represent it as a civilization ideally domestic, and founded on the sacredness of the family. The truth is that it was in many ways the very opposite of this. For instance, the English of this period were the only people in the world who prided themselves upon sending their boys far away from home, to be herded in undomestic institutions and taught to be rather ashamed of being fond of their own mothers. Some, by a similar reactionary illusion, have even described the Victorian Age as an Age of Religious Faith. If one thing is certain, it is that it was supremely the Age of Religious Doubt.

The true definition or distinction, I fancy, is something like this. The Victorian epoch was the epoch in which most respectable people still believed in liberty, because they still believed that no liberty would ever in *practice* invade respectability. Men believed that the consolidated commercial civilization of England, with its great wealth and its world-wide base, was already cast in a mould of manners and morals that could not really be shaken by any speculations. To take a personal example; the great Professor Huxley was as much of a sceptic or agnostic in theory as his grandson Mr Aldous Huxley. But if you had told old Huxley that some of young Huxley's literary works could be published and printed, he would have refused to believe it. Yet the grandson is in some ways more in sympathy with dogmatic Christianity than the grandfather. In short, the Victorian Age was one in which freedom of thought went with conservation of convention; that is why men like Dean Inge revere and regret it. The cheap way of putting it would be to say that one could attack the Deity without affecting the Deanery. But that would be unjust to the subtle sincerity in the Victorian and in the Dean. It was an age when a conservative could safely be a sceptic; but in these later days we must believe in order to conserve.

One result of this curious condition was this. The Victorians excelled in throwing off fancies, which were rather dreams relieving the general system than visions breaking it up. They were holidays of the intellect rather than (in the modern sense) emancipations of it.

Alice in Wonderland is not Alice in Utopia; she is not in an ideal country which challenges or satirizes her own country. Lear's landscapes and travels are really in the other end of Nowhere; not in Somewhere disguised as Somewhere Else. In this sort of bourgeois Saturnalia there could even be a great deal of satire; but not satire that could ever be mistaken for sedition. Perhaps that is what the Victorians really meant by talking so much about evolution; that the one thing quite inconceivable to them was revolution. They would never turn the world topsy-turvy in fact; but they would travel in topsy-turvydom in fancy; and they found it, as they did their annual journeys to Brighton or Margate, bracing and quite a change.

This special type of escape is well exemplified in Opera. *Le Mariage de Figaro* was a light opera; but it helped to produce the French Revolution; which was not a light opera. *H.M.S. Pinafore* in many respects made as much fun of British pride and prejudice as *Figaro* made of the pride and prejudice of the old régime. But we may safely bet that it never crossed the mind of any human being that *H.M.S. Pinafore* would ever produce, I will not say a revolution, but even the tiniest mutiny on the most minute gun-boat. The Victorians, for various reasons, felt secure from all practical results; and therefore their satire was all in the air and lacked both the malice and the force of more militant peoples. And, as I have said, there never was a more marked example than this great achievement of the Savoy Operas, which held the field for so long as a genuine creation of the national humour and hilarity; and which was the result of two men of genius, and as some held of serious genius, consenting to dedicate their lives to playing the fool. But they were British buffoons; they were only *playing* the fool; anything more practical they would have regarded as acting the lunatic.

Mr Maurice Baring has truly remarked that we, who grew up in the great days of the Savoy Operas, never realized how great they were till they ceased. With all the growth of theatrical technique and experiment, even with a certain amount of wit and intelligence lingering in the world, it has been found in fact impossible to do anything like the same thing again. Doubtless it was largely the coincidence that brought together two talents suited for a special tone and style of work. I must speak here mainly of the literary talent; for though even I could appreciate the popular fascination of Sullivan's work, I do not even know enough of music to describe my own pleasure in musical terms. But certainly, in any case, the work as a whole was very remarkable. A distinguished foreign musician said to me that it would be easy to find here or there, on the Continent, one or two particular comic operas as good or better; but of the Savoy Operas there are at least ten, if not twelve, of the first rank of invention; and we had come to count on their going on for ever, like the seasons of summer or of spring.

Some of Sir Arthur Sullivan's admirers, or perhaps some of his detractors who cunningly posed as his admirers, were in the habit of lamenting that he had lent himself (they sometimes said sold himself) to a lifetime of light opera music, when he was originally capable of doing something more serious. Curiously enough, the judgment upon Sir William Gilbert, his great colleague, must be almost the reverse. Sullivan began with work that was more serious and may have been better; Gilbert began with work that was broadly comic and was quite certainly his best. I know he had written some sentimental plays like *Broken Hearts*, and probably fancied himself as a pathetic writer; but that was perhaps no more than the recurrent anecdote of Grimaldi longing to create Hamlet. Gilbert was a mocker, if ever there was one; he knew much better what he wanted to deride than what he wanted to defend; on the negative side he was really a satirist, on the other side he would never have been dogmatic enough to be anything but a sentimentalist. The point that is not adequately grasped is that his satiric power appeared long before the Savoy Operas; and was at its wittiest when it was most wildly satiric. Nobody knows anything about W. S. Gilbert who does not constantly compare the Savoy Operas with *The Bab Ballads*. Unfortunately, while managers still find it worth while to revive the Operas, publishers and reviewers do not at the same regular intervals republish and review the *Ballads*. If they did, we should know all about the Savoy Operas; exactly why they succeeded and exactly where they failed. They succeeded because Gilbert had already accumulated in *The Bab Ballads* a dazzling treasure-house of fantastic and paradoxical ideas. They failed because even a man of genius cannot always repeat his best idea twice. He has very often forgotten what it was.

Oddly enough, there is a sort of symbol of this repetition and relative deterioration in his experiment as a caricaturist, as well as a satirist. To the first edition of *The Bab Ballads* he appended delightfully indefensible little pictures, grotesque and grimacing, figures with bodies like eggs and mouths like frogs' and little legs like dancing insects'. They were amateur drawings; but they were artistic drawings, in being apt and fitted exactly to their purpose. Afterwards, in a later edition and in a disastrous hour, in some dark moment of mental decline, he actually erased these right little tight little goblins, and laboriously went over the design again with a timid and tottering line, in the attempt to give some resemblance to real human figures; an attempt not merely amateur but amateurish. He actually said, with all solemnity, that perhaps the original figures were a little too grotesque; and this represented his attempt to make them a little more serious. Serious, if you please, as a quality slightly lacking in Calamity Pop Von Peppermint Drop or Mrs MacCatacomb de Salmon-Eye. The truth is that Gilbert had made the joke and forgotten the joke. It is a thing that does sometimes happen to humorists. And it is a thing that did most definitely happen to Gilbert, as can specially be noted by a comparison between *The Bab Ballads* and the Savoy Operas. Every single Savoy Opera is a splendid achievement as compared with every other attempt at such an opera in modern times. But every single Savoy Opera is a spoilt Bab Ballad.

There are several obvious cases in which this double operation occurred. I mean that Gilbert first went back to one of his ballads for an idea, and then came back with the wrong idea, because he had forgotten the right one. For instance, in some of his best operas, notably in *H.M.S. Pinafore* and *The Gondoliers*, he seems obsessed with the notion that there is something very funny about the idea of two babies being mixed up in their cradles, and the poorer infant being substituted for the richer. But there is nothing particularly odd or original, or even amusing, about the mere idea of a substituted baby. That baby has been a stock property of many tragedies and numberless melodramas. To blast it with a yet more withering bolt of criticism, it has even happened in real life. The truth is that Gilbert vaguely remembered having put the joke into a very good ballad, where it is a very good joke; but, in

searching for it again, found the ballad but could not
find the joke. He did not notice what it was that was
really funny in his original fancy. The real ballad, which
contained the real joke, which entirely withered in
being transplanted to the opera, is the admirably severe
and simple poem of *Private James and Major-General
John*. I hope that all readers will remember it; I fear
that most readers have forgotten it. Perhaps they dimly
recall that the Major-General was of a disdainful
disposition:

> "Pish" was a favourite word of his,
> And he often said "Ho! Ho!"

James, the private soldier was a sadder and more obscure being: "No characteristic trait had he of any
distinctive kind". But this gloomy ranker suddenly
addresses the General out of the ranks and says that
he has been visited by an intuition:

> "A glimmering thought occurs to me
> (Its source I can't unearth),
> But I've a sort of a notion we
> Were cruelly changed at birth."

Major-General John ungraciously sneers at the suggestion, though reminded that "No truly great or generous
cove...would sneer at a fixed idea that's drove in the
mind of a Private James"; whereupon the General, his
better nature prevailing, abruptly admits that the facts
are probably as suggested:

> So General John as Private James
> Fell in parade upon;
> While Private James, by a change of names,
> Was Major-General John.

Now that is the pure and holy spirit of Nonsense;
that divine lunacy that God has given to men as a
holiday of the intellect; has given to men and, if we

may say so, rather especially to Englishmen. It may be hard to talk about the point of something when its point is its pointlessness. But essentially the point of that nonsense rhyme is not in the rather stale and vulgar notion of mixing up the babies. The point is in the outrageous abruptness with which the brooding James mentions his intuition, entirely unsupported by reason; and the equally absurd abruptness with which it is accepted. That is a very funny idea, and yet it was not the idea which its own author thought funny. That error accounts for many of the defects which disfigure the general brilliance and fancy of the Gilbertian Operas. A man can borrow from himself; but a man does not really know himself. And Gilbert, when he borrowed what he thought was most grotesque, did not really know what was most Gilbertian.

It would be easy to give many other examples of the same truth; that the Gilbertian Operas, vivacious and inventive as they are, are not the first sprightly runnings of the Gilbertian fancy; and that he sometimes fished out the wrong things from those upper streams. In *H.M.S. Pinafore*, with the assistance of Sullivan's lively music, he makes an excellent musical comedy chorus of ladies of the refrain, "And so do his sisters and his cousins and his aunts". But in its very joviality it has lost the joke; the original joke suggested by the wooden solemnity of the stiff lines about Captain Reece:

> The sisters, cousins, aunts and niece,
> And widowed ma of Captain Reece,
> Attended there as they were bid:
> It was their duty, and they did.

Similarly, I think, his parade of coronets and the costumes of the Peerage in *Iolanthe* is partly a reminiscence of the beautiful inconsequence of the poem called "The Periwinkle Girl" and the two Dukes who "offer guilty splendour" to that discriminating young woman. But he leaves out the fine and delicate point about the adoring Dukes; which is the contrast between these exalted yet degraded aristocrats and the honest worth of the humble youth, who could claim no better social position than that of an Earl:

> Her views of earldoms and their lot
> All underwent expansion—
> Come, Virtue, in an earldom's cot!
> Go, Vice, in ducal mansion!

But perhaps the strongest example of all is to be found in *Patience*; which contains a typical example of this readiness to spoil a joke in order to repeat a joke. All the business about the one poet persuading the other poet to give up his poetical hair and habits, and put on the uniform of a stockbroker, is obviously copied from the notion of a similar rivalry in the magnificently absurd ballad of "The Rival Curates". In that touching story one curate, accounted the mildest for miles round, hears the hissing and poisonous whisper that there is another curate who is yet milder. He therefore sends assassins to force the meek usurper to assume a gay demeanour, and smoke and wink at the girls. But the seed of sublime nonsense is in the notion of men fiercely competing as to which of them is the more insipid. It is inherent in the idea of a mild curate being jealous of a milder curate. It evaporates altogether with the change to a wild poet being jealous of a wilder poet.

So much should be said to make clear that, if we are considering the Gilbertian literature as literature, and alone, the still fashionable Savoy Operas are not the first or the best work of Gilbert. But they are so very much better than any work of anybody else that has been done in the same medium then or since, that it is no wonder that his genius, when it had been so exactly fitted to the genius of Sullivan, produced something that was in every way unique; and not least unique in being united. It may be equally true, on Sullivan's side, that his earlier musical expression was yet more individual and promising than that which he showed in the great partnership; it is a point upon which I cannot judge even as tentatively as I judge the literary comparison. Some may tell me that The Lost Chord is more completely lost than Lost Mr Blake, that glorious but I fear largely forgotten sinner. But even if these two masters had each brought to the work only half his mastery, there was enough when taken together to make up a masterpiece. It is a masterpiece of a very singular and significant kind, both as a type of the things of its period and as a contrast to them.

Perhaps the first point to note is that Nonsense was here treated as almost a sacred thing, in the ancient sense of a thing fenced off and protected from intrusion. The history of what may broadly be called Pantomime, in modern England, based on the old Harlequinade with its clown and poker and policeman, ranging through various phases such as the fairy plays of Planché, and now transformed like one of its own transformation-scenes (not to say dissolving like one of its dissolving-views) into the form or formlessness of the Revue—that tradition of the Pantomime had many moods and changes, but it always possessed, both before and after Gilbert, a certain vague implication of infinite possibilities or impossibilities. It was a spirit not only of hilarity but of hospitality. In the old as in the new fairy-palace, all the doors of the stage stood open. In the Gilbertian fairy-palace all the doors were shut. They were shut so as to enclose and secure the separate dream of an individual artist; something that was nonsensical from the standpoint of reality, but was none the less serious from the standpoint of art. The atmosphere of the old Pantomime and of the new Revue implies, if not that everybody may turn up, at least that anybody may turn up. Incongruous figures from the ends of the earth may appear against any scenery, however conventional or local. The man in the top-hat in front of the Ogre's Castle, the man with the red nose in front of the Gates of Fairyland, was incongruous and was justified by his incongruity. He did not have to match his surroundings, but only to sing for his supper. This naturally led to the limelight being concentrated on the actor and not on the scenery; not indeed on the scene; or even on the play. This led to songs and speeches quite separable from the play, and much more connected with the world outside the theatre; songs that could be sung in the streets; topical songs; political songs; songs that one man could pick up from another without even seeing the play at all. It also led to gags; to infinite, incessant, irresponsible gagging. The player was ten times as big as the play. The Ogre and the Fairy were nothing; but Dan Leno and Herbert Campbell were everything.

W. S. Gilbert was accused, rightly or wrongly, of being a splenetic, acrid and fault-finding individual. However this may be, in the creation of his art, these vices, if they were vices, were also virtues. He would not permit anything really incongruous to mar the complete congruity of his own incongruity. He stopped all gags so despotically that one can only say that he gagged the gaggers. He would not allow a word of contemporary political or social allusion, beyond the few which he touched upon very lightly himself. His whole conception, right or wrong, was to make a compact artistic unity of his poetical play; and the fact that it was also a nonsensical play was not a reason, in his eyes, for anything being thrown into it; but, on the contrary, for everything else being kept out of it; because its very frivolity was fragility. It was not a potato sack into which the clown could poke anything with a poker; it was a coloured soap-bubble which would burst if tickled with a straw. In this matter of keeping the artistic unity of a comic play as a whole, Gilbert has rather an important position in the history of modern artistic experiments. It is all the difference between the levity of *Three Men in a Boat* and the levity of *The Wrong Box*. For the main point about The Wrong Box is that it is emphatically The Right Box; it is a box, in being a compact enclosure into which nothing *really* incongruous is allowed to enter; and Stevenson hits the right nail on the head every time, when he is hammering the box together. The scenery of the Gilbertian Operas has exactly the same quality of harmonious chaos or carefully selected senselessness.

Thus *The Mikado* is not a picture of Japan; but it is a Japanese picture. It is a picture deliberately limited to certain conventions of colour and attitude; it is, as is truly claimed in the first words of its first chorus, something to be seen "on many a vase and jar, on many a screen and fan". And it will be noted that its author was as autocratic as any Emperor of the Far East about the exclusion of sky-breakers and barbarians from other lands. There is not a single European character or costume in the whole of *The Mikado*; and there could not be, without destroying the whole fantastic conception and colour scheme. Imagine an old popular Pantomime about Japan, or for that matter a modern Revue about Japan; and the very background of Japan would be regarded as an opportunity for introducing everybody, or anybody who was not Japanese. A popular test was almost immediately provided by *The*

Geisha; the most famous, or rather the least utterly forgotten, of the string of Musical Comedies which so
rapidly attempted, and so completely failed, to fill the
place of the old Savoy Operas. In *The Geisha*, which
does glimmer faintly among my boyish memories, the
scene was also laid in Japan. But it was only laid in
Japan in order that Mr Hayden Coffin, or some such
gentleman in a naval uniform, should instantly land
from a British battleship in company with an equally
British young lady and attended by a comic Chinese
cook. In that Japan the ports were all open; in Gilbert's
Japan the ports were all closed; because it was the undiscovered island of a dream. Similarly in a play like
The Gondoliers, the Venice is not really Venetian; but
it is really artificial; one might say as artificial as Venice.
The author will introduce a Spanish Inquisitor in a
black cloak, because he fits into the same sort of Mediterranean masquerade. But wild horses would not have
driven him to introduce an English policeman, such as
lends a final inconsequence to the chaos of the Harlequinade. The thing may not be taking place in Venice;
but it is not taking place in Britain; it is taking place
in Barataria, the imaginary kingdom, the island of
Sancho Panza's dream. And the Two Kings are not
Pantomime Kings, or mere knockabouts with wooden
sceptres and crowns; all the setting is fitted to a certain
frosty eighteenth-century elegance; the mockery of a
Venetian romance. The same scheme of decorative
unity could be shown as running through each of the
operas in turn. The scene of *H.M.S. Pinafore* is in the
harbour, but it is never off the ship. Only one landsman
is allowed on board; and he in order to emphasize the
jest that the First Lord of the Admiralty is not a
landsman, but ought to be a sort of seaman. It is
amusing to think what vistas of varied scenery a modern

producer of Revue or Pantomime would see in such a story; what grand receptions at Sir Joseph and Lady Porter's town house; what riotous scenes in taverns to celebrate the adventures of Jack Ashore. But in the strict simplicity and concentration of the Gilbertian theme, Jack is never Ashore. He has taken the background of deck and rigging and blue sea; and he sticks to the note and the theme. It is perhaps amusing to reflect that the author of *The Bab Ballads* was the only Englishman who understood and observed the unities of the Greek Tragedy.

The next thing to notice is this; that it was precisely because he did keep this comic convention, as strictly and even sternly as if it were Chinese etiquette, that he was able to be a satirist of our own society; almost as airy and impartial as a voice from China. The gag, the topical allusion, the ordinary vulgar joke about the things most notorious in the newspapers, could never be thus deadly because it could never be thus delicate and detached. There was always something rowdy about it, because it was not only an appeal to the gallery, but a direct demagogic appeal instead of an indirect dramatic appeal. It was an appeal to people's momentary political feelings, and not to their permanent artistic tastes. Now I am very fond of demagogy in the right place, which is exactly where it is not allowed: in Parliament and the places of open debate, which are supposed to express the feelings of the democracy. But in a satire, especially an ornamental and elegant satire, there can never be any place for demagogy; satire and demagogy are direct opposites. For it is the very definition of demagogy that it deals with the obvious; sometimes with obvious and very valuable virtues; often with obvious and very noble ideals. But it is the very definition of satire that it is not obvious, and deals with points of view that are not obvious. And it needs a sort of unreal exactitude of setting and habit which is different from the rowdy reality of life. For instance, I do not in the least share the sickly and chilly reaction against the traditional passion of patriotism. I do not object to patriotism, at some passionate crisis, breaking out of the framework of art. If a popular actor happens to be acting Fauconbridge on the night of a great national crisis, when war is declared, I do not in the least object to his swaggering sword in hand down to the footlights, and bellowing to the gallery, without the slightest reference to the play:

> Come the three corners of the world in arms,
> And we shall shock them. Nought shall make us rue,
> If England to itself do rest but true.

I do not mind that, because I happen to hold the horrid heresy that the nation is more important than the drama; and even that England is more important than Shakespeare—a view in which Shakespeare would have warmly concurred. And if I do not mind this being done to Shakespeare, I naturally do not mind what anybody does to *The Geisha*; and should not in the least object if the gentleman in the naval uniform became on such an occasion a regular gatling-gun of gags, about British bulldogs assisting God in saving the Union Jack. This is demagogy; but it is also humanity; and it matters the less that it knocks the whole play out of shape, because the play was in any case shapeless. But for the purposes of satire we do emphatically want a shape; something sharpened and pointed and above all polished. If we want people to look at the unfamiliar side of patriotism, at the unpopular side of demagogy, we need a certain conventional calm over the whole proceedings, that people may have the patience to criticize themselves. If we want to point out what can really be stupid and irrational and dangerous about a vulgar and conceited patriotism, we need a sort of ritual of satire that the irony may have a chance. Thus we find it is against the almost monotonous background of blue waves and bulwarks, in the unreal rigidity of *H.M.S. Pinafore,* that the sailor is permitted to burst forth into that sublimely logical burlesque:

> He is an Englishman!
> And it's greatly to his credit.

And reaching the ironic heights of:

> But in spite of all temptations
> To belong to other nations,
> He remains an Englishman.

That knocks at one blow all the stuffing out of the stuffy and selfish sort of patriotism; the sort of patriotism which is taking credit instead of giving praise. It lays down for ever the essential and fundamental law; that a man should be proud of England but not proud of being an Englishman.

But the point is that we cannot get these detached or distinguished points of view listened to at all, in a general atmosphere of the rowdy, the fashionable or the obvious. They require something like an unusual atmosphere or a rather remote symbolism. A man might make any number of highly justifiable jokes about, or against, Mr Lloyd George or Mr Winston Churchill or Lord Birkenhead or Lord Reading; and the jokes might involve real criticism of our political inconsistencies or legal fictions. But in practice, the effect would simply be that everybody would howl his head off at the mere mention of Winston or Lloyd George. The people would not wait for the jokes; the names would be jokes enough. They certainly would not wait for the criticism; being altogether in too hilarious a mood of the public meeting. But Gilbert can criticize a hundred of such inconsistencies and fictions, if he puts the scene entirely in Japan or calls the politician Pooh-Bah.

It is certainly rather grotesque that the satire should have been understood so little that certain British officials gravely discussed whether the performance of *The Mikado* might not offend our allies in Japan. There is not, in the whole length of *The Mikado*, a single joke that is a joke against Japan. They are all, without exception, jokes against England, or that Western civilization which an Englishman knows best in England. I doubt whether it is an ancient and traditional Japanese habit to scribble on the window-panes of railway carriages; I think it improbable that any native Japanese peasants were "sent to hear sermons by mystical Germans who preach from ten to four"; it may be questioned whether even the habit of autograph-hunting is confined to the islands of the Rising Sun; it seems probable that "the judicial humorist" is more often an English judge than an Oriental official; and "the people who eat peppermint and puff it in your face" were not, I imagine, first encountered by W. S. Gilbert in the streets of Tokyo. But it is true to say that this sort of English caricature requires a Japanese frame; that, in order to popularize a criticism of our own country, it is necessary to preserve a sort of veil or fiction that it is another country; possibly an unknown country. If the satirist becomes more of a realist, he enters the grosser native atmosphere in which he is expected to be a eulogist. The satire bears no sort of resemblance to an Englishman criticizing Japan. But it has to assume a certain semblance of a Japanese criticizing England. Oliver Goldsmith discovered the same truth, when he found he could only talk truth-

fully to his countrymen in the stilted language of a
Chinaman.

In a word, the style must not be too familiar when
the moral is unfamiliar. The story is told of W. S.
Gilbert that he indignantly rebuked a leading actor who
had introduced a gag, that is a joke of his own, into the
dialogue. The actor defended himself by saying, "Well,
I always get a laugh for it"; and Gilbert answered,
"You could get a laugh any time by sitting down on
your hat". What is true about a man sitting on his hat
and getting a laugh is equally true about a man waving
his hat and getting a cheer. It is always possible to
appeal to the audience with success, if we appeal to
something which they know already; or feel as if they
knew already. But if we have to get them to listen to
a criticism, however light, which they have really
never thought of before, they must have a certain atmosphere of repose and ritual in which to reflect on it.
Now many of Gilbert's best points were in a sense
rather abstruse points. They asked the listener to think
about phrases which he had always used without
thinking; they pointed out something illogical in something that had always been thought quite sensible.
Men cannot so re-examine their own phraseology and
philosophy except in a world more detached, and perhaps more dehumanized, than that in which they roar
at an old chestnut or cheer at a patriotic toast. To take
only one example; there has crept into our common
speech and judgment a very evil heresy, one of the
dingy legacies of Calvinism; the idea that some people
are born bad and others born so solidly good that they
are actually incapable of sin; and can never even be
tempted to cowardice or falsehood. So long as this is
repeated as a sort of hearty and jolly compliment, in the
form of saying, "William Wiggins, Sir, could not tell

a lie if he tried", it all passes off well, in the atmosphere
of the fashionable toasts and the familiar jests. But that
notion of the impossibility of lying is itself a lie. It is
one of the worst lies produced by one of the worst
heresies. And Gilbert struck that heresy to the heart,
and nailed the logic of that lie as with a nail hammered
through its head, in two or three lines of the lightest
and most buoyant lyrical chorus:

> We know him well,
> He cannot tell
> Untrue or groundless tales,
> He always tries
> To utter lies
> And every time he fails.

That is a pure piece of logical analysis and exposure;
a great deal more philosophical than many that are
quoted among the epigrams of Voltaire.

It is true that Gilbert had no particular positive
philosophy to support this admirable negative criticism;
he had even less than Voltaire. For that reason he did
sometimes fall into mere expressions of prejudice; and
sometimes into expressions of bad taste. But the point
here is that the satire was often a really intellectual
satire; and that it could hardly have been expressed
except under certain formal and even fictitious conditions, which make it possible to appeal to the intellect
without arousing the prejudices, or even the more
obvious and vulgar of the really healthy sentiments.
People would hardly have followed the real satire of
H.M.S. Pinafore if it had been filled with real and rousing
patriotic songs; as an ordinary writer of pantomime or
musical comedy would certainly have tried to fill it.
This is not to say that anti-popular satires are necessarily better than popular songs. It is only to say that the
artist is generally a man who does one thing at a time.

It would· be easy to give numberless examples in which the Gilbertian wit did criticize things that need to be criticized, and even did so by the right negative standard of criticism; but it would still be true that there was an absence of the positive standard of perfection. The real power of the Sophist over the Philistine, of the pretentious person over the plain man, could hardly be better conveyed than in the limpid and flowing lines of the song about the man who had a Platonic love for a potato:

> And everyone will say,
> As you walk your flowery way,
> "If he's content with a vegetable love
> Which would certainly not suit *me*,
> Why, what a very singularly pure young man
> This pure young man must be."

But there is no heroic indignation behind the sarcasm, as in some of the great satirists; for nobody can feel a moral enthusiasm for three fatuous Guardsmen and an impossible milkmaid. There was no such prophetic satire as Aristophanes or Swift might have shown; and certainly no sort of prophecy of the path which the pure young man eventually followed, or the way in which Platonic love came to mean something different from admiration of a potato.

This relative lack of moral conviction did mark Gilbert as a satirist, and did to some extent mark all his epoch as an epoch. There were many men of conviction still active; Newman was still teaching and corresponding in his old age; Gladstone was still blazing away with his discovery of the case for Ireland; but Newman stood for something still almost alien; and perhaps even the case for Ireland was the first wedge of such alien things that broke up the Victorian solidity of England. The older Victorian prophets had been earnest enough; and though Matthew Arnold "was not always in all ways wholly serious", Ruskin was never anything else. But in the case of the mocker, it was already true (as he himself hinted) that the mockery had become something like a hollow mask. The original forces that had sustained the hope and energy of the nineteenth century were no longer at their strongest for the rising generation. The light of the great legend of the French Revolution had been darkened by the success of Prussian materialism in 1870; the men who had taken the humanitarian ideal simply and naturally were dropping out; like Dickens, the greatest of them, who died in the same year as the fall of Paris. Nor had any other or older ideas as yet taken hold so solidly of the human mind as to permit of natural laughter or of noble scorn. Hence there were not in this epoch any great convinced satirists, as Voltaire and Beaumarchais were on the one side, or Father Knox or Mr Belloc are now on the other. The typical satire of this period remained what Gilbert himself loved to preserve it, an airy, artistic, detached and almost dehumanized thing; not unallied to the contemporary cult of art for art's sake. Gilbert was fighting against a hundred follies and illogicalities; but he was not fighting for anything, and his age as a whole was no longer certain for what it was fighting. The moral of *The Pirates of Penzance* is in some ways exceedingly like the moral of a play by Mr Bernard Shaw; but there is not the moral fervour behind it which really belongs to Mr Bernard Shaw even when his moral is most immoral. For Mr Bernard Shaw, like Mr Belloc, belongs to a later period when the controversy has fallen back upon ultimates and reached the ends of the earth. It is not in these new struggles of our own time that we can find the clue to that curious and half unreal detachment, in which some of the Victorians came at last to smile at all opinions including their own. Perhaps the finest form of it is in a certain light version of the *Vanitas Vanitatum*, such as Thackeray so often suggested; and which is really not unlike a certain almost empty radiance in some of the later lyrics of the Renaissance. This would seem to have been the most serious mood of W. S. Gilbert; and it makes one entirely apt appearance in his most serious play. For one of his comic operas was very nearly a serious play. *The Yeomen of the Guard* is deliberately pathetic; and it marks exactly what I mean, when I say that if Gilbert had been serious he could only have been pathetic. He had not the positive moral resources to be heroic or mystic or dogmatic or fanatical. *The Yeomen of the Guard* is in a Renaissance period and setting and it contains one serious lyric really worth quoting, as having caught the spirit of the end of the sixteenth century; and perhaps in some sense of the end of the nineteenth. When the hero is going to execution, under Henry VIII, for his sixteenth-century scientific curiosity, he sings words which do prove, perhaps paradoxically, that the veteran song-writer could really write a song:

> Is life a boon?
>   If so, it must befall
>   That Death, whene'er he call,
> Must call too soon.
>   Though fourscore years he give,
>   Yet one would pray to live
> Another moon!
>   What kind of plaint have I,
>   Who perish in July?
>   I might have had to die
> Perchance in June!
>
> Is life a thorn?
>   Then count it not a whit!
>   Man is well done with it:

Soon as he's born
  He should all means essay
  To put the plague away;
And I, war-worn,
  Poor captured fugitive,
  My life most gladly give—
  I might have had to live
Another morn!

That is not unworthy of what it imitates; and might really have been thrown off by Raleigh, when he gave The Lie to all the vanities of this world, or by Chastelard, when he refused on the scaffold all the ministrations of religion and recited, standing alone, the great ode of Ronsard to Death.

THE COMING OF IBSEN

By Harley Granville-Barker

It was delayed till 7 June 1889, and the circumstances
were modest to a degree; but the production of *A Doll's
House* "for seven performances only" at the Novelty
Theatre—the name not inappropriate; it is now the
Kingsway—proved to be the most important dramatic
event of the decade. Ten years before the play had made
Ibsen renowned throughout Scandinavia and Germany,
his more literary repute already being high there, and
after it had come *Ghosts, An Enemy of the People, The
Wild Duck* and *Rosmersholm,* each in its kind a challenge
and an achievement. But to England, France, Italy and
America he was still hardly a name. William Archer
recounts suggesting *viva voce* to some editor (Edmund
Yates, was it?) an article on Henrik Ibsen. "Gibson!
Who on earth is he?" was the answer. By the time the
seven performances at the shabby little Novelty were
over—lengthened to twenty-four, such was the amazing
noise they made!—he was good copy at least. He was
"the talk of London"—of literary London, that is
to say, of the few dozen people who write, and the
few hundred who read its weekly reviews. Add a few
hundred more up and down the country and we have
the common measure of such sensations. But there was
an unwonted potency about this one. Something startling had happened in a theatre!

The Moral Shock

Ibsen's was a powerful and disturbing mind. Encountered in his own tongue—so they say that know —he ranks high as pure poet, but had the theatre not been his battleground his impact upon his time could hardly have been so violent as it was, in England, at any rate. *Ghosts*, one admits, must have been accounted scandalous in any guise. We flatten our voices a trifle and circumlocute the unpleasanter part of its subject even now, unless we are very strong-minded indeed. But why should Nora's exit from her doll's house, slamming the door, have given 1889 such a moral shock? In 1880 Germany, no doubt (I admit ignorance of the Scandinavian situation), Herr Schmidt und Frau —when she had helped him into his coat and handed him his hat—must have gone home with something to ponder over. But surely in 1889 England, land of an already flourishing Newnham and Girton, and of a seven-year-old Married Woman's Property Act, women were emancipated enough—if they wished to be. Surely that revolution was all over, bar the shouting. But this was just it! There is much conservative virtue in the if; and while in England we take our revolutions calmly, one, by process of law, every twenty years or so, what we do our best to bar is the shouting. Keep quiet about them, and the average man and woman, in a Devon or Hereford village, in the City, in Balham, in Middlesboro, busy with bread-and-butter affairs, will be long in realizing they have occurred. Newspapers are more bought than read, and who can quote last year's *Times*? But here was the shouting. The English theatre is the home, not of lost causes and their dignity, but of those that have been irrevocably and blatantly won. When you find a new idea in the theatre it must be current coin indeed.

This, partly at any rate, accounts for the shock and
the rumpus. There had been women enough in England,
before Ibsen's Norwegian Nora was born or thought of,
to whom her poor little revolution would have looked
very small beer. Nor, unless they were most provoking
—unless, that is to say, they insistently advertised their
opinions by their conduct: be a free-thinker or a free
liver, but not both at once, please!—did society always
conspire to hound them down. The Victorians were not
consistently Victorian. No age is consistent, except in
the smaller history books; and few human beings are,
fortunately, until they are dead. George Eliot was not
treated as, in more patently shameless times, Mary
Wollstonecraft had been. She saw to that; and distinguished ladies, irreproachably married, found themselves dropping curtseys to her when presented.[1]
Certainly, you did not give your fifteen-year-old daughter,
along with *The Mill on the Floss*, the information that
its authoress was living in sin with Mr George Henry
Lewes. But if you had to tell her story—she was a
genius; that fact was an important part of it, and her
conduct, therefore, bore no more relation to yours than,
say, Cleopatra's home life, so colourfully pictured by
the immortal Shakespeare, did, as the legendary old lady
said leaving the theatre, to that of "our own dear
Queen". This Nora, though, with her little household, her work-basket and her Christmas shopping, her
children and her bank-manager husband—caricature
though he might be, Norwegians all of them in their
outlandish ways!—this was still far too like Balham
to be pleasant. And was the flag of domestic revolt to be
set flying there?

[1] A fact, as the phrase is; for I had it from one of them.

The Theatre in the 'Eighties
—and William Archer

The English drama of the early 'eighties was really—
though one must never patronize the past, and the
theatre to-day is not offering over much to the adult
mind—a rather childish affair. The joyous idiocies of
Mr Vincent Crummles were no more, were at least
banished to even remoter nooks than the Theatre
Royal, Portsmouth. Robertson was dead, his chief legacy
to the theatre seemed to be a gentlemanly generation of
actors, and if cup-and-saucer comedy was still served,
the china was now second-hand, and apt to look rather
chipped and shabby. Irving, in his little kingdom of
the Lyceum, would have nothing to say to modern
drama at all. The Bancrofts had turned to Sardou, and
in 1885 they retired. John Hare and the Kendals did
what they could find to do. There was bowdlerized
French farce, with, at the best, Wyndham's deft charm
to cover its emptiness—or nakedness. There were Mr
Wilson Barrett and Mr William Terriss in melodrama,
the one, for preference, as a noble Roman with tunic cut
low in the neck (lower than was altogether "nice" perhaps; but what a neck![1]), the other as a Lieutenant R.N.,
his cap worn at the angle since made famous by Lord
Beatty. A fancy dress bazaar in the Vicarage garden,
with everyone enjoying it very innocently; suddenly the
wind veers to the east! Such was Ibsen's advent.

This, of course, is not the whole story of the dramatic
'eighties. We can find that fairly fully set out for us in
a couple of books by William Archer, whose critical
career more or less began with them, and who, as they
ended, was to be the sponsor of this same devastating

[1] See the early caricatures of Mr Max Beerbohm; though these, of course,
belong to the 'nineties, by when it was ten years more massive and monumental.

Ibsen. From first to last Archer's own influence upon
the English theatre was considerable. He meant little to
the larger public for he said little to them; he detested
daily journalism. He never wrote a play into success,
as managers piously believed that his contemporary
Clement Scott, who slashed and slushed his way through
long columns of the *Daily Telegraph*, could do. Success
or failure, in that sense, did not (except for kindness of
heart) concern him. If he thought a play good he would
say so, though the last act had found him sitting alone
in the theatre. If he thought it bad he said so, and it
might run for five hundred nights—what difference did
that make? But more than one dramatist, sure of his
manager and pretty sure of his public, has owned that
he never finished a new piece of work without asking
himself: What will Archer think of it?

His critics held that his attitude towards drama was
too rigidly intellectual. It may well have seemed so—
towards some of the stuff he had to criticize! He was
possessed, actually, by a boyishly romantic love for the
theatre, and this held him to the last, through forty
years and more of grinding labour for it. But he had
brought with him besides from the Edinburgh University of the 'seventies an integrity of commonsense,
which, undiluted, was certainly a very acid test indeed
for the popular pinchbeck of the day—would have been
for the drama of any day, perhaps, popular or unpopular.
Archer did, however, habitually and consciously, toler-
antly and encouragingly, dilute it. The British drama was
a backward boy; but with a little blindness and much
kindness meted out, and, above all, patience, it would be
a credit to school and country yet. For when in 1882,
he publishes a little book, *English Dramatists of To-day*,
the "recognized" men are Albery, Burnand, Byron
(Henry J., not Lord), G. R. Sims, Gilbert and W. G.

Wills, and he treats them with what must seem to us
now—glancing at such of their product as survives in
print, at the best of it, therefore—an amazing serious-
ness. There is also a chapter on Mr Alfred Tennyson
in which he maintains "...the paradox that of the four
plays...the best (*Harold*, one surmises) has never yet
seen the stage, the worst (*The Cup*, undoubtedly) has
been the most successful and the remaining two (*Queen
Mary* and *The Falcon*) have met with quite unmerited
neglect". But "He is a bold man, who, except in the
morning papers, dares to talk seriously of Mr Tennyson
as a dramatist"—a cryptic observation, across fifty
years! Then there are the young hopefuls. Mr Arthur
Pinero is a beginner with a lot to learn. Mr Henry
Arthur Jones "...seems to possess a good deal of
culture and a great deal of earnest aspiration which may
go far to supply the place of some more strictly dramatic
qualities in which he is rather lacking". And of Mr
Sydney Grundy we are told that he "...is as yet not
far on the wrong side of thirty; and if, as some of us
venture to hope, the tide of culture is setting slowly but
surely towards the stage, his opportunity must ulti-
mately arrive". But with that the tale ends.

1886: *The Theatre advancing*

Hardly four years later, however, in another book,
About the Theatre, in the long buoyant chapter "Are we
advancing?" one at least of the young hopefuls, we
find, has more than fulfilled his hopes. Mr Arthur
Pinero has become "the most original and remarkable
of living English playwrights, with a possible exception
in favour of Mr Gilbert". (Less the Gilbert, this, of the
operas—and not at all of the "serious" plays *Dan'l
Druce*, *Gretchen*, and *Pygmalion and Galatea*—than

of the excellent farces, *Tom Cobb, Engaged,* and *The Wicked World.*) And here already is Archer the critic in quiddity. Of the plays which beget such praise *Lords and Commons* has had something of a success at the Haymarket Theatre, but *The Rector* and *Low Water* have been admitted fiascos. That does not matter. The public is wayward, actors are uncertain, the theatre is all hazard. Good plays succeed and bad plays succeed, good plays fail and bad plays fail. The business of criticism is to be discerning. These three have long lain forgotten. Mr Samuel French's charitable catalogue does not contain them, possibly their very author could not lay his hands on a copy now. For unquestionable success soon came, and in a year or so "our leading dramatist" was a commonplace in Pinero's ears. But one wagers he remembered and still remembers what the worth to him was of the praise of the frustrate effort.

Another young hopeful had made strides, Mr Henry Arthur Jones. He and Mr Henry Herman had produced between them one melodrama, among others, *The Silver King,* which won public praise from no less a person than Matthew Arnold. On his own account, too, he had turned out a three-act dramatic study of country chapel-folk called *Saints and Sinners,* which was not, perhaps, startlingly good, which had no great success, but in which, again, Archer's discerning eye saw promise of "the real thing". Jones himself came of Welsh farmer stock that had settled in Bedfordshire, and he knew his subject at first hand, the smug, lower-middle-class world of the little market town, in which all that is dankest in the notorious "nonconformist conscience" breeds. Unluckily, if inevitably, he knew it only to hate it, with the hate which is unforgiven fear, as a prison from which he had freed himself; and to the end this withers the theme for him whenever he touches it. He could hardly, it is true, have won popular success in the theatre of that day—or of this—by painting even quite idyllic pictures of lower-middle-class (the damnation is in the lower-) provincial life. For the actor-manager had then to be reckoned with, who, whatever his artistic virtues, did not see himself, and simply could not have let his faithful audiences see him side-whiskered, reach-me-down suited, with pepper-and-salt trousers slightly baggy at the knee. In the popular play, too, pretty ladies must parade in smart frocks, half a dozen at least, and as many more as the playwright could provide for and the management afford. Women went to the theatre as much for the dresses as the drama; they must have their money's worth. Not lowest of the barriers between Ibsen and the "recognized" London theatre was the distressing fact that there is hardly a fashionably dressed woman to be found in his plays. Hedda Gabler, to be sure; but heaven help us, even she *walks* home after a party!

"Henry Arthur", as he came familiarly to be, was an able craftsman. He wrote plainly and well. He had a vigorous if not very distinguished mind, which ran to humour rather than wit, which set, with the safeguards of a quite British decency and honesty and with a softening of manly sentiment, a frankly sensual value upon things. Too self-confident and self-respecting to be an intellectual snob, he was, as Archer had quickly divined, a realist in grain. But, for all his acquired knowingness, Dukes and Prime Ministers (the Victorian brand) and their womenkind of the right hand or the left, remain romantic figures to him still, and he makes woolly work of them. Whereas the butchers and bakers and candlestick makers of Market Parbury are convincing even in caricature. The vividest impressions and the truest, which we redraw into pictures, are those bitten into the consciousness of our sensitive years. Now that Henry Arthur Jones's work is done, one would give the lot of it for the single play he might have written, had circumstances with him and the theatre of his day been a little different—some mellower, more charitably humorous enshrining of the little world which was native to him. For such things live.

A Doll's House *with Ibsen left out*

But, indeed, the theatre of the 'eighties was not asking for actuality. Jones and Herman, besides collaborating in melodrama for Mr Wilson Barrett, had produced a certain play in three acts called *Breaking a Butterfly*. It did not pretend to be original; it was drawn—*via* the German, one supposes—from *A Doll's House*. Its vicarious authors probably only thought of the job as an honest piece of hack-work, and the result was no better nor worse than half a hundred other plays of the time. What is interesting is to see the changes they were inspired to make. The scene is laid in some English country town. Nora becomes Flora, and to her husband, rather terribly, Flossie. He is Humphrey Goddard and we find him gifted with a mother (quite unnecessarily) and a sister (wanted for the piano playing *vice* Mrs Linden, who disappears). The morbid Dr Rank is replaced by a Charles-his-friend, called, as if to wipe out every trace of his original, Ben Birdseye! He is not in love with Nora-Flora, of course; that would never do. But Dunkley, alias Krogstad, had loved her as a girl, when Humphrey Goddard stole her young heart from him; so love has turned to hate and revenge is sweet. Observe the certainty with which our operators in the English market fasten on the flawed streak in Ibsen's play and cheapen it still further. The tarantella

episode, of course, will be the making of the whole
affair (such was many people's judgment then, and
now we rather find it marring) and this is left intact.
But the third act sees the parent play deliberately stood
upon its head, and every ounce of Ibsen emptied out
of it. Burlesque could do no more. Torvald-Humphrey
behaves like the pasteboard hero of Nora's doll's-
house dream; he *does* strike his chest and say "I am
the guilty one". And Nora-Flora cries that she is a
poor weak foolish girl, "...no wife for a man like you.
You are a thousand times too good for me", and never
wakes up and walks out of her doll's house at all.

Amazing! But yet more so, at first sight, Archer's
comment upon the outrage. "It falsified, or rather
ignored, the whole ethical import of Ibsen's play...
and converted the tragedy into a commonplace comedy-
drama. All this manipulation—I had almost said
stultification—was necessary to make Ibsen tolerable
to the English playgoer, and even then the piece failed
to attract." One is tempted to read irony into it. But
that was not Archer's way. No, it is a candid estimate,
by a critic convinced that the English theatre and its
public are advancing, of the standard of dramatic intelligence they have reached. Not so long after he is
writing of a performance—somewhere in Scandinavia
probably—of "the even more extraordinary drama of
Ghosts which followed *A Doll's House*...I have never
experienced an intenser sensation within the walls of
a theatre. It proved to me the possibility of modern
tragedy in the deepest sense of the word, but it also
proved to me the impossibility of modern tragedy on
the English stage".

1889

Yet the advance was patent, and it even quickened a little; and at any time the dramatists could have pleaded that they went as fast as their public would let them. 1889 saw the opening of the Garrick Theatre by Mr John Hare with "a new and original play by A. W. Pinero". Note the claim in that "and original". London is no longer to be counted as a mere dowdy dramatic suburb of Paris. But for some years yet it was customary—and necessary—to make it. The play was *The Profligate* and the occasion was admitted to be important. *The Times* gave a column on the leader page to its review. "The English playgoer has long sighed for novelty", we are told, "and although it may not be irreproachable in form as here presented, it is not unwelcome judging by the flattering reception accorded last night to actors, author, and all concerned." Since the action of the play passed in an "atmosphere of fashionable libertinage" this was as far as one could expect *The Times* to go. Did Mr Walkley, who was just about then hitching his well-sprung waggon to Mr T. P. O'Connor's new risen *Star*, read these solemnities that morning at breakfast and smile? Before not so many years were past he was to be wearing the majestic mantle himself—with a difference!

"Sentimental puritanism" is the reproach we should be likelier to find levelled against *The Profligate* to-day. The young wife implacable towards her husband's past, the irretrievably "ruined" village maiden, the repentant libertine's suicide—though for this was temporarily substituted a more theatrically moral "happy ending"; 1930 sniffs at such a scheme of things. But in 1889 here was a daring deed; and the *Saturday Review*, remarking that "on previous occasions Mr Pinero has almost invariably shown a desire before all else to break with convention", thanks him for discussing "a difficult subject with such remarkable delicacy". If Mr Walkley read his *Times*; did Mr Shaw and Mr Beerbohm, the one then "doing" music for the *Star*, the other modestly emerging from Charterhouse, take a weekly look at their anonymous predecessor on the *Saturday*, and what did they make of him?

He was not so complaisant towards Henry Arthur Jones, whose *Wealth* had just been produced by Beerbohm Tree at the Haymarket with a cast which, itself, one thinks, should have drawn London. He calls this "a very poor play". He was wrong, if a recent reader of its shabby manuscript may belatedly tell him so. A crude and slapdash and at times a quite preposterous play, but by no means poor. For Henry Arthur had pluckily tackled a big and imminent subject, and had spread his canvas wide and laid on his colour boldly. The *Saturday* shakes a schoolmaster's finger. "Many things are desirable in a play, and their presence or absence affects the result; but there is one thing that is absolutely indispensable and that is a plot." To the post-Ibsen and post-Tchekov reader *Wealth* will seem all plot, and empurpled at that.

But the play's subject, one suspects, was the real trouble. Capital and Labour, and Labour demanding its rights; far more objectionable this than Mr Pinero's "fashionable libertinism". Nor did Mr Jones treat it with his rival's remarkable delicacy. "...Davozen [the young hero] displays bad taste in advocating Socialistic doctrines in Mr Ruddock's drawing-room (incidentally it may be added that political discussions, and in particular discussions in the politics of a rabid and ridiculous little knot of mischief makers—for audiences are not composed of Conybeares, Cunning-

hame Grahams and William Morrises—are very much
out of place on the stage)." No, indeed, audiences were
not, and are not; one wishes to heaven they were!
Search in the shabby manuscript discovers nothing but
a little mild advocacy of profit-sharing. The actor must
have made a great deal of it or the Saturday Reviewer
have been a very, very timid person. But the Trafalgar
Square riots were not three years old, and perhaps he
had been in his club when the unemployed marched
down Pall Mall and broke a few windows. The play
was a failure, however; Mr Jones would know better
than to try that sort of game again. By no stretch of
charity can *Wealth* be called a good play. Compare it
to John Galsworthy's *Strife*, another essay on the
Capital and Labour question written only seventeen
years later, and it is fustian. But the welcome for the
one owed something to the courage that had faced the
failure of the other. Henry Arthur once asked me
not to go and see a revival of yet another early play of
his. "You young men", he said a little wistfully, "have
a smoother road to travel than I had."

For the rest it was a yet more incongruous company
that Ibsen came so modestly to join. If the playgoer
wanted simple—oh, very simple!—thrills, he went to
The Harbour Lights at the Adelphi or *The True Heart*
at the Princess's. That sort of thing, somewhat robbed
of its innocence, survives now in the Cinema. It must
probably always survive in one form or another. There
was farce played by nobody very distinguished at the
Strand, by Hawtrey and Lottie Venne at the Comedy
and by Toole in a little rat-trap of a theatre named after
him—it had once been the Folly, I think—that was
wedged somehow into one side of the cellars of Charing
Cross Hospital. There was sentiment at Terry's;
Pinero's *Sweet Lavender*, a great success, with Edward

Terry himself (excellent comedian by night, kindly if thrifty man of business, good citizen and churchwarden by day) as the Dickensian Dick Phenyl. Over the road at the Vaudeville Robert Buchanan's *That Doctor Cupid* promised more sentiment, less competently compounded, probably. Mr and Mrs Kendal proffered slightly stiffer fare at the Court with *A White Lie*; and one could see Charles Wyndham turned from admirable ease in farce to an ease and distinction yet more admirable in an even then dowdy and ridiculous deodorization from the French, which is still on record (evidence of our one-time shamelessness in such matters) as "an original comedy by Tom Taylor, Esq.", called *Still Waters Run Deep*. There was Grand Opera at Covent Garden and at Her Majesty's, the spacious old arcaded house in the Haymarket; and for Comic Opera, much in vogue, one had, besides the unrivalled *Yeomen of the Guard*, *Doris*, *Mignonette*, and *Paul Jones*, all very pretty and romantic. At the Gaiety Coquelin and Jane Hading were playing French comedies for a week or so. Fred Leslie and Nellie Farren had finished their season there; they were soon, untimely, to finish altogether, and with them the true lamp of burlesque went out. It flickered in corners for a few years more, but one suspects *Lancelot the Lovely*, occupying the Avenue at the moment (which stood where the Playhouse stands; Charing Cross station finally fell on it), to have been rather a sad affair. Irving and Ellen Terry were playing *Macbeth* at the Lyceum.

The Gate to Hell

There were people who went to the Lyceum and to no other theatre; even so, perhaps, only to see Shakespeare there. They might further yield—to amuse the children

—to the Drury Lane pantomime at Christmas, for this was not precisely a play. Savoy opera came to be considered safe too. Their difficulty was not aesthetic but moral; the theatre was, by Puritan tradition, a gate to hell, one of the many. They would not have called themselves Puritans, there would be little else positively puritan about them; but a creed's taboos outlast all the rest of it, and man has long proved "Thou shalt not" to be the only practical form of commandment. Puritan tradition in England is still very far from dead. It no longer stands strongly on its own square-toed feet; it must make compromises and strange allies. Mr Saklatvala votes against the new Prayer Book. Sir William Joynson-Hicks may plead that he could not ask him not to, and a vote is a vote. The Lord's Day Observance Society has seen Museums and concerts and even Cinemas thrown open in spite of its teeth, but Drama pays it formal tribute still. There are excellent arguments against the general opening of theatres on Sunday; actors and scene shifters want a day of rest and Trade Unions must have their say. But such difficulties could all be disposed of; it is the Puritan tradition keeps the theatres closed. They are closed, of course, by law. Ask any Home Secretary, Conservative, Liberal or Labour, to bring in an amending act. It will not be long before the Chief Whip warns him to let sleeping Puritanism lie.

Outside the Gate

In the London of 1889 there were also a few odd little shanties grouped round the gate to hell, buttressed against the wall of it, so to speak; theatres that were not theatres, giving plays that were not quite plays, the innocuous near-beer of drama. There was Mr and Mrs German Reed's Entertainment, which consisted

of an "Operetta" and a "Comedietta", with Mr
Corney Grain besides, gigantic and blandly comic,
sitting at the piano singing "You should see me dance
the Polka". No deadly sin in enjoying that surely?
There was England's Home of Mystery and Imagination, the Egyptian Hall—how one still misses the
queer sight of it in Piccadilly!—where Messrs Mas-
kelyne and Cook (Mr Cook, though, was already but
a name) presented you, after a prelude of plate-spinning
and card-tricks and conjuring, with a play which could
be relied upon to have at least two ghosts in it; and
far better ghosts they were than Banquo's at the
Lyceum. Terrifying to the very young, but little that
was morally deleterious about them! Then there were
the Moore and Burgess Minstrels at the St James's
Hall—the *small* St James's Hall; if you got into the
large one by mistake you might have to stay through
the first movement of a Brahms symphony before you
could be let out again. They sat in a slightly curved
row, four and twenty gentlemen in evening dress,
"blacked up" (such was the technical phrase) with
burnt cork, and wearing woolly wigs. For an hour or
more they sang songs, sentimental and comic, some
with chorus, some without; not all negro songs by any
means, though many a now famed melody may have
had its forgotten hour there. The blacking up was a
tradition, and, like all traditions, had its value. It
swamped personalities in a common personality; that
unshifting array of expressionless masks fairly hypnotized you. Between the songs there would be witticisms
contributed by the "corner-men" who were allowed
fuzzier wigs, frills to their shirts, and more widely,
pinkly hippopotamic mouths. But the ritual went
forward with all dignity. The gentleman sitting in the
centre, who directed the proceedings, who should

have been either Mr Moore or Mr Burgess but who
was usually, if I remember right, a Mr Johnson, would
turn towards one corner with "Mr Bones, would you
be good enough to tell the company, if you happen to
know: Why is *a* raven like *a* writing-desk?" Whereupon Mr Bones, really for the benefit of the inatten-
tive but seemingly for his own assurance, would solemnly
restate the problem. "You ask me, Mr Johnson, why a
raven is like a *writing*-desk?" And Mr Johnson, to make
all sure, would repeat with studied, but now slightly
ironic courtesy, "Yes, Mr Bones, please tell us—if you
can!—why is a RAVEN like a WRITING-DESK?" Mr
Bones would let a moment elapse and then say, "Because,
sir, there is a B in both". At which most of us would
laugh. But Mr Johnson (so that nobody should miss it)
would retort, "Mr Bones, I studied spelling at school
and I think I can assure you that there is no B in either
Raven or Writing-desk". Mr Bones would then neatly
finish him with "I never said there was, sir. I said there
was a B in both". At which everybody would laugh except Mr Johnson. He would smile ruefully and say, "We
will now sing 'Massa's in the cold, cold ground'".

The second part of the entertainment provided a
simple rough-and-tumble sort of farce, in which too, by
tradition, everybody was "blacked up". Did this somehow cleanse it from original dramatic sin? It was all
very jolly, whether you sought it for its own sake or as
a safe half-way house to the devil.

The true Puritan Standpoint

Is there anyone left in England to-day who will tell us
flatly that plays and play-acting are the devil's own?
Just three months before Ibsen came to flutter our
already mildly fluttered dramatic dovecote Dr Teape,

the incumbent of St John's Episcopal Church, Edinburgh—I am quoting again from the *Saturday Review*
—had been invited by Mr Walter Bentley to witness
a performance of *Hamlet*. Why, we are not told. Probably Dr Teape was a known discountenancer of theatre-
going, and the innocently wily Mr Bentley thought to
trap him by this challenge; for surely no one would
dare to blaspheme against the immortal Shakespeare!
He mistook his man. As well have expected Elijah to
say civil things about Baal-zebub the god of Ekron!
One only hopes that he, in turn, is among the Sunday
congregation at St John's when Dr Teape, impregnable
in his pulpit, lets fly. This play, said the Doctor, exhibited "...vice of a revolting character, a son driven
almost insane, a usurper, three people poisoned, and
the dead lying about as one left the scene. It was
horrible". This will surprise Mr Bentley, who, even
as Hamlet himself, has long been lost in the clouds of
"To be or not to be..." and "What a piece of work
is man?" and will almost have forgotten the plot.
But the facts of it, so stated, are undeniable; and,
adds Dr Teape, "such a mode of influencing the public
mind is thoroughly ruinous....*The Newgate Calendar*
bears ample testimony to the fact that the manner in
which vice is represented, instead of being repellent,
exercises a powerful and deadly attraction on those who
come under the spell of theatrical amusements". That
"*Newgate Calendar*" goes rather far perhaps. Mr Bentley
will have protested silently. Had he been passionate
for his cause, there was precedent for a hassock flung
at the preacher's head. And, indeed, against such
didactic what other sort of argument is effective? One
cannot prove the contrary. But Dr Teape compels
respect. Even in 1889, even in Scotland, it probably
took courage to talk like this about Shakespeare. He

would have dealt as roundly—one doesn't doubt it—
with Burns himself. Nor is he one of your merely
destructive critics. Towards the sermon's end comes
promise of a plan for "a new kind of exercise, amusement
and recreation that would add strength to the constitution, give pleasure in performance and that would
conduce to the well-being of body and soul". What was
it? Some highly spiritualized sort of golf? We are left
guessing, for the *Saturday Review* laughs Dr Teape out
of its cultured columns.

But, really, the nonsense about Ibsen and his work
that was to flood the press during the next few years was
little if any less ridiculous. It is true that after a century
of varnished poverty, such a picturing of life—and, for
all its Norwegian furnishing, of the sort of life lived by
most of the audience, no dukedom or millionairedom
as far removed from their actualities as the Britain of
King Lear!—such drastic judgment upon it, and that
hammer-blow method of his which at last compelled you
to listen, found our parochial puppet show of a theatre
and its sleepier critics very unprepared. But even so!

Then and Now in the Theatre generally

This, at least, one supposes, could hardly happen again.
No Ibsen to-day could become famous over one half
Europe while the other half ignored him. The Paris of
the 'eighties was content with French drama, with, for
the time being, rather poor drama very well acted.
For one thing it was then still a French city. Now the
thousands of its South Americans and North Americans,
its Russians (those of them that are not starving),
Japanese, Chinese, English, Germans, Italians, Rou-
manians, Greeks, Turks, Czechs, Yugo-Slavs and lesser
breeds without the law, who will pay well for enter-

tainment, who need it as they need food, since they
have often little social life to sustain them, make an
omnivorous public. And even the French themselves
have come to take a defiant interest in the natural
history of these detested invaders and welcome cus-
tomers as far as books and plays and music will exhibit
it to them. The Cinema shows them the home life of
America as the Cinema sees it, and the truth about
England is to be discovered at the Odéon in *Le Rosaire*
and *La Châtelaine de Shenstone* by Mrs Florence Barclay.

The London of the 'eighties welcomed French, but few
other foreign actors, and, as we have seen, was beginning
to pride itself upon producing a drama of its own. Italy, as
far as modern drama went, was poverty-stricken. And in
America it was the dark ages, though certain fine figures,
native and alien, moved luminously through the void.

One of these, it should be noted—Helen Modjeska;
the sound of the name can stir memories still—did
actually, as early as 1883, "try out" some translation
of *A Doll's House* in Louisville, Kentucky. What did
the Kentucky Colonels make of it? Not very much
apparently, for Modjeska played it no more. But
Louisville, for all that, may have seen the light shining.
Kentucky in the 'eighties may have had as good an eye
for the real thing as now, when Ibsen's name is in
its every High School library text-book. It may even
have had a better one. Was the rest of America robbed
of the play for another ten years or so only by some
terrified manager rushing round to beg "Madame",
for the love of Mike, to give them no more of—whatever was the 1883 equivalent of "this highbrow stuff"?

Nor, if we are to be accurate, was England left totally
without its Ibsen. Archer records "a quaint performance" in 1885 of Miss Lord's translation of the play
by "an adventurous amateur club" at a hall in Argyle

Street. One takes off one's hat to the adventurous amateurs across the years. Then at last, as we know, in 1889 comes Archer's own translation, produced by Charles Charrington and his wife, as adventurous an enterprise every whit. They have a hundred pounds to spend, possibly, and the courage of their convictions; and the Ibsen "movement", with much more of consequence to the English theatre, begins.[1]

The Charringtons

Let us then take off our hats to Charles Charrington and Janet Achurch too. He was a mild Irish idealist, with a love for whatever was fine in literature and drama, but with an incapacity for business, and too often a conscienceless recklessness in the transaction of it, which drove his friends and apologists to despair. He was not a good actor and perhaps never thought himself so, but by sheer intelligence he could often make the part more interesting than many a supposedly far better one would. He was unselfish and single-minded, his ambitions were for his wife; and here he was justified, for in her part and on her day she could challenge comparison with any actress in Europe. I never saw her Nora. The later scenes, apparently, were better than the earlier, the last scene of all the best. But as here is the making of the play, when what has so far seemed the play being over: "Sit down", says Nora, "we have much to talk about"—and, as has been said, modern drama begins—nothing mattered in comparison.

Having set London talking, she and Charrington

[1] The play was talked of and written about—mainly abusively, it is true —as no play had been for years. The performances were extended from seven to twenty-four. The takings were apt to be between £35 and £45 a night. Charrington only lost £70. This was not bad for an epoch-making venture in the higher drama. It would cost more to-day.

disappeared on a two years' tour round the world. This, one exclaims, was how business-like they were! But it was more a measure, probably, of the chances theatrical England offered to two people who had just made history for it. Later however, besides much else, I did see her play Rita in *Little Eyolf*, and I am not likely to forget it. The tragedy of the sensual incarnate, and "They said—the crutch is floating!" perhaps the most tremendous single moment I have ever experienced in a theatre. Later still (Mrs Theodore Wright had been the first English actress to play it) her Mrs Alving in *Ghosts* had force and quality, even if it was too little the woman of that one tragedy, and too much a Mrs Alving with a mission.

The Ibsenites

But self-consciousness was the bane of the Ibsen "movement". There never need have been such a thing, in its more aggravating aspects, had we only possessed—as we still do not possess!—a sensibly organized "theatre for adults" where the plays could have found a normal place. Not, for a while, *Ghosts*; here, as we said, there was bound to be trouble. Though Ibsen protested, as did his saner interpreters, that he had no social mission, that he was a poet and so to be judged, this one play had been a deliberate challenge, a dramatic challenge, at any rate. He meant, and he boasted it, "to move some boundary stones", to stake out the drama's claim to deal frankly with the darkest tragedies of this modern life that it pretended to picture. Significantly, he cast the play into austerely classic form, and behind their mask of commonplace the characters are as heroic as any Greek could have made them. Moreover, he took particular pains, he tells us, to keep the author as chorus, or any shadow of him, out of the scheme. Not for two years, even in the one half Europe that acclaimed him, would any theatre face its staging. Then its challenge was won, and it became the emblem of the drama's new freedom. In England in 1891, it was given a technically private performance at the Royalty Theatre, Soho; and the wrath of God and the Police was called down by an indignant press upon author, translator, actors and everybody concerned in sullying that chaste district and England's atmosphere with this "drama of the Lock Hospital"—one of the choicer phrases flung at it. The Lock Hospital itself—did the critic observe?— happens to stand, a stark sardonic reality, a few yards up the street. The Lord Chamberlain, the last of our autocrats, not merely condemned the play but later committed himself, through the mouth of his Reader, to the omniscience of "*Ghosts* will never be licensed". But when the war came someone suggested that here, for the many young men we were daily thrusting into a desperate world, might be a wholesome object lesson upon this subject, which preachers, clerical or lay, so temptation proof as they themselves must seem, find it hardest to tackle convincingly—and the play was acted "by command" to our troops in France!

A thousand pities that the English theatre of the 'eighties was still too feeble of constitution to absorb the new strong wine of the Ibsen drama, for its own sake and for Ibsen's also. The plays were driven into corners where it was the harder to protect them from the hungry enthusiasms of that intellectual jackalry which hangs—a scurvy pack!—upon the skirts of all new departures.[1] "What does the thorough-going Ibsenite care", asks our Saturday Reviewer when, a

[1] Needless to say, I hope, that this does not refer to the many able men and women who genuinely admired and discriminatingly praised them.

little tardily, he gives his attention to *A Doll's House*, "about works of art whether they be plays, poems, or pictures? He has just one idea, Woman's Suffrage, Anti-Vivisection, or Social Purity—as the case may be." The years revenge themselves upon such gibes. Ibsen and the suffrage, at least, are free of their jackalry for ever; and "What on earth was Social Purity?" asks the bright young savage of to-day. But there were in fact such Ibsenites, short-haired women (thirty years before the fashion) and long-haired men (some thirty years behind it) who doubtless cared little enough for the plays as plays. The worst was that a mere handful of them, self-consciously intense, could colour and infect a whole audience. One wished them to the devil. Inevitably there sprang up "Ibsenite" actors too, though not many of them, and never the best. And a ridiculous fiction became current—much encouraged by others who had no use for the unwholesome stuff—that Ibsen was easy to act. He is, of course, as easy to act badly as Shakespeare and Aeschylus are, and as the silliest farce is. He was then, for highly professionalized actors, much harder to act well. And perhaps, in their hearts, they knew this. For he asked a humility of approach, and a new schooling in that packed dynamic method of his. Airs and graces avail little for the assault on our consciousness meant to be made by Mrs Alving and Oswald, Rosmer and Rebecca; and Nora, Hialmar Ekdal and Hedda Gabler are tuned to a pathetic, a ridiculous, and, for the last, to a deadly mockery of them. There was no such snobbish nonsense about Janet Achurch, who was an able professional actress when Ibsen made her career for her, and she went to school to him whole-heartedly. But thereafter the stigma of Ibsenism did very much to ruin it.

The Middle Class View

There was just one antidote to Ibsenism, Ibsen himself, and full knowledge of him as the great dramatic poet which above all else he was. But this was not easily imparted; the British public, indeed, has hardly attained it yet. The plays—the important earlier work too, *Peer Gynt, Brand* and the historical tragedies—were, thanks to Archer, mostly translated and published within four or five years. But few people will read plays, and fewer still *can* read them with much profit. The new ones and those simpler to stage were given sporadic performance. The rest stayed within their book covers, and mostly do so to this day.

The "recognized" theatre, with its actor-managers —whose passing we mourn!—would have none of Ibsen.[1] This seems mere stupidity, and largely it was; they did not find much in him except to dislike. But had they thought him a god among dramatists worldly wisdom would have warned them to let him alone. The great Victorian middle-class was then still at the height of its prestige (it has disintegrated since; part is now plutocratic and the other part pretty well ruined) and they and their theatre had only recently become re-spectable in its eyes. It was their chief paymaster and they could not afford to offend it. Besides, they were middle-class themselves, and respectability was rightly dear to them. Their own social status was improving. Irving's knighthood was in the future; but, for ex-ample, people would no longer address letters to "Mr John Hare" (not that he would have cared, and his knighthood was coming, too) as they once had to "Mr

---

[1] Beerbohm Tree was an honourable exception. Truly, he only ventured upon *An Enemy of the People*, and at matinées, and he "clowned" the produc-tion outrageously. But still!

W. Macready" who used to destroy them in a rage
unread. If anything seemed solid in the structure of the
England of that day—and most things did!—it was
this prosperous and contented middle-class; and both
interest and inclination brought the theatre to appeal to
its tastes and to flatter its prejudices, which were to be
found reflected in its representative organs—such a
fittingly sonorous word for them—in *The Times*, of
course (but *The Times* cost threepence, and the middle-
class preferred to pay a penny for its newspaper), the
Globe, the *Morning Advertiser*, the *Standard*, and, above
all, in the *Daily Telegraph*, its secular bible. This was
why theatre managers read Mr Clement Scott's pro-
nouncements in those columns with such awe. He was
—not to speak it unkindly—a person of no intellectual
account whatever; but he spoke to, and (supposedly)
for the great middle-class.

The drama was advancing, even daringly. Everyone
—Mr Archer included—owned it. Had not Mr Pinero
just written this "new and original" play, in which he
had treated the "difficult subject" of the seducer and
his wife and his victim "with such remarkable delicacy"? But where was Mr Ibsen's delicacy—over the
affairs of Captain Alving, of Mr Werle and Mrs
Ekdal? And as to Rosmer and Miss Rebecca West, if
that unpleasant business was somewhat more decently
handled it was only at the price of complete incom-
prehensibility. Nor, as with the amusingly, tradition-
ally indelicate French author, could you square the
Lord Chamberlain by any such simple devices as the
turning of *maîtresse* into *fiancée* and the writing in of a
shadowy chaperon, the suppressing of *cocu* and the
setting of the second act in the lounge of a seaside hotel.
These plays of Ibsen's were stubborn, self-respecting
things. Nor were their unpleasant events palliated even

by being let pass in any "atmosphere of fashionable libertinism". Quite the contrary, they persistently pictured and, as the *Saturday Review* remarked, were obviously "in a great measure written in order to satirize the detested middle-class". Why then, one's own taste apart, should one at the bidding of a small crew of noisy revolutionary intellectuals, insult one's chief patrons and quarrel with one's bread-and-butter by producing them?

The Critics

No, the theatre may be excused. But what of the critics? Not the Clement Scotts, from whom nothing better could be expected, but the men—the critics proper—whose business it was to know and welcome the new thing that was the real thing when they saw it. One blushes for them still. For Mr Frederick Wedmore, who is patronizingly glad in the *Academy* "to have had an opportunity of seeing a play of Ibsen's . . . upon the stage in London, even though the conclusion one draws after having seen it is, that it is not particularly likely one will see it again". For the innominate monitor of *The Times*, who found *A Doll's House* boring—and was within his rights!—but who considers that it suffers from an "almost total lack of dramatic action". For the *Scots Observer*—the most brilliant review of its time, still remembered and quoted—which was permitted by its Editor to announce, when the first two volumes of the collected plays appeared, that "the four volumes promised will be a neat monument beneath which the remains of Ibsenism will no doubt be decently interred"; to decide that Ibsen is not a master of dialogue, "nor is it (his) skill in stage-craft that has endeared him to his admirers. It is scarce possible to believe that the author of *A Doll's House* and

The Wild Duck has spent many years of his life in theatrical management. In the composition of his own dramas he has resolutely declined to profit by an experience of the stage sufficiently long to furnish a dozen ordinary playwrights with technique. Now and then, it is true, he has lapsed into effectiveness...". And as if here were not obliquity enough we are next informed that Ibsen cannot draw character either. This reviewer turns from the reading of Torvald and Nora, Oswald and Manders and Mrs Alving, of Dr Stockmann, of Hialmar, Gina, Hedvig, Gregers and Relling to tell us that Ibsen cannot draw character! Then, for a finish, that soon, when he is no longer dealt with by the critic of morals but the critic of literature, "...his later prose plays will pass into the limbo of dead books".

Our much quoted Saturday Reviewer, belatedly noticing *A Doll's House* and premising, with suitable superiority, that as to "the controversy which has raged round the production" he does not "pretend to have followed it very closely", goes on nevertheless to discuss the play with comparative intelligence. True, he finds that Torvald towards the end "is made to talk in a tone of selfishness which reminds one very much of Mr Gilbert's satiric strain. This is amusing enough in its place; but here it fails to effect its object, which is to reconcile the audience to the heartless and immoral conduct of the wife"—which would seem to show that Ibsen's main dramatic purpose had still more or less escaped him. Nora's second act scene with Dr Rank and its pitiful ironies he finds most unpleasant; it leaves him wondering whether "we have a licenser of plays at all". Is it the episode of the silk stockings that so upsets him and Rank's mischievous little joke about not knowing whether they will fit her or no? Dress Nora in the fashion of 1929 and the point cannot even be made. But 1960 may be shocked by it again, who knows! Lastly he very much wishes that in "re-furnishing the Doll's House for England Mr Archer had moved the marriage couch out of the drawing-room". This must refer to Torvald's champagne-charged bout of love-making. What *did* Mr Herbert Waring and Miss Achurch do? There was a sofa probably. Did they sit, or did Miss Achurch, for a brief moment, even recline on it? Or is the reproof purely metaphorical? Alas, such critical delicacy is no more. Couches—marriage and other—are the common furniture of the stage nowadays. It is not Ibsen, however, who has introduced them there.

We can pass by the grosser stupidities, outcries against "The Socialistic Nora" (one would rather have thought that extreme individualism was her failing; but Socialistic was—as Jacobin had been to 1889's grand-fathers, as Bolshevist is to its sons—less a word that meant anything in particular than a useful stick for the beating of anyone you might find on the left of you) and against Ibsen himself as a "muck-ferreting dog". It was *Ghosts*, however, that inspired this last effort in criticism.

The plain fact was that the coming of Ibsen struck fear into the hearts of the parents and guardians of the yet invertebrate British drama. There was the easy-going journalist crew who knew—as the actors of the old school did, though neither could confess it—that they were incompetent to deal with him. Once grant there *was* something in the stuff, clearly it was not the sort of thing you could dispose of in a dashed-off thousand words without danger of making a fool of yourself. There were the critics proper, competent and cultured enough, but resentful of this attempt to cut through the well-baked crust of their minds. They felt, what was more, and they had readers in plenty to

agree with them, that on the whole the theatre had
better not deal with vexed and vital questions, had
better not "take itself too seriously".

The Neo-Puritans

For this was the dominant intellectual attitude towards
the theatre in England, nor, perhaps, is it greatly
changed to-day. It may be called the neo-Puritan
attitude, and it is a more noxious, not to say a far more
aggravating one than was the old uncompromising
frown. A Dr Teape would simply close the theatres if
he could, as did his forefathers when they ruled the
roost. He cannot, so he avoids them, and for once will
speak his mind about them. And as it is the conscience
of an honest man speaking, who does not fear to sound
ridiculous, there will be profit in considering what he
says. He could perhaps have found a better case than
Hamlet's to argue. So few of us are confronted with the
doubtful duty of killing our stepfathers. But it is true
that people may be prompted to say and do all sorts of
foolish and wicked things by the mimic spectacle of
them. Doubtless many a Torvald (and there is Torvald's side to that business too) has repented, if only for
an hour or so, that his Nora ever saw *A Doll's House*.
But these will be people of crude and cramped imagination. And the question is, since life itself also presents
tempting spectacles—are we to cultivate their imagination and give them good of it in the freedom of it, or
no? The consistent Puritan says no; safety from sin is
in the milk of the Word and nowhere else at all. The
artist, and those that believe in the morality of art, only
go a longer way to work. Incidentally, Dr Teape, could
he have suffered him at all, would have found Ibsen
far more to his mind than Shakespeare!

The neo-Puritan has little faith in art, and more than a little fear of it. He will allow us painting and sculpture (not too much of the nude), music, and literature as long as he may hold it in leading-strings. But there is something less candid, something really rather sinister, in his view of the theatre.

To begin with he only grudgingly admits the drama to be an art at all; it is, at any rate, not a fine art.[1] He still carries in his memory an echo of his forefathers' outcry against it as a place of sin and shame. But that sort of thing, he now says, within the bounds of decorum, a pull at the leading-strings always possible, is a useful safety valve for compressed virtues. Let it alone, then, as long as it merely plays the fool. It may even play the harlot a little if it will play the helot as well. But don't let it take itself too seriously. This was also the opinion of the larger part of the liberal-minded "men of the world", who gave evidence before the Joint Committee on the Censorship in 1909, of the then Speaker of the House of Commons in particular. The late Lord Morley of Blackburn, through whose cultured scepticism the Nonconformist conscience sometimes spoke, was accustomed occasionally, I believe, to take a tired mind into the stalls at the Gaiety—and why not? But he had no use whatever for higher flights in drama. Mr Gladstone, on the other hand, who remained in many things a high church Tory to the end and never, certainly, became a "man of the world", liked, when he was old, to have a chair placed in the O.P. corner at the Lyceum, and Irving would give him royal welcome there.

[1] Here I speak by the card. The Royal Academy of Dramatic Art has for years been applying for a rebate in its rates under an act which accorded this grace to institutions devoted to the Fine Arts, and the application has been rejected on the specific ground that acting was not a Fine Art—till at last, a month ago, a bench of justices was found to say "What perfect nonsense!"

The theatre (this is the argument), if it takes itself too seriously, if its public takes it seriously, may well become a nuisance and a danger. Is the authentic moralist—and your neo-Puritan sees himself as that— to encourage a rival whose morals may by no means be his, and set him up in such a powerful pulpit? Again, is the glamorous theatre a fit place for the ventilating of embarrassing questions? Lord Morley, seeing in the average audience only a lot of intellectual children, avid for excitement, being there himself to indulge the child in him, shakes a wise head. But what is to be done? You cannot prevent your dramatists—misguided fellows!— from writing such plays. You can, as the law stands, forbid their public performance. (It was amusing, when the Censorship was on trial, to hear some Liberals, pledged to liberty under the law, justifying its exercise —and by an officer of the King's Household too!) But that only advertises forbidden fruit and stimulates appetite; and in one way or another the most potent of them seem to get performed. Is there at last anything you *can* effectively do except make your theatre a fit place for the posing of every sort of question which the terms of its art can compass—add, if you like, which the manners of the time allow to be discussed in a public assembly; then, by experience and the help of stern criticism, educate your audiences in the taste and judgment that will tell them whether such a question is artistically (and this means honestly) posed and resolved or no. With a high standard set him, the dramatist's art is a difficult one; you need not be afraid you will be overrun with such plays. More-over it is one which strangely revenges itself, even upon the most accomplished dishonesty of purpose. The dramatist cannot cheat us as readily as the novelist can. For he must have human beings to interpret him, and their reality will show up his unrealities. They may conspire with him, but since this flesh and blood medium is pretty familiar to us it is not very hard, if we have a mind, to see through their falseness, and his.

The Movie and the Talkie

We can respect a Dr Teape even while we smile over him, but it is hard to be patient with the neo-Puritan, who must merely confess, in the last analysis, that he prefers bad drama to good. Since Ibsen's day there have arisen the Movie and the Talkie to make, so to speak, bad drama worse, more efficiently and elaborately and alluringly worse. The European theatre, somewhat shaken by the war, sits gazing distractedly at this striving young monster with the American accent, this amazing Benjamin of the family. What is to be done about him? As a partner he will not leave his elders much to live on; he embraces them affectionately and picks their pockets of the few talents they have left. As a rival, can they hope to compete with his prosperous democratic enterprise of making cheap what is most dear, all the art that money can buy him ground in his mill, with his binding of the whole world together in the bonds of a common vulgarity? Do I *want* to compete with him, asks the poor harassed theatre; and answers pathetically: If it weren't for the bread and butter difficulty, good heavens, no! Our neo-Puritans have now begun—a little diffidently, for a lot of capital has been invested in him, and there are Interests to offend—to shake their heads over the monster and to talk, not only of offences against morality, which they have appointed a few "men of the world" to control, but of bad taste and the degradation of English culture and things like that. They have even

passed a law to enable England to bring up a monster
of its own!

The Condition of the Theatre Question

The remedy for every evil is innate in it. Towards what
precise scheme of better and worse the costly chaos of
the Cinema itself is evolving I do not pretend to know,
nor—except that the coming of the Talkie has so far
robbed me of some restfully amusing afternoons—very
greatly to care. It is its compromising partnership and
rivalry with the theatre which concerns me. Well, the
antidote to bad drama is good drama, and I do not
believe there is any other. Not solemn drama, nor, of
necessity, serious drama, not of the Ibsen brand in
particular, nor of the Shakespeare brand exclusively;
but just good drama of its kind, and of pretty nearly
any kind that is not quite infantile. Train it up, see fair
play, and let the good stuff fight the bad for the suf-
frages and—if we want to talk solemnly—for the souls
of the people. There is no other way. But the bulk of
the people will still prefer the bad! It may well be so;
and if that were the end of the matter, of this and of
kindred matters, civilization itself would soon be throwing up the sponge. But it obviously isn't. Where the good
does not win outright, the bad only ostensibly beats it by
becoming not quite so bad. And the taste of the better
thing imperceptibly spoils our appetite for the worse.

Such, to a degree at least, is the history of Ibsen's
influence in England and of its native sequel. He gave
modern drama its intellectual liberty. The theatre that
would have none of him soon found itself setting out to
emulate him. The actors who had sneered at "Ibsen
actors" learned a lesson from them, and the critics
who had abused him began to measure plays by his

standard. This is the revenge which genius takes. And while his true followers, playwrights and actors, won no popular success, and but a begrudged reputation, on their work the best work of the next generation was built; and now another generation builds diversedly on that.

The Ibsen "movement" is now of no more account except to pious historians; but his plays have their place, which, by every test, is among living drama still, and is likely for long enough to remain so. There are, we may say, two sorts of drama, that to which the theatre gives a transient life and that which gives life to the theatre. Whatever the first may bring in pleasure or profit, it is as well to recognize the difference; for in a crisis, such as the present one, it may be only the second sort, and our sense of the vital worth of it, that can pull the theatre through.

Ibsen as he is Translated

When an Ibsen play is revived one may sometimes hear a little grumbling at Archer's translation; it is too literal or too stiff, or what not. The problem of play translating admits of no one solution, is always troublesome, and Ibsen, with his close packed lines, his choice of words for both their sound and sense and his complexity of meaning, presents it at its worst. Archer never pretended that his versions were impeccable and he would always labour, if the occasion came, to improve on them. One hopes that his critics have his familiar knowledge of the plays as Ibsen wrote them and have faced their difficulties as squarely as he did.

Should anybody fancy quite another version of *A Doll's House* here are extracts from one which Archer himself delighted in and, in a magazine article, partly presented to the public. Let me do something more to preserve it.

It was first published in 1880 by Weber's Academy at Copenhagen and it is dedicated

To
Her Royal Highness
Alexandra
Princess of Wales.

Here is one of the earlier passages between Torvald and Nora:

Helmer. . . . Has my thoughtless bird again dissipated money?

Nora. But Thorvald, we must enjoy ourselves a little. It is the first Christmas we need not to spare.

Helmer. Know that we cannot dissipate.

Nora. Yes, Thorvald; we may now dissipate a little, may we not? . . .

Helmer. Nora! (*goes up to her and catches her in jest by her ear*) Is thoughtlessness again there? Suppose that I borrowed £50 to-day, and you dissipated this sum during the Christmas week, and a tile fell down on my head New Year's eve, and I were killed—

Nora. O fy! don't speak so badly.

Helmer. Yes, suppose that such happened, what then?

Nora. If such bad were to happen, it might be indifferent to me either I had debt or no. . . .

Helmer. What do we call the birds that always dissipate money?

Nora. Gamblers, I know it, indeed.

Helmer. . . . The gambler is sweet, but it uses up excessively much money. It is incredible how expensive it is to a man to keep a gambler. . . .

Nora with Mrs Linden is hardly less happy:

Nora. O, Kristine, how flighty and happy I feel! It is charming to have excessively much money and need not to give one's self any concerns, is it not?

Mrs Linden. It must at any rate be charming to have the necessary.

Nora. No, not only the necessary, but excessively much money!

·   ·   ·   ·   ·

Mrs Linden. . . . My poor mother needs me no longer, for she has died. Nor the Boys; they have been employed and can shift for themselves.

Nora. How flighty you must feel!

Mrs Linden. No, but so much abandoned.

·   ·   ·   ·   ·

And when Ibsen warms to his work so does Mr Weber.

Helmer. He has written counterfeit names. Have you any idea of what such means?...Only imagine how such a guilty man must lie, play the hypocrite, and dissemble in all ways, must be masked in presence of his nearly-related, even in presence of his wife and children. And as to the children, that is just the most terrific of all, Nora.

Nora. Why?

Helmer. Because a such atmosphere, containing lie, causes contagion and disease-substance in a home. Every breath the children draw in a such house contains germs of something ugly.

Nora (nearer behind him). Are you sure of that?

Helmer. My dear, as an advocate, I have often learned so. Almost all early depraved men have had lying mothers....Therefore, my sweet little Nora must promise me not to plead his cause. Give me your hand as an affirmation. Well, what's that? Give me your hand. Well, thus decided, I assure you it would be impossible to me to work conjointly with him. I feel literally indisposed in the presence of such men.

Mr Weber's crowning effort, however, says Archer, is reserved for the last words of the act:

Nora (pale with horror). Deprave my little children! Poison my home? *(a short pause; she turns up her nose[1])* This is not true. This is in the name of wonder not true.

There are gems towards the end of the play. Helmer, warm with wine, has brought his wife back from the ball.

Helmer. And when we are to go, and I am laying the shawl on your tender, youthfully fresh shoulders—on this charming nape—then I imagine that you are my young bride....

And the climax of the famous scene is a climax indeed.

Helmer. Nora—may I never more become but a stranger to you?

Nora (takes her portmanteau). Alas, Thorvald, then the most wonderful must happen—

Helmer. Tell me the most wonderful.

[1] *Tosses her head,* one regrets to say, is the correct translation.

Nora. That both you and I changed ourselves in such a manner that—O, Thorvald, I no longer believe in anything wonderful.

Helmer. But I will believe in it. Tell it me! Change ourselves in such a manner that—?

Nora. That cohabitation between you and me might become a matrimony. Good-bye.

I am not indisposed to offer a prize at the Royal Academy of Dramatic Art to the student who could manage to speak the last line without making her audience laugh.

MARTIN TUPPER

By John Drinkwater

In 1886 Martin Tupper published his autobiography, *My Life as an Author*. It is a remarkable book. Tupper was then seventy-five years of age. He had enjoyed, exuberantly enjoyed, astonishing success. *Proverbial Philosophy* had appeared in its original form in 1838. For many years it had brought him in a steady income of between £500 and £800 annually, and the profits would have been very much larger had he received any compensation for the pirated editions that circulated in enormous numbers in America. For more than a generation the book was an easy best-seller in two continents, and portions of it were translated into several European languages. Tupper's appearance in any public place was the likely signal for an emotional display on the part of some stranger whose life had been redeemed by the revelations of *Proverbial Philosophy*. He was the favourite poet of thousands of readers who knew nothing about poetry. Learned societies, church dignitaries, philanthropic zealots, regimental messes, antivivisection leagues and boards of directors, united in his praise. And they not only praised him, they read him. When he visited a hospital for the feeble-minded he found his ballad *Never give up* on every door, and was "surrounded by kneeling and weeping and kissing folks, grateful for the good hope my verses had helped them to".

Never give up! it is wiser and better
  Always to hope than once to despair;
Fling off the load of Doubt's heavy fetter
  And break the dark spell of tyrannical care:

Never give up! or the burden may sink you,—
  Providence kindly has mingled the cup,
And, in all trials or troubles, bethink you
  The watchword of life must be Never give up!

Tupper in his life story gives a full account of his poetical career and its triumphs. It is true that although he had at least a passing acquaintance with many of his great contemporaries, Tennyson, Browning, Arnold, Longfellow, Holmes, Dickens and Thackeray, he is never able to cite a compliment from these, be it never so mild, nor do we hear of any critic whose authority has survived testifying in his favour. Nevertheless, responsible journals of the time acclaimed him without misgiving. N. P. Willis may cut little ice in these days, but he was a power in his time. There is a story of an American enquiring of a compatriot "Who is Go-ethe?" and receiving the reply, "I guess he's the German N. P. Willis". It was, then, no small recommendation when Willis wrote in his *Home Journal* that Tupper's "words form an electric chain, along which he sends his own soul, thrilling around the wide circle of his readers". The *American Courier* announced that Tupper was a man "whose name will eventually be one of the very noblest on the scroll of fame"; and the *New York World*, more solidly, that a million and a half copies of *Proverbial Philosophy* had already been sold in America. The *Episcopal Recorder* of Philadelphia had "rarely met a volume so grateful to the taste in all its parts, so rich in its simplicity, so unique in its arrangements, and so perfect in all that constitutes the perfection of style.... It must live like immortal seed, to produce a continual harvest of profitable reflection". These were American journals of note and influence, but in case the reader should suspect American culture in the Victorian age, we may find these views supported in our native contemporaries. The *Church of England Journal* and the *Court Journal* may be negligible witnesses, but their opinions should not be lost. Said the one, "*Proverbial Philosophy* is poetry assuredly; poetry exquisite, almost beyond the bounds of fancy to conceive, brimmed with noble thoughts, and studded with heavenward aspirations"; and the other, "A book as full of sweetness as a honeycomb, of gentleness as woman's heart; in its wisdom worthy the disciple of a Solomon, in its genius the child of a Milton". The *Glasgow Examiner*, beyond proclaiming *Proverbial Philosophy* to be "a work of standard excellence", was chiefly informative. The book "has met with unprecedented success, and many large editions of it have been sold. It led to the author's being elected a Fellow of the Royal Society; and the King of Prussia, in token of his Majesty's high approbation of the work, sent him the gold medal for science and literature". The *Morning Post* with great ingenuity said much in little: "Were we to say all we think of the nobleness of the thoughts, of the beauty and virtuousness of the sentiments contained in this volume, we should be constrained to write a lengthened eulogium on it"; a seductive example for reviewers. The *Saturday Review* pledged its credit boldly thus: "If men delight to read Tupper both in England and America, why should they not study him both in the nineteenth century and in the twentieth? The judgment of persons who are more or less free from insular prejudices is said in some degree to anticipate that which is admitted to be the conclusive verdict of posterity". And the chorus was nobly joined

by the *Spectator* with "Martin Farquhar Tupper has
won for himself the vacant throne waiting for him
amidst the immortals, and after a long and glorious
term of popularity among those who know when their
hearts are touched, without being able to justify their
taste to their intellect, has been adopted by the suffrage
of mankind and the final decree of publishers into the
same rank with Wordsworth, Tennyson, and Browning".

It all sounds fantastic, doubtless, but our own
journals to-day, if the paper upon which they are
printed has not perished, will afford as much matter
for a May morning to investigators fifty years hence.
When Tupper as an old man took stock of his career
he was serenely unconscious of any miscalculation in
these estimates. As frontispiece to his volume appears
a photograph of himself taken by Messrs Elliot and
Fry. A refined and sensitive hand holds a quill pen,
the braided black frock-coat sets off beautifully laun-
dered linen, and the head, with a full white beard and
crowned with a snowy mass of locks revealing an ample
forehead, is mildly magnificent. Mild because of a
certain transcendental docility in the eyes, but splendid
in its front and contours. Tupper as he here faces us
might well be Longfellow's competent twin brother.
He is, in fact, a fine-looking old fellow.

He was happy in his ripe age, confident that his
fame with posterity was secure. He closed his book
with a translation from Ovid:

My name shall never die; but through all time
Whenever Rome shall reach a conquer'd clime,
There, in that people's tongue, shall this my page
Be read and glorified from age to age:—
Yea, if the bodings of my spirit give
True note of inspiration, I shall live!

Three years later, in 1889, he died in his eightieth year
with the illusion undispelled. For illusion incontestably
it was. Martin Tupper's verses are dead beyond all
hope of resurrection. Nothing perhaps in our mortal
terms is so surely immortal as the genuine spark of
poetry. However feebly or fitfully it may inform a man's
work, however obscured it may be by brighter lustres,
sooner or later someone will come along again to discern
it and do it a moment's homage if no more. But nowhere in Tupper is the genuine spark discoverable.
His rewards were lavish, but the account is closed.
Nevertheless there is something likeable about that
venerable figure, and the autobiography is not without
significance, if not always the significance that its
author intended. It has after all the conspicuous merit
of being readable, which *Proverbial Philosophy* is to-day
only under compulsion. Moreover, it helps us to divine
the secret of that poem's sensational vogue.

Tupper's name, says the *Dictionary of National
Biography*, "in due time became a synonym for the
common-place". The observation, if adroit, is no more
than suggestive. The strange and rather disturbing fact
about Tupper is that if he had been a poet at all he
might have been a great one. Since he decisively was
not a poet at all, it may be held that the question does
not arise, but I think that it does, and pertinently.
Tupper addressed himself to great themes. A list of his
poems might well be taken for a list of essays by
Emerson or Carlyle. Further, he had a certain kind of
logical force, and he had courage. A confirmed op-
timist, he could advance by no means negligible arguments for his faith in a universal benevolence, and when
Gladstone, whom he knew and whom he had praised,
took what he conceived to be a wrong turning, he could
say so plainly and in public. His mind was generous;

he was not afraid to lend his considerable influence to unpopular causes. He loved virtue and had on the whole a liberal and lucid conception of what virtue really was. His character, for all its naïvety, was not without a certain toughness, and he attempted in his thought to take a large view of life. All this may be said well enough of a man for whom poetry does not exist, but they are the kind of things that in a poet make for something considerable. And for Tupper poetry was a constant and lifelong preoccupation. To be a great poet was his steady ambition, and from first to last he convinced himself that it was being realized. Also he convinced tens of thousands of readers to the same effect. How was it that with material not unpromising and a purpose so resolved he was so entirely a victim of self-deception? And, further, how came it that the deception was so widely shared?

The resolution of purpose is important. Great numbers of people with amiable sentiments turn for expression, especially in their youth, to inadequate verse. But in default of all inspiration the efforts are sporadic and usually fade away altogether. Tupper presents a much more uncommon spectacle. For something like sixty years he wrote with unabated fertility. He had the incentive of success, and it is clear from his autobiography that he felt himself to be fulfilling a great destiny. But of genuine creative satisfaction, which alone commonly sustains a man through the determined effort of a long career, he can have known nothing. I cannot profess to have read all that Martin Tupper wrote, but I have read a great deal of it, enough to make it clear that the delight of subduing difficult or profound comprehension to significant expression can never for a moment have been his. The one astonishing thing about his work is how even applause so lavish could induce him year after year to go on with it. But the fact remains, and it needs some explanation.

The explanation must be sought without any reference to the real achievement of Victorian poetry. With this Tupper's work had no contact, and in his autobiography there is no suggestion that he was conscious of its existence. A personal compliment here and there to Tennyson or Browning is the only indication of any knowledge of the poetic age in which he was living, and of poetry in any other age there is hardly a word. Either of two reasons might account for this isolation. The one that Tupper was an original poet sufficient unto himself clearly does not apply. We are left with the other, which is simply that Tupper did not know what poetry was. And still he remained sufficient unto himself. His readers also did not know what poetry was, but they found in him an inexhaustible source supplying comfort and encouragement to the sort of aspiration that characterized the ethical religion of the age. Tupper, on all the evidence, was a good man, and he was not doctrinal. He professed himself a Christian, but he attacked priestcraft. What passed for his liberal intellectual position gave him the appearance of exploring life in all its aspects with great candour, and he was able to come back from the adventure with a ringing message of hope. That as a prophet he had no imaginative or intellectual foundations did not matter; the great thing was that he prophesied, and in a mood very congenial to the time. People who had sensitive minds or sharp wits were not taken in, but earnest people in their thousands, who had neither, were lifted up. Tupper could not write poetry, but he could write this, which may be taken as a single and sufficient example of *Proverbial Philosophy*:

For the enemy, the father of lies, the giant Upas of creation,
Whose deadly shade hath blasted this once green garden of the
     Lord,
Can but pervert the good, but may not create the evil:
He destroyeth, but cannot build; for he is not antagonist deity:
Mighty is his stolen power, yet is he a creature and a subject;
Not a maker of abstract wrong, but a spoiler of concrete right:
The fiend hath not a royal crown: he is but a prowling robber,
Suffered, for some mysterious end, to haunt the King's highway;
And the keen sword he beareth, once was a simple ploughshare;
Yea, and his panoply of errors is but distortion of a truth:
The sickle that once reaped righteousness, beaten from its useful
     curve,
With axe, and spike, and bar, headeth the marauder's halbert.
Seek not further, O man, to solve the dark riddle of sin;
Suffice it, that thine own bad heart is to thee thine origin of evil.

This is a favourable specimen of a work that approaches *Paradise Lost* in length. It has qualities that for nearly half a century took a huge public by storm. Its reasoning is something better than specious, its temper is firm, and its expression directly intelligible without being entirely banal. But as we read it the explanation for which we are looking seems to reveal itself. "It will be considered", says Tupper in his autobiography, "that my public versifying was quite extempore, as in fact is common with me." That is it; all his versifying was improvised. In another place he says "ideas are ofttimes shy of the close furniture of words". The self-revelation is complete. An improviser of quite astonishing energy who spent his entire life writing with no sense of words, in the belief indeed that words were an embarrassment to ideas. The phenomenon in itself is a common one, but on this scale it is hardly to be matched in literature.

The accomplished improviser who employs his gifts not derisively but sympathetically has a great pull on people, and when he can give his incantations a literary

turn the spell and the prestige are complete. As Tupper
went through life he could rise in verse—if rise be the
word—to any occasion at a moment's notice. If he
stays in a historic house, and if his host calls at dinner
for a rhyme in honour of its associations, delivery is
made before bedtime, if not indeed before the port has
finished circulating. During his triumphant American
tours *Aves* and *Vales* flow from him in a tropic profusion
of rhyme.

> Ho! brother, I'm a Britisher,
>   A chip of heart of oak,
> That wouldn't warp or swerve or stir
>   From what I thought or spoke;
> And you—a blunt and honest man,
>   Straightforward, kind, and true,
> I tell you, brother Jonathan,
>   That you're a Briton too!

The sentiment would hardly do now, but it seems to
have gone very well then. Impressed by a visit to a
stained-glass works, he walks to the Royal Society, calls
for paper, and deposits in the archives of that institution
a record of his experience in forty lines. An amateur
inventor himself, he is bidden to a feast to celebrate the
completion of the Atlantic Cable, and after dinner when
the first message is to be flashed to America he has
ready in his pocket seven eight-line stanzas, of which,
however, one only is deemed sufficient for the purpose.
A request from the rifle clubs for a poetic slogan pro-
duces six ballads. Words like Jubilee, Coronation,
Review, Wedding, Installation, went straight to his
head.

As this is the Jubilee year, and I may not live to its completion,—
for who can depend upon an hour?—I will here produce what has
just occurred to my patriotism as a suitable ode on the great occasion.
If short, it is all the better for music, and I humbly recommend its
adoption as *libretto* to some chief musical composer.

Victoria's Jubilee: for Music

I

(*Major forte*)

Rejoice, O Land! Imperial Realm, rejoice!
   Wherever round the world
   Our standard floats unfurl'd,
Let every heart exult in music's voice!
   Be glad, O grateful England,
   Triumphant shout and sing, Land!
     As from each belfried steeple
      The clanging joy-bells sound,
     Let all our happy people
      The wandering world around,
Rejoice with the joy this jubilee brings,
Circling the globe as with seraphim wings!

Asked at Hereford by the S.P.C.A. for help in an anti-vivisection campaign, he completes a sonnet before he leaves the train at London:

   If ever thou hast loved thy dog or horse,
     Or other favourite affectionate thing...

a work supplemented on another occasion by

   Worn, jaded, and faint, plodding on in the track,
   I praise your great patience, poor omnibus hack....

The recovery of bad verse merely to make a Roman holiday is a graceless task, but it is beguiling to consider the enormous impression that was made by verse so bad as this. Tupper's genial nature, his easy, well-intentioned mind, bustled along with an endless facility of expression. Thought and word were correspondingly shallow, but they were reinforced by ponderable impulses. The ethical urge that clung to faith while rejecting dogma was, after all, a great manifestation of the spirit, and Tupper voiced it for his age, without distinction, but not altogether without point. Also he

believed, again without vision, in the goodness of God
and in the goodness of man, and here he was fighting
in a field which, however fluctuating its fortunes have
been, has never yet been surrendered to the forces of
cynicism or malice or despair. His gospel, in short, was
a great one, and he attempted high terms in its argument. When we turn from his occasional trifles to the
crowded wastes of *Proverbial Philosophy*, we find that
in the result his major musings are no less occasional
and no less trifling. The pedestrian standard is absolute,
and we wonder how the miracle can ever have happened. But it did, to the tune of hundreds of thousands
of copies in England and over a million in America.
And these things never happen quite for nothing. The
truth is that Tupper, who was a demagogic poetaster
of unexampled success, might have been a great
popular poet. Might have been, that is to repeat, if he
had been a poet at all. He set his face from the first
in the right direction by instinct. He believed throughout a long life that he was marching steadily forward.
His belief was shared by cheering crowds of readers.
Something very energetic undoubtedly was happening.
But the first step as a poet was never taken.

Tupper's work did not belong to the 'eighties, but
it was in the 'eighties, as we have seen, that he was able
to persuade himself that its purpose had been accomplished and that its influence would be abiding. He
died with no suspicion of the gloomy truth, and the
most avid realist could hardly wish it to have been
otherwise. Let us turn for a short time to the man
himself. Martin Farquhar Tupper was born in 1810,
and died in 1889; that is to say, his life to within a year
or two was contemporaneous with those of Tennyson
and Browning. Among his ancestry he counted an
Ironside officer in Cromwell's cavalry, and at a nearer

date Arthur William Devis, the historical painter. He remembered his father in powder, and he remembered walking in the meadows of Regent's Park "in search of cowslips and new milk". He was taken as a child to see Winsor's Patent Gaslights at Carlton House, and he was also taken to call upon George III, "his kind-hearted Majesty, who patted my curls and gave me his blessing!" He endured a bullying master at Charterhouse, and at the age of nineteen he went to Christ Church at Oxford, where he published anonymously *A Voice from the Cloister*, "being an earnest appeal to my fellow-collegians against the youthful excesses so common in those days". He won the prize for a theological essay, and the donor when presenting him with £25 worth of books desired that Mr Gladstone might be allowed to have £5 worth of them "as he was so good a second". He was a member of a Greek class which was to provide the world with Gladstone, two Dukes, a Viceroy, three Governor-generals, three Bishops, a Professor of Poetry, several Earls, and not only Liddell but also Scott. He was greatly afflicted by a stammer, which disqualified him for the church, and it was only in late middle life that he cured himself by what appears to have been sheer pertinacity of will.

The failure of his church candidature was followed by failure at the law, and he decided upon authorship as a profession. When his first book was published, Landon, editor of the *Literary Gazette*, and brother of L. E. L., told him to review it himself. This he did, but so unfavourably that Landon rejected the notice, substituting a laudatory one from his own pen. From these beginnings Tupper proceeded to a life of uninterrupted success. It is true that, owing to the unsatisfactory conditions of authorship in those days, his material rewards were often disappointing, and he complains more than once of philanthropic publishers who supply the public with books at the author's expense. Towards the end of his life he sustained reverses which induced his friends to organize a testimonial for him, an episode of which he speaks with some tartness:

> Everybody knows (so I need not blink it) that some time ago a few friends kindly got up a so-called testimonial for my benefit; but that sort of thing had been over-done in other instances; and it is small wonder that...the trouble and care and humiliation are scarcely compensated where the costs and defaults are considerable: however, I desire heartily to thank its promoters and contributors, one and all; even those who promised but never paid.

These anxieties, which seem to have been momentary, alone disturbed the equable course of his public career. It would be unfair to charge Tupper with "the devil's darling sin, the pride that apes humility", but never did a man so modest in his professions enjoy so child-like yet so secure a self-esteem. As between Gladstone and himself he had

> ever tried to hold the balance equally too, according to my lights, and if at one time (on occasion of the great Oxford election, 1864) I published a somewhat famous copy of verses ending with
>
> > Orator, statesman, scholar, wit, and sage,
> > The Crichton,—more, the Gladstone of the age...
>
> my faithfulness must in after years confess to a well-known palinode (one of my "Three Hundred Sonnets") commencing
>
> > Beware of mere delusive eloquence....

Record is left of "a small chamber in the turret of No. 19 Lincoln's Inn Old Square, on the second floor of rooms then belonging to my late friend Thomas Lewin...where I used to dream and think and jot down Proverbial morsels on odd bits of paper". Some of these, by the poet's prodigality, found their way into the wastepaper basket and were saved for the world by the vigilant Lewin. Going through his old papers when writing his book the poet finds a manuscript written at the age of nineteen, *A Vindication of the Wisdom of Scripture in Matters of Natural Science.* He now can give it no attention, but "Some day a patient scribe may be found to decipher this decayed manuscript and set out orderly its miscellaneous contents". Reports of controversies on his work are "duly pasted down for future generations in my Archive Book". And for posterity, too, was designed the many volumes of *My Literary Heirloom,* which contained "newspaper cuttings, anecdotes, and letters and scraps of all sorts relating to my numerous works". In "picking out... a few of the plums of praise wherewith my early publication was indulged", he takes comfort to himself that "no one of my reviewers all my life through has ever been bought or rewarded". And when the originality of *Proverbial Philosophy* was impugned, he retorted that the *Pilgrim's Progress* and *Paradise Lost* had been similarly libelled. "I have spoken of all this at length, that if anyone hereafter finds this 'Politeuphuia' [the book from which he was alleged to have drawn] in the British Museum...and years hence accuses my innocence of having stolen from it, he may know that I have thus taken the bull by the horns and twisted him over." When it was suggested to him that in the interests of impartiality he ought in his autobiography to print some of his adverse as well as his favourable notices, he preferred

now to appear one-sided, as a piece of common sense; quite indifferent to the charge of vain-gloriousness: all the good verdicts quoted are genuine, absolutely unpaid and unrewarded, and are matters of sincere and skilled opinion; so being such I prize them: the opposing judgments—much fewer, and far less hearty, as "willing to wound and yet afraid to strike"—may as well perish out of memory by being ignored and neglected.

Printing complimentary lines from his own pen *To my Book "Proverbial Philosophy", before Publication*, he adds, "There were also two others afterward, in the jubilate vein; but I spare my reader, albeit they are curiously prophetic of the wide good-doing since accomplished". He thought it

only just to the many unseen lovers of "Proverbial Philosophy" to show them how heartily their good opinions have been countersigned and sanctioned all over the English-speaking world by critics of many schools and almost all denominations. It is not then from personal vanity that so much laudation is exhibited (God wot, I have reason to denounce and renounce self-seeking)—but rather to gratify and corroborate innumerable book friends.

The sonnet, he tells us, is "a form of metrical composition which has been habitual with me.... The best always come at a burst, spontaneously and as it were inspirationally". When living for a time in the Channel Islands, Tupper fell out with Victor Hugo, but at a later date "Mr Sullivan of Jersey published on his decease some splendid stanzas in French, which by request I versified in English: so that our spirits are now manifestly *en rapport*". A display of revivalist emotion on the part of Jenny Lind when meeting him, stirred him to the reflection: "God has blessed my writings to millions of the human race! And from prince to peasant good has been done through this hand, incalculable.—God alone be praised". Happy Martin Tupper; he was praised too.

He liked fishing, and it was his pleasure to see a guest take a trout from the brook by his carriage gate at Albury. Two or three of his fishing sonnets have a happier touch than is common in his verse. He was a liberal host, an affectionate and dutiful head of his family. In 1855 he took his household of eleven on an extended continental tour, spending £40 a week, taking personal care for everybody's comfort. He was, it seems, favourably regarded at Court. On the death of John Brown he wrote:

> Simple, pious, honest man,
>   Child of heaven while son of earth,
> We would praise, for praise we can,
>   Thy good service, thy great worth;
> Through long years of prosperous place
>   In the sunshine of the Crown,
> With man's favour and God's grace
>   Humbly, bravely, walked John Brown.

A similar tribute on the occasion of the Princess Royal's marriage brought an invitation to Buckingham Palace, where he enjoyed "the honour of personal conversation with Her Majesty", and Prince Albert commanded, "Wales, come and shake hands with Mr Tupper". The Queen's Jubilee inspired the gratifying reflection that the same versifier who in his youth fifty years ago saw the coronation from a gallery seat in Westminster Abbey, overlooking the central space, and wrote a well-known ode on the occasion, to be found in his Miscellaneous Poems, is still in full force and loyalty, and ready to supply one for his Queen's jubilee,—whereof words for music will be found anon.

When his "little Masques of the Seasons, and the Nations—wherein Corbould was pictorially so efficient, and Miss Hildyard so helpful in the costumes" were performed "both at Osborne and at Windsor", a grateful sovereign rewarded the poet with Winterhalter's engravings of all the royal children.

It was characteristic of Tupper that he should think his fugitive interests worthy of permanent record. He was a man of many inventions, some of which were patented by others, none by himself. He gives us a list of them.

1. A simple and cheap safety horse-shoe,—secured by steel studs inserted into the ordinary soft iron shoes.
2. Glass screw-tops to bottles.

3. Steam-vessels with wheels inside; in fact, a double boat or cata-maran, with the machinery amid-ships.

4. The introduction of coca-leaf to allay hunger, and to be useful here as in Chili.

5. A pen to carry its own ink.

6. The colouring of photographs on the back.

7. Combined vulcanite and steel sheathing.

He also interviewed Sidney Herbert at the Ordnance Office about "a composite cannon missile of quoits tied together", and the commercial success of essence of coffee suggested to him that there might also be a market for essence of tea. Finally, he declared, with prophetic vision, in the 'fifties:

> To fly as a bird in the air
> Despot man doth dare!
> His humbling cumbersome body at length
> Light as the lark upsprings,
> Buoyed by tamed explosive strength
> And steel-ribbed albatross wings!

"That ode", he tells us, "is extinct, but will revive." He enjoyed the honours that came his way, though with some apologetic piety. On going to the Prussian legation to receive his medal, he reflected in his best manner:

An author, if he be a good man and a clever, worthy of his high vocation, already walks self-ennobled, circled by an aureola of spiritual glory such as no king can give, nor even all-devouring time, "*edax rerum*", can take away. He really gains nothing by a title—no, not even Tennyson; as in the next world, so in this, "his works do follow him", and the "Well done, good and faithful" from this lower world which he has served is but the prelude of his welcome to that higher world wherein he hears the same "good and faithful" from the mouth of his Redeemer.

Of his social no less than of his poetic successes he tells us with disarming ingenuousness: "Of course, like everybody else who may be lifted above the crowd,

I have experienced, almost annually, the splendid hospitalities of the Mansion House and most of the City Companies". Although he belonged to no club, he was careful to explain to an eager public that he had been "sometimes specially tempted by indulgence as to terms, more than once having been offered a free and immediate entry". He might well, at the close of his career, testify "seriously and practically to the fact (disputed by too many from their own worse experience) that it is quite possible to live from youth to age in many scenes and under many circumstantial difficulties, preserving still through them all the innocent purity of childhood".

The innocence never failed him. Of one of his works he wrote:

> In this volume, commencing with Abel, and ending with Felix Neff, I have greeted both in verse and prose threescore and ten of the Excellent of the earth. Probably the best thing in it is the "Vision Introductory"....If an author can be accounted a fair judge of his own writings, this is my best effort in the imaginative line.

If that "imaginative line" is startling, it is far from the limit of his capacities. Writing of old Lady Cork, he hoped that her Diary might soon be published "as probably a more spicy record of past celebrities than even Pepys's". In one of his prefaces he wrote:

> I feel Malthusian among my mental nurslings; a dire resolve has filled me to effect a premature destruction of the literary populace superfaetating in my brain,—plays, novels, essays, tales, homilies, and rhythmicals; for ethics and poetics, politics and rhetorics, will I display no more mercy than sundry commentators of maltreated Aristotle. I will exhibit them in their state chaotic,—I will addle the eggs, and the chicken shall not chirp.

This project, he tells us, was undertaken in order to effect "a most wholesome, a most necessary relief" by "the emptying out of my thought-box".

And at last, it is no unfriendly figure of whom we take our leave. As in his old age he recalled some of his verses, there was a hardly conscious suspicion that somehow they had no beginning nor ending, and that it did not very much matter. He writes down a stanza from his version of *King Alfred's Poems*:

> Lo, I sang cheerily
> In my bright days,—
> But now all wearily
> Chaunt I my lays,—
> Sorrowing tearfully,
> Saddest of men,
> Can I sing cheerfully
> As I could then?

And then, without guile, he adds, "etc., etc." Nevertheless, he was confident of the future: "When I am [dead] all these old works of mine will rise again in a voluminous complete edition". It is impossible not to warm a little towards the man who could write this:

An odd thing happened to me in the church, where at the vestry I had just signed my name as other visitors did. An American, utterly unknown to me as I to him, came eagerly up to me as I was inspecting that unsatisfactory bust and inscription about Shakespeare, and said, "Come and see what I've found,—Martin Tupper's autograph,—he must be somewhere near, for he has just signed: do tell, is he here?" I rather thought he might be. "I've wished to see him ever since I was a small boy. Do you know him, sir?" Well, yes, a little. "Show him to me, sir, won't you? I'd give ten dollars for his autograph." After a word or two more, my good nature gave him the precious signature without the dollars,—and I shan't easily forget his frantic joy, showing the document to all around him, whilst I escaped.

And yet very occasionally there is just a word of misgiving, almost of resignation. Speaking of one of his "most notable prose pieces", he tells us that he could "fill many pages with the critiques pro and con this queer book has provoked, but it is useless now the world has let it die".

The world has let it die, and the innumerable musings besides. During his life Tupper's fame came upon no adversity that touched him; the critics who spoke ill of him were bad men, and that was an end of it. His contacts with the real achievement of his age were, as we have seen, of the slightest. Even anecdote is scanty in his pages. His lecture agent told him that "Dickens, though with crowded audiences, was not liked, nor nearly so good as Mr — expected: he carried about with him a sort of show-box, set round with lights and covered with purple cloth, in the midst of which he appeared in full evening costume with bouquet in button-hole, and, as Mr — said, very stiff", and among his literary acquaintances he mentions Lady Wilde, "admirable both for prose and poetry on Scandinavian subjects, and her eloquent son Oscar, famous for taste all the world over". His success came easily and it lasted long. In 1842, the poet's father wrote:

> My dearest Martin,—Anything that I could say, or any praise that I could give respecting your last volume would, in my estimation, fall very far short indeed of its merits. I shall therefore merely say that I look upon your chapter upon Immortality, not only as a most exquisite specimen of fine, sound, and learned composition, but as combating in the most satisfactory manner the *wisdom* of infidelity, almost perfect. I only hope that you may receive the just tribute of the literary community: your own feelings as the author of that chapter must be very enviable. God bless you, dearest, dearest Martin.—Believe me, ever your affectionate father and sincere friend,
>
> Martin Tupper.

With the letter, as a more tangible token of approval, was enclosed a cheque for £2000. The paternal fondness found an echo in countless homes. That was when the proverbial philosopher was a little over thirty; when he was seventy-five and writing his autobiography his "own feelings as the author" of many chapters were enviable still. He was at peace with the world, with which, indeed, he had never begun to be at odds. It was not unfitting that in one of the more agreeable passages of his book he should tell of the bees in his house:

Amongst other specialities of ancient Albury House, which has 1561 on a weathercock and 1701 on a kitchen wing, is the same peculiarity which Tennyson told me at Farringford vexes him in his own less ancient dwelling,—and which Pindar of old declared to be the privilege of poets. We are, and have been for generations, a very house-hive of bees: the whole front of two gables has them under its oak floors and panelled walls throughout,—and when guests sleep in certain rooms they have to be forewarned that the groans at midnight are not those of perturbed spirits, but the hum and bustle of multitudinous bees. We cannot drive them away, nor destroy them utterly,—as often has been attempted; and if we did, the worry would be only worsened, as in that case hornets would come and succeed to the sweet heritage of bee-dom. When the stuccoed front of our house was demolished, to show the oaken pattern (but it had to be re-roughcast to keep out the weather), there were pailsful of honey carried off by the labourers, of course not without wounds and strife: but in ordinary times it is a strange fact that our bees never sting their hosts; be careful only to remain quiet, and there is no war between man and bee. Two years ago a great comb was built outside an eaveboard, probably because there was no room for more comb inside. It is curious that it should have survived two hard winters. Is not all this apposite, as suited (let Pindar and Tennyson bear witness) to a poet's home?

Somehow Tupper's own mind, or his bonnet, seems to come into the picture. As we look over *Proverbial Philosophy* a somewhat somnolent buzzing takes our ears, though there is perhaps an apter figure. Just now and again we come across lines that quicken our attention, as

The flash that lighteth up a valley, amid the dark midnight of a storm,
Coineth the mind with that scene sharper than fifty summers.

But it is for a moment only. As we read on the words become quicksands, and we are lost.

LEWIS CARROLL

By WALTER DE LA MARE

Every century, indeed every decade of it, flaunts its own little extravagances and aberrations from a reasonable human standard. Passing fashions in dress and furniture, in plays, music and pictures, and even in ideas and sentiments, resemble not only the caprices of our island climate, but also the extremes made manifest in English character, both of which in spite of such excesses yet remain true to a more or less happy medium. And so too with literature.

The Victorian age was rich in these exotics. It amuses us moderns, having dried and discoloured them, to make little herbariums of them. We may be on easier terms with the great writer of the 'eighties with whiskers for symbol, though less so perhaps with feminine dignity trailing a crinolette. But there is one Victorian wild flower which makes any such condescension absurd—and it is called Nonsense. Unlike other "sports" of its time, this laughing heartsease, this indefinable "cross" between humour, phantasy and a sweet unreasonableness, has proved to be of a hardy habit and is still living and fragrant. And we discover it suddenly in full bloom under the very noses of Martin Tupper and of Samuel Smiles.

None even of its kindliest apologists would deny that in the earlier years of the nineteenth century the attitude of mind towards children tended to the over-solemn—a state which resembles a lantern without any light in it.

Excesses may secrete their own antidotes. The mothers
and fathers who had been brought up on Scotch oats
with a pinch of salt for savour were to realize that
honey is also a provision of nature. Yet writers who
had the nursery in view, and even long after William
Blake had sung of innocence, remained for the most part
convinced that what is good for the young must be
unpleasant. Their rhymes like their prose were "nearly
always in a moral, minor or miserable key". They prescribed not simples, syrups and cordials, but brimstone.
And even the treacle that accompanied it was spelt
theriaca, and was connected with vipers. A reaction,
it is clear, was bound to follow, and that reaction has
perhaps reached its extreme in a good deal of the
nursery literature of our own day, which is as silly, if
not worse, as theirs was dismal.

Not that all the books intended for children in the
early nineteenth century were concerned solely with the
cautionary and the edifying, which as Charles Lamb
said only "starved their little hearts and stuffed their
little heads...". And while moralisms like, "'My dear
child', answered her father, 'an ox is not in the world
for nothing'"; like, "Oh, dear Mamma, if I had done
as you bade me I should not have had all this pain!";
like,

> ...When up the ladder I would go,
> (How wrong it was I now well know)
> Who cried, but held it fast below?
> MY SISTER.
>
> Once too I threw my top too far,
> It touch'd thy cheek, and left a scar:
> Who tried to hide it from Mamma?
> MY SISTER...;

and

> ...Papa, who in the parlour heard
> Her make the noise and rout,
> That instant went to Caroline,
> To whip her, there's no doubt;

—while moralisms and menaces of this order, with an occasional reminder that God's anger has no respect for persons, and far, far less for little persons, and such wolflets in lamb's clothing as *Useful Lessons for Little Misses and Masters*, and *Paul Pennylove's Poetical Paraphrase of the Pence Table*, were prevalent, we must not forget the many merry heart-free exceptions like Dame Wiggins of Lee which was the joy of John Ruskin, or the benefactions of Dame Partlet:

> ...That cold a fever soon brought on,
>   The fever brought on death,
> So, after having made her will,
>   She yielded up her breath.
>
> Yet stop your grief, for she has left
>   Each little girl and b'y
> Who gets by heart this little hymn
>   A cheesecake and a pie.

"The interesting and the amusing moreover were then supplanting the improving." Many of the chap-books for children (even of the severe order) were illustrated with admirable cuts by artists almost as gifted as Bewick himself, and that can hardly be said of some of our own nursery pictorialisms. And the pattern of versicle of the Dickory-dock order—called a Limerick because it is said to have emanated from Ireland—was already familiar to young ears even in the eighteen-twenties:

> There liv'd an Old Woman at Lynn
> Whose nose very near touch'd her chin,
>   You may easy suppose
>   She had plenty of Beaux,
> This charming Old Woman of Lynn.

That—both in form and content—is at least towards Nonsense bound.

But even M. Emile Cammaerts in his *Poetry of Nonsense*—a little book as rich in appreciation and interest as it is original in theme—has been able to cite very few specimens of true Nonsense of a date prior to the nineteenth century. And the practice of the art seems to be as clearly localized in space as it is in time. The French word *non-sens* has not this particular nuance; and the German *Un-sinn* is in meaning, I gather, to madness nearer allied.

In fact M. Cammaerts has not only declared that Nonsense is wholly English in origin—"I have tried in vain to discover anything similar in French or German literature"—but he is also convinced (and seemingly with satisfaction) that it would have received a very cold welcome if it had made its appearance abroad. Only a poet could have written M. Cammaerts' book; and since he has, as it were, crossed the sea to discover this precious little autochthon, his tribute to it as "one of the most valuable contributions to the development and happiness of mankind" may condone a natural family pride in it and incite us to appreciate it as we should.

Whatever its origin, no little tiny boy of any time or clime who was ever dandled to the strains of *Old Mother Hubbard*, *Hey*, *diddle*, *diddle* or *Three Blind Mice*, or listened at his mother's knee to such ancient tales as *The Three Sillies*, *Teeny Tiny* and *Mr Vinegar* can have been positively untouched by its influence. Its full "showery, flowery, bowery" summer, however, continued from the 'forties into the 'seventies. With Kate Greenaway, it hid its face in a poke-bonnet; though such recent literary lucky-bags for the nursery as *The Adventures of Dr Dolittle*, *The Pirate Twins*, *Mr Tootleoo* and *Millions of Cats* are proof that it still flourishes.

Its acknowledged masters were two in number. Two years after the appearance in 1810 of Jane Taylor's *Hymns for Infant Minds* Edward Lear came into the

world. He was followed twenty years later, and two
years before the death of Charles Lamb, by Charles Lutwidge Dodgson, who having latinized his Charles and
transmogrified his Lutwidge, was destined at last to be
known (and beloved) all the world over by his pen-name
Lewis Carroll.

Lear's first *Book of Nonsense* was published in 1846,
a year after the death not only of the author of *The
Ingoldsby Legends* but also of Thomas Hood, a poet who
because, perhaps, he was also a punster, has not even
yet had his due. *The Rose and the Ring* followed in 1855.
Hood, like Lear and Thackeray, could fit pictures to
his rhymes as amusing as themselves, but Lear was an
artist by profession. He contributed the handsome
plates to one of the earliest of the lavishly illustrated
English books about birds; and it is as appropriate that
its title should have so alluring a flavour as *The Family
of the Psittacidae* as that the first published pamphlet in
which Dodgson collaborated with his *alter ego* should
have been called *The New Method of Evaluation as
Applied to* Π.

Lear left this world—much the poorer by his absence
—in 1888, four years after Calverley. Lewis Carroll, the
veritable pied piper, having visited "valleys wild" on
his way from Hamelin, vanished from its ken a little
later, while Dodgson himself lived on until a year after
Queen Victoria's Second Jubilee.

The rich sheaves of pure Nonsense had by then been
garnered. While *The Hunting of the Snark* was of 1876
and Prince Uggug had edged into being at Hatfield to
amuse Princess Alice in 1872, by 1889, when *Sylvie
and Bruno* was published, another order of nonsense
was in flower. *The Green Carnation*, and *The Yellow
Book*, are symptomatic of a very different and a wholly
adult species. Satire and parody in themselves are

mortal enemies of true Nonsense; and though such sallies as "On an occasion of this kind it becomes more than a moral duty to speak one's mind. It becomes a pleasure"; or "A little sincerity is a dangerous thing, and a great deal of it is absolutely fatal"; or "Punctuality is the thief of time"—though pleasantries of this nature may faintly echo (and may even have been inspired by) Humpty Dumpty, Oscar Wilde would not perhaps have greeted the kinship with a cheer, and Humpty Dumpty, quite apart from his setting, conversed in a far less worldly English.

As compared with wit, too, Nonsense, in M. Cammaerts' metaphor, is what bubble is to needle, though wit itself is powerless to prick the bubble. Twinkling on in its intense inane, it is as far out of the reach of the ultracommonsensical, the immitigably adult and the really superior as are the morning stars. That flat complacent veto—"This is nonsense" (in the cast-iron sense of the word), while intended as a sentence of death, means little more than "We are not amused".

But what *is* this Nonsense? How does it differ from the merry, the comical, the frivolous, the absurd, the grotesque and mere balderdash? Take the Limerick. There are two distinct orders of them: the mere Limerick and the Lear Limerick. They differ as much as mushrooms from moonshine. Mere Limericks, harmless, orthodox and amusing, may be scribbled with an effort at the rate of about two a minute. Funny, and even witty, Limericks are fairly common. A genuine Lear Limerick—and that only derivative—is unlikely to be the reward of a precious moment more than once or twice in a lifetime!

> There was an Old Man of the West,
> Who wore a pale plum-coloured vest;

When they said, "Does it fit?"
He replied, "Not a bit!"
That uneasy Old Man of the West.

Again:

There was an Old Man in a boat,
Who said, "I'm afloat! I'm afloat!"
When they said, "No! you ain't!"
He was ready to faint,
That unhappy Old Man in a boat.

Now the most apparent thing about these old gentlemen is that they are not merely respectable, they are irreproachable. Are they irrational? Surely not. Those of us who in questions of pure matter-of-fact decline to heed the *No! you ain'ts* of our fellow creatures are to say the least of it guilty of the indiscreet. And what irrationality is there in being uneasy in vests that fit not a bit, or in having the candour to confess that they don't? As for the crisis in either rhyme, it is little short of Aristotelian: a (seemingly) just soul endures an undeserved stroke of adversity. And could fewer words more vividly present that unhappy Old Man in a boat, whose rapture in a situation so ordinary is followed by physical symptoms so extreme after a surrender to public opinion so meek and so magnanimous? And last, where *is* this Old Man? In a region and a state of being solely his own, and in an Everlasting Now. Is not "pure poetry" itself in a similar relation to actuality?

While, then, there is in these rhymes a sort of vacuum where the "sense" should be—and the mere alteration of "pale" into *new* in the first of them will show how delicate the literary poise is—there is plenty of meaning. And what we call their Nonsense is nothing purely negative but lies in some celestially happy medium between what is sense and what is not sense. This being so, are not these two old gentlemen and their exceedingly nebulous "they" triumphantly, and up to their eyes, *in* that medium? And "*well* in"? In what then does it consist?[1]

> They hunted till darkness came on, but they found
> Not a button, or feather, or mark,
> By which they could tell that they stood on the ground
> Where the Baker had met with the Snark.

That unfortunately is the position. None the less a glance at *Alice in Wonderland*—with its bright full moon of Nonsense for lantern, may help to enlighten it a little. And first, Lewis Carroll.

Of what in the deeps of our sub-consciousness we owe to our ancestors only the confidants of Unkulunkulu, perhaps, are fully aware. We know, however, that Charles Dodgson's father was renowned for his wit and humour. He delighted in any amusing joke or anecdote provided its text was not in the Bible. His father, a Captain in the 4th Dragoon Guards, was shot in the dark by an Irish rebel from the window of his cottage as he came on alone and unguarded to the appointed meeting-place where the Irishman had promised to give himself up. *That* gallant gesture is neither humorous nor nonsensical, but there is a touch of the sublime in it that is part and parcel of both.

Dodgson's great-grandfather not only loved a joke but like his great-grandson was a character. It was very cold in the winter in the vestibule, a "low stable",

---

[1] This is only of course to skirt the fringe of the subject. Lear sometimes lost on his rhymes what he made on his pictures, and if pure Nonsense be our test, one essential feature of which is that—so swiftly that we cannot possibly perceive the *process*—it shall instantly secure the hospitality of our sense of humour, his shafts are not always on the mark. Opinions must differ, but the Old Man with a nose, the Old Man with a beard, the Old Man with a gong and the Old Man in a tree perhaps fall a little short of it. The Young Lady of Wales, the Old Lady of Chertsey, the Old Person of Ems and the Old Man who said, "Hush!" are exemplary; while *Rheims* and *Wrekin* and even *The Courtship of the Yonghy-Bonghy Bô* may leave one debating. And so with the rest of his rhymes.

as he described it, of the castle which in 1762 he was compelled to use as a temporary parsonage:

"Above it", he wrote to a friend, "is the kitchen, in which are two little beds joining to each other. The curate and his wife lay (lie) in one, and Margery the maid in the other. I lay in the parlour *between* two beds to keep me from being frozen to death, for as we keep open house the winds enter from every quarter, and are apt to sweep into bed to me."

Again:

As washing is very cheap, I wear *two* shirts at a time, and, for want of a wardrobe, I hang my great coat upon my own back, and generally keep on my boots in imitation of my namesake of Sweden.

A mind capable of this hospitality to life—and I am quoting from Mr Collingwood's *Life and Letters of Lewis Carroll*—had ample room in it for a window overlooking Nonsense Lane. But whatever Charles Dodgson owed to heredity, he himself, as a small boy, was exactly the *kind* of small boy we should have expected Lewis Carroll to have chosen to grow up from. He was born in a little village called Daresbury, seven miles from Warrington. So peaceful was his father's vicarage that even the creaking of a passing farm-cart was something of an event. Here Charles spent his first eleven years. He made pets of toads and snails. He carried out little martial experiments on earthworms. He peeled rushes in the belief that the pith might be of use to the poor, though he never explained precisely how. Before he was in his teens he expressed an interest in the *looks* of logarithms, and at twelve was skilled in the invention of games. Mantled in wig and robe, and wand in hand, he practised as a parlour conjuror. He made a toy theatre and marionettes, and wrote their plays himself. And from his preparatory school in 1844 we have tidings of his first "little girl". "The boys that I think that I like the best are Harry Austin and all the

Tates of which there are 7 besides a little girl who came down to dinner the first day, but not since."

His first schoolmaster reported that Charles had become skilled in Latin verse, had a "very uncommon share of genius" and showed a "love of precise argument". He warned his father however against letting his son realize his superiority over his fellows. "The love of excellence", he remarked, "is far beyond the love of excelling." That Charles *did* occasionally realize his superiority over his fellows, and that he even thought it desirable at times to be candid concerning the dear, is revealed by a remark he made about a relative who was for some years a resident in the Island of Tristan da Cunha. He said that he was well-intentioned but vulgar. Three months afterwards he changed his opinion. He said, "He is now less well-intentioned and more vulgar."

Long before he went up to Rugby in 1846—and eleven years after he had left his schooldays behind him he confessed that "no earthly consideration" would induce him to go through them again—he set up as editor (and chief contributor) of one or two of those home-made magazines which are apt to be ephemeral but none the less give excellent opportunity and practice to the budding author. And in the shade of *The Rectory Umbrella* of 1849 appeared not only his first nonsense rhymes but his first humorous drawings. They explore a world of the grotesque entirely his own and are unmistakably in the manner of the pictures he afterwards made for *Alice in Wonderland*, and shared with Tenniel. And never surely were author and artist in a closer and happier partnership.

So punctilious, too, was Carroll in the choice of a frontispiece for *Through the Looking-Glass* that he consulted "about thirty of his married lady friends before finally deciding to bestow this honour on the White Knight". As for his early rhymes:

> Fair stands the ancient Rectory,
>   The Rectory of Croft,
> The sun shines bright upon it,
>   The breezes whisper soft.
> From all the house and garden
>   Its inhabitants come forth,
> And muster in the road without,
> And pace in twos and threes about,
>   The children of the North.

It is the unspecified *looks* of these inhabitants, quite apart from the dulcet air they breathe (or the stair-cased family pews and preacher's hourglass they shared in their parish church), that show how many miles Carroll had already ventured as a boy over the border-line of his Wonderland. The first four lines of *Jabber-wocky* too, which were afterwards expanded to twenty-eight at an evening party, first appeared in the *Umbrella* with the title "Stanza of Anglo-Saxon Poetry" and with a full glossary of its terms.

Seldom has any child shown himself so clearly the father-to-be of the man. This roving ingenuity, this skill in the use of words, this delight in logic and mathematics, this passion for invention, this penchant for puns, puzzles, parodies and palaver—such things as these were to occupy Dodgson's long working days and his absorbed leisure during the forty-seven years, from 1851 onwards, which he spent at Christ Church. He positively "belonged to the 'house'", says Mr Dodgson Collingwood, his biographer, "never leaving it for any length of time" from the day when on Pusey's Nomination he won his studentship there until his death. He "became almost a part of it", the conditions of this initial privilege being celibacy and the taking of Holy Orders. He was ordained deacon in 1861, but

"never proceeded to priest's orders", says Mr Collingwood, "partly, I think, because he felt that if he were
to do so it would be his duty to undertake regular
parochial work". "He was essentially a religious man
in the best sense of the term."

In spite of a little impediment in speech which he
shared with Charles Lamb and which added a flavour
all their own to *his* witticisms also, he sometimes
preached, and always anxiously prepared for these
occasions. But, "it is not", he wrote to a friend, "good
to be told (and I never wish to be told), 'Your sermon
was so *beautiful*'". His one object in preaching was
that of "serving God". "His generosity was bound-
less." He never failed in patience when folly and error
came to him for counsel, nor in acts of kindness.

He had pronounced views, and expressed them
vigorously. And he was a precisian. If anyone even
of his little girls slipped in grammar when writing to
him he corrected it in his reply. Though he was wine-
taster to his College, and kept a record of all the *menus*
of all his little private dinner-parties, he was far from
being an epicure, at any rate in food for the body. His
usual lunch consisted of a biscuit or two and a glass of
sherry; but he tolerated less stringent habits in others,
and especially in his small guests. And when one day
at one o'clock he found himself at a newly made friend's
house, though he refused to eat anything, he gallantly
offered to carve the mutton. But it was a joint strange
to him and it mocked his efforts.

His views on reviewers were also inclined to be
abstemious. He assured them in one of his prefaces,
first, that no doubt their remarks on his last book had
been of service to it, and next, that he had refrained
from reading them, since their good opinions might
only have made him vain, and their chidings would

have dejected him. There were occasions, however, when he risked dejecting others. For when any biblical or dubious joke was uttered in his presence on the stage, he was not content, as are most sensitive souls, to blush unseen; he rose to his feet and stalked out of the theatre. Playgoers nowadays would enjoy exceedingly active evenings in the theatre if they followed his example.

Though he was the acknowledged wit of the Common Room at Christ Church when the elect were entertained, he was naturally shy and retiring. By no means a bear in company, he hated being lionized and detested publicity—a term which it is surprising though hardly reassuring to learn was "in common use" as far back as 1837. He generally declined to welcome any tribute to Lewis Carroll. If his morning postman brought messages of joy and gratitude in a strange handwriting to the explorer of *Wonderland*, Dodgson returned a printed and rather frigid reply: "Mr C. L. Dodgson...neither claims nor acknowledges any connection with any pseudonym or with any book not published under his own name". And when one afternoon at tea a genial Dean at a friend's house referred with buoyant approval to the author of the *Alices*, he was so much vexed by this intrusion that he entreated his hostess to give him warning when next the Dean threatened, in order that he might retreat to his bedroom in good time. The practice sounds a little austere and yet might in many circumstances prove grateful and comforting. He was of opinion, perhaps, that though a book is public property, its author is not; and that books best speak for themselves.

Mr Collingwood suggests that some shadow of disappointment hung over his life; and certainly the face that is looking away from the observer in one of the best known of his photographs has a shade of the disastrous in its aspect; and even in one taken when he was twenty-three there is a tinge of melancholy. Like Edward Lear, like most jesters, he had his hours of depression; and it may be to this natural reserve that a tribute to his memory in *Punch* referred:

> The heart you wore beneath your pedant's cloak
> Only to children's hearts you gave away. . . .

One is conscious, too, of a certain primness, a slight stiffness in his later letters; and his prefaces to *Sylvie and Bruno* are oddly deficient in the good humour that may make a man tolerable company to himself even when he has a pen in his hand. In these Dodgson himself, "tall and dark", is at times Victorian and solemn. And even the solemn, however excellent in sentiment it may be, takes a queer glint in such a sentence— thus emphasized—as "Would you kindly do *no* sketches, or photos, for *me*, on a Sunday?" The editor of *The Rectory Umbrella* in fact had very little share in either volume of *Sylvie and Bruno*, at which Dodgson laboured, he said, for "seven or eight hours a day".

Lewis Carroll was himself a punctilious craftsman, but even if he had insisted on spelling *can't* with two apostrophes and *traveller* with one "l", he would not have rather petulantly pointed this out, nor would he have tabulated page by page the "psychical states" of his characters or given a list of the scraps of talk he had borrowed for his story from real little girls and boys. "Theories" concerning the transference of one's "immaterial essence" may be engrossing in the proper place, but that is not a preface to a fairy-tale.

Nor perhaps would he have set his elfin Sylvie straying over the sandy themes of "Drink", teetotalism, matrimony, epidemics, cheating at croquet, conduct in church, Sunday observance and dinner-party talk. A

proper interest in such matters befits a sober citizen.
But while the insertion of little essays on these themes
in a nursery book may have been characteristic of the
retiring don—who was so little known to the public in
his later years that a "special correspondent" in Oxford
spelt his name *Dogson* throughout an obituary article
that appeared in a leading London newspaper—it was
not characteristic of the Dodgson who when a fond
Victorian mamma invited him to admire a not easily
admirable infant would exclaim with well-feigned
rapture, "He *is* a baby!"

Not that *Sylvie and Bruno* was intended merely as
new lamps for old. The author definitely excused himself from attempting the "old style" again, not for the
sufficing reason that self-imitation is usually disastrous,
but because "all the wayside flowers of Wonderland"
had long ago "been trampled into the dust by others".
He does not seem to have realized that it was *his*
clarion alone "o'er the dreaming earth" that could have
raised them from that dust. He apologizes too for
mingling grave thoughts on human life with what he
hopes will be "acceptable nonsense". Acceptable! It
is the mingling that is hazardous. Grave thoughts may
be wholly at their ease in pages devoted to Nonsense if
only they share its medium; and even the solemn is
palatable at a Mad Hatter's tea-party when it has the
flavour of its austere bread-and-butter. "If you knew
Time as well as I do," said the Mad Hatter, "you
wouldn't talk about wasting *it*. It's *him*"; "... The
rule is jam to-morrow and jam yesterday—but never
jam to-day..."; "What does it matter where my body
happens to be? My mind goes on working all the
same";—haven't such little remarks as these a rather
compelling *inward* ring?[1]

---

[1] Positively to trace, however, the fine degrees by which *sense* progresses

But the White Knight is not the only character in the
Alices whom one notices looking pensive. "Never imagine

towards either of its two extremes, Wisdom and Nonsense, would be a task of
the utmost difficulty and delicacy. Where shall we look for an analogy?
Possibly in the region of Pure Mathematics? This and the mood of the mind
that is at home in it may resemble and even neighbour the region and mood
of pure Nonsense. The sun that was shining in the middle of the night on
the sea and the Walrus and the Carpenter and the oysters may at any rate also
have beamed with its own seraphic radiance into the mind of the small boy
who made the following attempt to define a vacuum:

"A vacuum is nothing shut up in a box. They have a way of pumping out
the air. When all the air and everything else is shut out, naturally they are
able to shut in nothing, where the air was before."

And again:

"A circle is a line of no depth running round a dot for ever."

Such ventures as these are known as *Howlers*, and have been taken from the
mirthful book of that title by Mr H. Cecil Hunt. Nevertheless they have the
vivid limpidity of Nonsense itself. Indeed, with

"Infinity is a place where no one can get to but all lines meet,"

are we not veering into the azure of pure poetry? While as for "Ice = Water
that went to sleep in the cold", that comes straight from where Ariel sings
a dirge over the relics of him of whose bones coral was made. There is
indeed more pure poetry in Carroll's "You are old, Father William" than
there is even of pure prose in Southey's *The Old Man's Comforts*, though in
the cantering anapaests of the last two lines in the following stanza Southey
almost attains the true *Nirvana*:

"You are old, Father William," the young man cried,
    "And life must be hastening away;
You are cheerful, and love to converse upon death,
    Now tell me the reason I pray."

Here, there is no need to await "the reason", since it is implicit in the verbal
picture—sober in intention however otherwise in effect. Its moon-faced
"young man" indeed has come straight out of Lear. And yet Southey was
the author of that nursery classic *The Three Bears*!

A poem of Mr F. W. Harvey's in *September* tells of two small children who
having found a dead robin in their garden gave it gentle burial, scattering
their flowers over the mound they had raised to remember it by. As they
turned again to play, one of them remarked earnestly to the other, "I *hope*
he will have a *happy* dead life". That too perhaps was Nonsense, but of such
is the kingdom of heaven.

yourself not to be otherwise than what it might appear to others that what you were or might have been was not otherwise than what you had been would have appeared to them to be otherwise." Or, as Polonius preferred to put it, "To thine own self be true...". "In *this* Style 10/6", perhaps; yet if in general Polonius had kept to the other kind of counsel he might also have kept not merely on the safe but on the right side of the arras.

But apart from all "grave thoughts", the lovely harmonics of any page of the earlier books are only occasionally audible in *Sylvie and Bruno. Their* gravity is in as supreme a solution as are the sun and rain and light and chemicals of the soil in a vintage Burgundy. When, too, the mind is at peace in that rare and serene state we call serious—which is as little like the mock solemn or even mere composure as the fool in *Twelfth Night* is like a bore at a dinner-party—it is safe from folly. So also with true Nonsense.

There are memorable gleams and glimmers of the old true magic in these later books; but they are few. Yet, when the first *Sylvie and Bruno* was written Dodgson was not so old as Defoe when he began *Robinson Crusoe*, and that also has moral intentions. And Serge Aksakov was in his middle sixties when he wrote perhaps the truest, as it is certainly the fullest, of all records of childhood. Whatever the explanation may be, some time after 1871, when *Alice through the Looking-Glass* was published, Lewis Carroll's visits to his old friend unquestionably became fewer. *The Hunting of the Snark*, of 1876, is in the old vein. But even at that, it is not all pure Carroll. And here the flaw is the combining of a nonsense which may to some minds seem a little *too* nonsensical with references which, while nonsensical, are not completely assimilated. The pearl of the *Alices'* oyster reposes in the Snark's shell, but there are also traces of its primal grit:

> But oh, beamish nephew, beware of the day,
> If your Snark be a Boojum! For then
> You will softly and suddenly vanish away,
> And never be met with again!

There gleams the orient pearl. But this?—

> You may seek it with thimbles—and seek it with care;
> You may hunt it with forks and hope;
> You may threaten its life with a railway-share;
> You may charm it with smiles and soap—. . . .

Here, surely, apart from the less flawless melody and rhythm, the grit obtrudes, whereas in *Alice* even Father William's indirect reference to his wife's jaw-bone, even talk in a railway train (with Disraeli in a cocked hat in one corner and a gnat for fretful counsellor) shimmers on with the rest. Not that the first draft even of *Alice* itself was all pure *Alice* as we know it now, for it contained a chapter about Wasps which, on the candid and unsolicited advice of Tenniel, Carroll afterwards decided to omit.

These are, of course, critical needle-points, and of no less delicate an issue, in relation to their context, than the attempt to compare the poetical merits, in *their* context, of "O what can ail thee Knight at arms" and of "Ah, what can ail thee, wretched wight"; an issue more delicate yet when we have to choose between "Many a summer's suns have shone" and "Many a summer's sun has shone"; but easier again when our choice lies between,

> With never a whisper on the main
> Off shot the spectre ship,

and

> With far-heard whisper o'er the sea
> Off shot the spectre-bark.

A parallel example may be suggested. Coventry Patmore told Dodgson that Wordsworth once assured his friends that, so far as he was aware, he had made only one joke in his complete mortal existence. Out one morning on a solitary walk he met a carter who stopped him and enquired if he had seen his—the carter's—wife. "My good friend", said Wordsworth, "I didn't know you *had* a wife." Not to be able to *see* this joke (as Wordsworth saw it) is nothing of course but a misfortune. And so it may be with the soap in the *Snark*.

But whatever may have happened to Lewis Carroll in these later years, the small boy in Dodgson who had fallen in love at first sight with logarithms, who armed earthworms with tiny sections of clay pipe, and revelled in puns and puzzles, lived on. He was his own happiest company in his solitude at Christ Church; and college life, he said, is "by no means unmixed misery". There this recluse indulged in more hobbies than the king in the story in the *Arabian Nights* had horses. The foremost of them was being methodical. He first summarized, then filed, all his letters. He kept lists of the unanswered—containing sometimes as many as seventy or eighty names—and to such admirable effect that he once apologized to a friend for not acknowledging a letter twenty-four months old, and sent his thanks to another for a present that had reached him five years before.

He was a skilful amateur photographer ("in the wet process"), his portraiture being remarkable for his original attempts at "pictorial effects", and he particularly enjoyed practising his art on a distinguished sitter. He invented a system of mnemonics and of electoral reform, a postage-stamp case, poetical acrostics and the nyctograph, and he improved the game of backgammon.

He published a volume of parodies, chiefly of Tennyson and even of Longfellow, but none quite equal to "Will you walk a little faster?" or "Beautiful Soup". He wrote a little treatise on Reading. Feed the mind, at intervals, he advised, as you should the body, on a diet not too rich or too miscellaneous, and let it be *consciously* digested. As with a bun and a small boy so with a good book and the deserving grown-up; he will devour it at *any* moment.

> O what fun!
> A nice plum bun!
> How I wish
> It never was done!

In *Wise Words about Letter Writing*, again, the author counselled his reader to write clearly and therefore slowly—his own graceful handwriting and ingenious monogram being exemplary; to address the envelope *first*; not to *seem* in earnest when writing in jest; and in the event of relations with a friend becoming a little strained, always to go one less in severity and one better in friendliness. And last, he said, never post an angry letter on the day it is written.

His own letters, even when playful, were apt to be a little dry. And though he once played a joke on one of his little girls which was not quite successful, he kept the rules which he himself laid down—rules that are easily elastic enough to welcome the very far from dry—the inexhaustibly Queery-Leary epistles, for example, of the author of *There was an Old Man who said, "Hush!"*:

> ...So then I hope to hear your ways
> Are bent on English moves
> For that I trust once more to gaze
> Upon the friend I loves....

But if you are not coming now
  Just write a line to say so—
And I shall still consider how
  Ajoskyboskybayso.

No more my pen: no more my ink:
  No more my rhyme is clear.
So I shall leave off here I think—
  Yours ever,
                        Edward Lear.

Dodgson was actively interested in public affairs, too. When the erection of a belfry in Tom Quad was proposed he made witty sport of the design—in both senses of the word: "Its chief architectural merit is its simplicity—a simplicity so pure, so profound, in a word so *simple* that no other word will fitly describe it". He thus transported the hated belfry into the atmosphere of *Wonderland*. In *The Dynamics of a Parti-cle*, on the other hand, the fancy of the mathematician is at play. This pamphlet appeared in 1865 when Mr Gladstone was contesting (in vain) the seat he had held at Oxford University for eighteen years, and it proved to be not of a kind that appealed to his sense of humour.

Apart from *A Game of Logic* and *A Tangled Tale* with ten stubborn "knots" in it, Dodgson invented also no less than four parlour paper pastimes, which he called Misch-masch, Doublets, Lanricks and Syzygies, the last so ingeniously elaborated that even intelligent novices might spend hours in heated argument over its rules for scoring.

Mathematics indeed and her sister science Logic were not only his serious occupation but the delight of his leisure. He was at times a poor sleeper and to while away the lagging hours and, as he confessed, to keep trespassing thoughts at bay, he set himself "Pillow Problems", and invented a method of recording them in the dark. Alas, even these, quite apart from his *Euclid and his Modern Rivals*, lie far beyond the scope of this paper, and, that being so, a friend who insists on remaining anonymous has very kindly allowed me to quote his remarks on them.

These problems were intended, he says, for those who possess the necessary intellectual equipment to tackle them and would all probably be classed by mathematicians as "elementary" because their solution does not require the use of the Calculus, but only Arithmetic, Algebra, Geometry and Trigonometry; but this is not to say that they are easy; that would hardly be expected of the author. Many of them are of a somewhat unusual character, and require the use of some ingenious device which would not readily occur to most solvers, even with the aid of paper and pencil. In some cases the construction of the problem[1] is an almost more remarkable performance than its solution, for the author must have foreseen the details as well as the method of their working,

---

[1] The following may be quoted as an example:

"Five friends agreed to form themselves into a Wine-Company (Limited). They contributed equal amounts of wine, which had been bought at the same price. They then elected one of themselves to act as Treasurer; and another of them undertook to act as Salesman, and to sell the wine at 10% over cost price.

"The first day the Salesman drank one bottle, sold some, and handed over the receipts to the Treasurer.

"The second day he drank none, but pocketed the profits on one bottle sold, and handed over the rest of the receipts to the Treasurer.

"That night the Treasurer visited the cellars, and counted the remaining wine. 'It will fetch just £11', he muttered to himself as he left the cellars.

"The third day the Salesman drank one bottle, pocketed the profits on another, and handed over the rest of the receipts to the Treasurer.

"The wine was now all gone; the Company held a meeting, and found to their chagrin that their profits (i.e. the Treasurer's receipts, less the original value of the wine) only cleared 6d a bottle of the whole stock. These profits had accrued in 3 equal sums on the three days (i.e. the Treasurer's receipts for the day, less the original value of the wine taken out during the day, had come to the same amount every time); but of course only the Salesman knew this.

"(1) How much wine had they bought? (2) At what price?"

In this problem the *number* of friends would seem at first sight to be immaterial; but this is not the case. The answer to the problem as proposed is that 60 bottles were bought at 8/4d each; but if there had been *four* friends in the Company instead of *five* the answer to the same problem would have been 48 bottles at 10/- each.

otherwise he would not have been able to arrange his figures so that the answers "come out".

Whimsical touches appear occasionally; two of the problems, for example, postulate the existence of a triangular billiard-table. A few are put into the form of a tale; and sometimes an essential element of the problem is concealed in a casual and apparently unimportant reference.

The author had a fondness, also, for the problem of probabilities, and the most startling example of this is the following: "A bag contains two counters, of which nothing is known except that each is either white or black. Ascertain their colours without taking them out of the bag". The author proved—to his own satisfaction at least—that one of the counters must have been white and the other black.

Compared with this short cut to euthanasia, such passing references as "The Apodoses of these two Hypotheticals are incompatible", in a playful little puzzle concerning Uncle Jim and Uncle Joe and their three barbers, are mere child's play. But there must be many devotees of Lewis Carroll who would find themselves faltering in the presence of the mathematical don.

The well-known story, for example, that Queen Victoria, captivated by *Alice in Wonderland*, sent for the rest of its author's works, and was thereupon presented with copies of *The Condensation of Determinants*, and *A Syllabus of Plane Algebraical Geometry*, is untrue. It was denied by Dodgson in *Symbolic Logic*. But there is another little story of Queen Victoria and Alice, both of them supreme characters in their several spheres, which is true beyond question. And it is a pleasure and privilege to be permitted by the friend who shared in it, but who, alas, withholds her name, to record it here.

When she was a little girl of three and a half, before she could read, that is, though not before she could be read to, she was sitting one winter's afternoon on a footstool by the fireside looking at the pictures in *Wonderland*, while a favourite and favoured aunt conversed with the Queen and her ladies at the adjacent tea-table.

Noticing presently this rapt doubled-up little creature in the fire-light so intent over her book, the Queen asked her what it was. She rose and carried it over, and standing at the royal knee opened it at the page where tinied Alice is swimming in the flood of her own tears. Five years had gone by since the Prince Consort's death, but the Queen was still attired in widow's weeds, in solemn black. Putting two and two together (as only Dodgson with the help of Carroll could), this little girl, pointing at the picture, looked up into the Queen's face, and said: "Do you think, please, *you* could cry as much as that?"

The profound hush that followed while the ladies in the room pondered this bold enquiry was broken by the Queen's reply—which, now, I fear, is no longer recoverable. Next day, however, a tiny locket, with a design of intertwined horseshoes in coral and seed pearls and with a minute portrait of the widowed Queen within, and this packed in a charming little box with the royal monogram on the lid, was despatched from Windsor by a special messenger in a most resplendent uniform. It remains a precious souvenir of those few tense moments.

The point of this little incident, if anything so childlike and tender can be said to have anything as sharp, is that the author of a book so remote from the realm of phantasy as *Leaves from a Journal of our Life in the Highlands* could share her delight in *Wonderland* with one of the youngest of her subjects. But that is precisely its supreme achievement. It is, in the words[1] of Sir Walter Besant, one of the very few books in the world

---

[1] These I have taken from a letter to a friend, Mrs Herbert Fuller, herself one of Lewis Carroll's little girls and also the mother of one whose happy thought it was to endow a cot in the Children's Hospital, Great Ormond Street, to his memory.

"which can be read with equal pleasure by old and young....It is the only child's book of nonsense that is never childish". And not only that; it admits us into a state of being which, until it was written, was not only unexplored but undiscovered. Nevertheless like other rare achievements it was the fruit apparently of a happy accident. For once in a while the time and the place and the loved one came together.

On the afternoon of 4 July 1862, in the Long Vacation, a minute expedition set out from Oxford up the river to Godstow. It returned laden with a treasure compared with which that of the *Golden Hind* was but dross. It consisted of Canon Duckworth, then a tutor at Christ Church and the "duck" in the story itself, of Dodgson, and the three little Liddells, whom Dodgson had nicknamed Prima, Secunda and Tertia. They were, each in her own degree, members of a happy band of children who were the delight and solace of Carroll's long years at Christ Church. A few of them remained his intimate friends. But in general they reigned in turn as briefly as the Aprils that have followed one another throughout the centuries. He collected them wherever he had the good fortune to find them, especially, so it seems, at the sea-side and in railway trains. It is related that, bound for the beach, he would leave his lodgings at Eastbourne armed not only with puzzles but with a supply of large safety pins, in case any little girl intent on paddling should be in need of one. Unlike most other dons, he provided not cakes or goodies for their entertainment in his "large, lofty and extremely cheerful-looking study", where he insisted on keeping all his furniture and carpets in precise alignment, but a musical box, toys and an old Woolly Bear, not to mention home-made devices for lighting his gas and for boiling his kettle. In London he took them to plays and pantomimes, and blessed any small actresses who shone behind the footlights with a like generosity and kindness. However brief the reign of these (occasionally fractious) little princesses, he was faithfully fickle to one and all of them—each in turn. Not so with small boys. Bruno may be a compound of imp, elf and infant Samuel, but for small boys in general Dodgson and even Carroll professed an aversion "almost amounting to terror". But then, as Mrs Meynell has pointed out, small boys in Art have never been neglected. It was Carroll's prerogative "to make great amends to little girls".

Of the three children who accompanied him to Godstow that afternoon, it was Secunda—Alice Pleasance Liddell—"courteous, trustful, wildly curious... loving as a dog and gentle as a fawn", who was destined as "Alice" to be immortal. She was the mistress jewel in his carcanet. They paddled on; Duckworth was stroke of the "pair", Dodgson bow, and *Alice's Adventures Underground* were told, on and on, over stroke's shoulder to Secunda who, with her sisters, and ropes in lap, sat at the tiller. "Yes", the skipper agreed, on the question being put to him, "I am inventing as we go along." Carroll was then thirty, Blake being two years older when *Songs of Innocence* was published.

Now afternoons in July, if fair and cloudless, are apt to be narcotic. The rhythm of sculling quiets the mind and sets the workaday wits drowsing. The low secret chuckle of the water, the lovely light on its surface, rimpling up into those three rapt little faces, would have decoyed any imagination into activity. And Carroll's voice flowed gently on to the accompaniment of the whispering of the river, the dipping swallows and the faint stir of the wind in the branches at the water side.

It was at Duckworth's suggestion that he laboured

16-2

on into the small hours that evening, pen and paper for company, and midnight oil for illumination. "His memory was so good", said his friend, "that I think the story as he wrote it down was almost word by word the same as he had told it in the boat." The manuscript was bestowed on the Deanery, and here Henry Kingsley chanced on it. Why should such a treasure remain hidden under a bushel? He urged Mrs Liddell to persuade its author to publish it, and suggested Tenniel as illustrator. *Alice's Hour in Elfland* having been discarded as a title, it appeared exactly three years afterwards, and in spite of its temporary withdrawal from circulation owing to the poor reproduction of its pictures, it instantly enchanted the sedate Victorians and has never since suffered the faintest eclipse.

Of few masterpieces have we so particularized a birthday. "Up the river", ran Carroll's Journal for 4 July, and then, "I told them the fairy tale." "Alice" herself, moreover, has not only recorded her belief that the story was begun one summer afternoon "when the sun was so burning hot" that the little party took refuge in a meadow down the river in the only bit of shade to be found under a new-made hay-rick", but has explained that she herself persuaded Carroll to write it down. Dr Paget, on the other hand, could recall a mathematical Reading Party at Whitby as far back as the summer of 1854, when the story, he said, was "incubated" by Dodgson, then only twenty-two, to amuse a circle of eager youngsters of both sexes:

> 'Twas there he rested on a rock
> Conveniently low:
> And all the little Oysters stood
> And waited in a row.

Yet another version is that he wrote *Wonderland* to amuse and comfort a remote little relative of his when she was ill. And the moral of *that* is, it couldn't be so; since only one paragraph of such a panacea would have sufficed to make her quite better.

And last, while in the *Life* it is recorded that George MacDonald persuaded Carroll to publish his story, yet another account avers that it was the wild applause of six-year-old little Greville MacDonald, to whom with his sisters Carroll read *Wonderland* from its manuscript, that had this effect. As for the weather, *The Times* of 5 July 1862 maintains that the previous day was occasionally rainy, and its temperature only 53°.

These varying accounts, however, are no doubt easily reconcilable and, like Homer's many birth-places they are a telling tribute to the poet who was the adequate cause of them.

What they have in common is evidence that the tale, rhymes and all, and "finished" to the finest edge of craftsmanship, seems for the most part to have floated into Carroll's mind as spontaneously as did one of the best known lines in English verse: "For the Snark was a Boojum, you see". "Every word of the dialogue", he said, "came of itself." And though he confesses elsewhere that his "jaded muse was" at times "goaded into action...more because she had to say something than because she had something to say"; and that he despatched Alice down the rabbit hole not knowing in the least what was to become of her; and though, whenever the crystal wellspring ceased to flow, he could always pretend to fall fast asleep (whereas of course he had actually come wide-awake)—all this little affects the marvel, and is interesting mainly because Dodgson in *Sylvie and Bruno* expressed his contempt for any writing that was chiefly the result of taking pains. He maintained that all such writing cannot but remain unimpassioned and uninspired.

What, then, of the scorned delights, and the laborious days; what of the loading of every rift with ore; and that midnight oil in the study of Christ Church? Are these the sighs of a Dodgson weeping over a lost Carroll? Or was it merely that, with advancing age, he himself, like most elderly writers, when recalling the light that shone upon their youthful achievements and the dews that dropped on them from heaven, forgot the care, the patience and the pains? Yet another marvel is that *Wonderland* should have been followed by so consummate a sequel as *Through the Looking-Glass*. They are twin stars on whose *relative* radiance alone literary astronomers may be left to disagree.

Both stories have a structural framework—in the one playing cards, in the other a game of chess, the moves in which Dodgson only to some extent attempted to justify. These no doubt suggested a few of his chief characters, or rather their social status; but what other tale-teller could have made Carroll's use of them? All that he owed to the device of the looking-glass, except that it is one which has perplexed and delighted child, philosopher and savage alike, is that the handwriting in the story is the wrong way round, and that when Alice wished to go forwards she had to walk backwards—a method of progression that is sometimes of service even in life itself. Both stories, too—and this is a more questionable contrivance, particularly as it introduces a rather sententious elder sister—turn out to be dreams; and one little girl I know of burst out crying when the awakening came.

All this, however, affects the imaginative reality—the supreme illusion—of the *Alices* no more than its intricate chronology and knowledge of the law affect that of *Wuthering Heights*, and these have been proved to be unassailable. In reading the Carroll stories, that is, we scarcely notice, however consistent and admirable it may be, their ingenious design. And that is true also of *As You Like It*. Quite apart from any such design, at any rate, they would still remain in essence perhaps the most *original* books in the world. Indeed the genius in Carroll seems to have worked more subtly than the mind which it was possessed by realized. It is a habit genius has.

Then again, the Queen of Hearts, he said himself, was intended to be "a blind and aimless Fury", the Red Queen was to reveal "the concentrated essence of all governesses", the Mad Hatter was once a don, the White Queen strongly reminded him of Mrs Wragg in Wilkie Collins's *No Name*, and the White Knight was intended to characterize the speaker in Wordsworth's *Resolution and Independence*. But if he had been merely as successful as *that*, where would these immortals be now? The reason is in service to the imagination, not *vice versa*. "Please never *praise* me at all", Dodgson entreated a child who had written to him about the *Alices*. "I just feel myself a trustee, that is all." So might Nature herself reply if one commended her for the inexhaustible versatility of design revealed in her hippopotamus, her camel, her angel-fishes and her flea!

So too with the *Snark*. "I am very much afraid", said Dodgson, "I didn't mean anything but nonsense. ...But since words mean more than we mean to express when we use them...whatever good meanings are in the book I am very glad to accept as the meaning of the book"—a remark which is not only modest and generous but well worth pondering.

The intellectual thread, none the less, which runs through the *Alices* is the reverse of being negligible. It is on this that their translucent beads of phantasy are

strung, and it is the more effective for being so consistent and art-fully concealed. As in the actual writing
of poetry the critical faculties of the poet are in a supreme and constant activity, so with the *Alices*. Their
"characters", for example, in all their rich diversity are
in exquisite keeping with one another. And it is curious
that though—a remark that applies to Lear's limericks
but not to most books aimed at the young, however
wide they may fall of the mark—they were written for
children, the only child in them is Alice herself. The
Mad Hatter is perennial forty, the Carpenter is of the
age of all carpenters, the Red King is the age Henry
VIII was born, while the Queens and the Duchess—
well, they know best about that.

Alice herself, of course, with her familiar little toss
of the head, with her serene mobile face, courteous,
amiable, except when she *must* speak up for herself,
easily reconciled, inclined to tears, but tears how swiftly
dashed away; with her dignity, her matter-of-factness,
her conscientiousness, her courage (even in the most
outlandish of circumstances) never to submit or yield;
and with one of the most useful of all social resources,
the art of changing a conversation—what a tribute she
is not only to her author but to Victorian childhood!
Capable, modest, demure, sedate, they are words a
little out of fashion nowadays; but Alice alone would
redeem them all. And even if now and then she is a
trifle superior, a trifle *too* demure, must not even the
most delicate of simple and arduous little samplers have
its wrong side?

She might indeed have been a miniature model of
all the Victorian virtues and still have fallen short if it
were not for her freedom from silliness and her saving
good sense—a good sense that never bespangles itself
by being merely clever. However tart and touchy, how-

ever queer and querulous and quarrelsome her "retinue" in Wonderland and in Looking-Glass Land may be, and she all but always gets the worst of every argument, it is this sagacity of mind and heart that keeps her talk from being merely "childish" and theirs from seeming grown-uppish, and, in one word, prevents the hazardous situation from falling into the non-nonsensical. She wends serenely on like a quiet moon in a chequered sky. Apart, too, from an occasional Carrollian comment, the sole medium of the stories is *her* pellucid consciousness: an ideal preached by Henry James himself, and practised—in how different a setting—in *What Maisie Knew.*

It is this rational poise in a topsy-turvy world (a world seen upside-down, as M. Cammaerts says, and looking far more healthy and bright), that gives the two tales their exquisite balance. For though laws there certainly are in the realm of Nonsense, they are all of them unwritten laws. Its subjects obey them unaware of any restrictions. Anything may happen there except only what can't happen *there.* Its kings and queens are kings and queens for precisely the same reason that the Mock Turtle is a Mock Turtle, even though once he was a real Turtle—by a divine right, that is, on which there is no need to insist. A man there, whether he be Tweedledum or the Carpenter or the White Knight, apart from his being a gentleman so perfect that you do not notice it, is never "a man for a' that", simply because there isn't any "a' that". And though "morals" pepper their pages—"Everything's got a moral if only you can find it"—the stories themselves have none. "In fact", as Carroll said himself, "they do not teach anything at all."

Instead, they stealthily instil into us a unique state of mind. Their jam—wild strawberry—*is* the powder—

virgin gold-dust—though we may never be conscious of
its cathartic effects. Although too Carroll's Nonsense,
in itself, in Dryden's words, may be such that it "never
can be *understood*", there is no need to understand it.
It is self-evident. Besides, haven't we, like the Red
Queen herself, heard other kinds of nonsense, and in
very sober spheres, "compared with which *this* would
be as sensible as a dictionary"? It lightens our beings
like sunshine, like that divine rainbow in the skies
beneath which the living things of the world went out
into radiance and freedom from the narrow darkness of
the Ark. And any mind in its influence is freed the
while from all its cares. Carroll's Wonderland indeed
is a region resembling Einstein's in that it is a finite
infinity endlessly explorable though never to be ex-
plored. Its heavens are bluer, its grass grass-greener,
its fauna more curiously revivifying company not only
than any but the pick of *this* world's but than those of
any other book I know. And even for variety and precision, from the Mad Hatter down to Bill the Lizard,
that company is rivalled only by the novelists who are
as generous as they are skilled—an astonishing feat
since Carroll's creations are not only of his own species
but of his own genus.

Just, too, as in the talk in the *Alices* we realize the
meaning of a remark made by a writer in the old
Spectator: "Nothing is capable of being well set to
music that is not nonsense", contrariwise, to invert a
reference to the law in *The Antiquary*, what sounds like
flawless sense in them may be flawless *non*sense for all
that. "*Must* a name mean something?" was Alice's
first question to Humpty Dumpty. "Of course it
must", said Humpty Dumpty with a short laugh. "*My*
name means the shape I am. . . . With a name like yours,
you might be any shape, almost."

Whose is the nonsense here, Humpty Dumpty's or the London Directory's—where Smiths may be grocers, Coopers haberdashers, and Bakers butchers? And what (on earth) would any man look like if he looked like a Wilkinson, a Marjoribanks or a John James Jones? Charles Dickens alone could say. Then again Humpty Dumpty's "Let's go back to the last remark but one" (an unfailing resource in any heated argument), his "If I'd meant that, I'd have said it", his "*One* can't, perhaps, but *two* can", and his righteous indignation with a person who doesn't know a cravat from a belt—well, not even a Lord Chief Justice in a black cap could be more incisive and more to the rational point.

What, too, even from a strictly conventional point of view, is unusual, unpractical, amiss in the Duchess's kitchen? She is gracing it with her presence, and these are democratic times; she is nursing her baby, and *Noblesse oblige*; and the kitchen is full of smoke, which Victorian kitchens often were. What do we expect in a kitchen? A cook, a fire, a cat, and a cauldron with soup in it. It is precisely what we get—and, to give it flavour, someone has been a little free with the pepper. The cook, it is true, is throwing frying-pans and saucepans at her mistress, but nowadays there's many a lady in the land who would forgive the fusillade if only she could secure the cook. As for the Duchess's remarks, they are as appropriate as they are peremptory. And do we not expect the high-born to be a little high-handed? Alice enquires why her cat grins like that.

"It's a Cheshire cat", she says, "and that's why."

Alice smiled that she didn't know cats *could* grin.

"They all can", said the Duchess, "and most of them do."

Alice didn't know of any that did.

"You don't know much", said the Duchess, "and that's a fact."

She goes on to remark that the world would be much improved if everybody in it minded his own business; and the only defect in that little grumble is that it is a counsel of perfection. Surely too when cosmological explanations of "how the earth rotates on its axis" are about, one's sole resource is to chop off somebody's head.

As for the lullaby the Duchess sings as she sits —long-coated, broad-grinned infant in lap—in that marvellous head-dress, square knees apart, dour and indomitable, it preaches justice in the first stanza and proves her personal practice of it in the last:

> Speak roughly to your little boy,
>   And beat him when he sneezes:
> He only does it to annoy,
>   Because he knows it teases.
>   *Wow! wow! wow!*
>
> I speak severely to my boy,
>   I beat him when he sneezes;
> For he can thoroughly enjoy
>   The pepper when he pleases!
>   *Wow! wow! wow*

Such discipline—those nursery *wows*—may sound a little harsh in the kindergartens of our own baby-ridden age, but it was on this basis Victorian mothers brought up the pioneers of our Empire!

So far, so practical. But it must not be forgotten that this "large kitchen" into which nine-inch Alice had so unceremoniously intruded belonged to a little house in a wood only about four feet high, nor that the Duchess's grunting infant as soon as it breathes the open air in Alice's arms turns placidly into a small pig. And that, except metaphorically, children don't do. Not in real life, that is. Only in *dreams*.

And it is here that we stumble on *the* sovereign

element in the *Alices*. It consists in the presentation of what is often perfectly rational, practical, logical, and, maybe, mathematical, what is terse, abrupt and pointed, in a state and under conditions of life to which we most of us win admittance only when we are blessedly asleep. To every man his own dreams, to every man his own day-dreams. And as with sense, nonsense and un-sense; as with me, you and a sort of us-ishness; as with past, future and the all-and-almost-nothing in between; so with Greenwich time, time and *dream* time; good motives, bad motives, and dream motives; self, better self and dream self. Dreaming is another state of being, with laws as stringent *and* as elastic as those of the world of Nonsense. And what dream in literature has more blissfully refreshed a prose-ridden world than the dream which gently welled into Dodgson's mind that summer afternoon, nearly seventy years ago, when, oars in hand and eyes fixed on little Alice Liddell's round-orbed countenance, the Lewis Carroll in him slipped off into Wonderland?

Who can say what influences one silent consciousness may have upon another? May it not be to some magical suffusion and blending of these two, the mathematician's and the child's, that we owe the *Alices*? Even the technical triumph of the two books consists in having made what is finally declared to be a dream actually and always *seem* to be a dream. Open either of them at random; ask yourself any one of the questions on the page exposed; endeavour to find an answer not merely as apt and pungent as are most answers of the *Alice* order, but one that will at the same time fret by not so much as a hair's breadth the story's dream-like crystal-line tissue: and then turn back to the book for *Carroll's* answer. That alone, though a trivial one, will be proof enough of the quality of his genius.

And what of the visionary light, the colour, the scenery; that wonderful sea-scape, for example, in *The Walrus and the Carpenter*, as wide as Milton's in *Il Penseroso*—the quality of its sea, its sands, its space and distances? What of the exquisite transition from one setting on to another in a serene seductive discontinuity in—for but one example—the chapter entitled "Wool and Water"? First the little dark shop and the hunched-up placid old sheep, with her forest of knitting needles, who but an instant before was the White Queen; then the cumbrous gliding boat on that queer glutinous water, among the scented rushes—"dream rushes" that melt away "almost like snow" in Alice's lap; and then, without the faintest jar, back into the little dark shop again—Platonic original of all little dark shops. All this is of the world of dreams and of that world alone. The *Alices* indeed have the timelessness, the placelessness, and an atmosphere resembling in their own odd fashion not only those of the *Songs of Innocence* and Traherne's *Meditations*, but of the mediaeval descriptions of paradise and many of the gem-like Italian pictures of the fifteenth century. This atmosphere is conveyed, as it could alone be conveyed, in a prose of limpid simplicity, as frictionless as the unfolding of the petals of an evening primrose in the cool of twilight; a prose, too, that could be the work only of a writer who like John Ruskin had from his earliest years examined every word he used with a scrupulous attention.

What relation the world of our dreams has to the world of our actual, who can say? Our modern oneiromantics have their science, but the lover of the *Alices* is in no need of it. What relation any such dream-world has to some other state of being seen only in glimpses here and now might be a more valuable but is an even less answerable question. In any case, and even though

there are other delights in them which only many years'
experience of life can fully reveal, it is the child that is
left in us who tastes the sweetest honey and laves its
imagination in the clearest waters to be found in the
Alices.

How the books fare in translation I cannot say. It
would be insular, in any case, since their "nonsense" is
solely their own, to flatter ourselves overmuch that it
is not only English of the English but how strangely
verdant a Victorian oasis also amid such quantities of
sand. May that nonsense in all its varieties continue to
blossom like the almond tree; the oaks of the forest will
flourish none the less bravely in its floral company.
Indeed there are times and crises in affairs not only
personal, but public, political and even international,
when the following tribute from M. Cammaerts may
first serve for a solace and then for a solemn warning:

> The English, he says, speak, in an off-hand way, of "possessing a
> Sense of Humour" or of not possessing it, little realising that this sense,
> with the meaning they attach to it, is almost unique in the world, and
> can be acquired only after years of strenuous and patient effort. For
> many foreigners, Einstein's theories present fewer difficulties than
> certain limericks....

Than certain limericks! We can at need, that is, while
still we keep the mint, dole out these precious coppers
whensoever the too, too intellectual alien proves in-
tractable, while for our own precious island currency
we can treasure the gold of the crystal-watered land of
Havilah—Carroll's and the *Alices'*. And if at any time
we ourselves need an unfaltering and unflattering critic,
which is not unseldom, there is always the Cheshire Cat.

INDEX

For EU product safety concerns, contact us at Calle de José Abascal, 56–1°,
28003 Madrid, Spain or eugpsr@cambridge.org.

www.ingramcontent.com/pod-product-compliance
Ingram Content Group UK Ltd.
Pitfield, Milton Keynes, MK11 3LW, UK
UKHW010348140625
459647UK00010B/904